Maybe You Know
My Kid

Maybe You Know My Kid

A Parents' Guide to Identifying, Understanding, and
Helping Your Child with Attention Deficit
Hyperactivity Disorder

THIRD EDITION

Mary Fowler

III

A BIRCH LANE PRESS BOOK
Published by Carol Publishing Group

A Birch Lane Press Book
Published by Carol Publishing Group
Birch Lane Press is a registered trademark of Carol Communications, Inc.

Editorial, sales and distribution, and rights and permissions inquiries should be
addressed to Carol Publishing Group, 120 Enterprise Avenue, Secaucus, N.J.
07094.

In Canada: Canadian Manda Group, One Atlantic Avenue, Suite 105, Toronto,
Ontario M6K 3E7

Carol Publishing Group books may be purchased in bulk at special discounts
for sales promotion, fundraising, or educational purposes. Special editions can
be created to specifications. For details, contact Special Sales Department,
Carol Publishing Group, 120 Enterprise Avenue, Secaucus, N.J. 07094.

Manufactured in the United States of America
10 9 8 7 6 5 4 3 2 1

Library of Congress Cataloging-in-Publication Data

Fowler, Mary Cahill.
    Maybe you know my kid? :   a parents' guide to identifying,
understanding, and helping your child with attention deficit hyperactivity
disorder   /   by Mary Fowler.—[Updated ed.]
        p.   cm.
    "A Birch Lane Press book."
    Includes Index.
    ISBN 1-55972-490-0 (pbk.)
    1. Hyperactive children. 2. Attention deficit hyperactivity disorder.
3. Attention deficit disordered children. I. Title.
RJ506.H9F68   1999
618.92'8589—dc21   98-48109
                                                                          CIP

For my sons,
David and Jonathan—the spirit behind the words—
and my mother

Contents

Acknowledgments

I am especially grateful to the researchers and practitioners who graciously contributed their time and knowledge to me. Their devotion and work in attention deficit hyperactivity disorder (ADHD) has made significant differences in the lives of those challenged by this disorder:

Russell Barkley, Ph.D., director of psychology and professor of psychiatry and neurology at the University of Massachusetts Medical Center, where he established the Center for Attention Deficit Hyperactivity Disorder. Dr. Barkley is the author of numerous books and articles, including the gold-standard text for practitioners. A clinical practitioner, scientist, and educator, Dr. Barkley is internationally recognized for his work in the field.

C. Keith Conners, Ph.D., professor of medical psychology in the Department of Psychiatry at Duke University Medical Center, where he is director of the ADHD Clinic and codirector of the Research Training Program. Dr. Conners has written numerous books, articles, and the Conners' Rating Scales. His work has received international acclaim.

Sam Goldstein, Ph.D., a psychologist in private practice specializing in child development, school psychology, and neuropsychology. He has written numerous books and created an award-winning video.

Melvin Levine, M.D., professor of pediatrics and director of the Clinical Center for the Study of Development and Learning at the University of North Carolina, Chapel Hill. Dr. Levine has published extensively.

Bennett Shaywitz, M.D., professor of pediatrics and neurology at Yale University Medical School and director of a federally funded center to study learning and attention.

Sally Shaywitz, M.D., associate professor of pediatrics at Yale University Medical School.

Paul Wender, M.D., professor of psychiatry and director of pediatric research at the University of Utah Medical School. Dr. Wender, author of numerous books and articles, pioneered much of the work in both child and adult ADHD.

I also wish to thank the following experts who contributed to the second and third editions:

Edward Hallowell, M.D., faculty member at Harvard Medical School, a child and adult psychiatrist in private practice who specializes in ADHD and has published a book on adults with the disorder.

Dr. Howard Margolis, coordinator of reading for the Educational and Community Programs department at Queens College of the City University of New York and specialist in dispute resolutions between parents and schools.

Kevin Murphy, Ph.D., chief of the Adult Clinic on ADHD at the University of Massachusetts Medical School.

Charles Popper, M.D., faculty member at Harvard Medical School and editor of the *Journal of Child and Adolescent Psychopharmacology.*

Ron Reeve, Ph.D., a psychologist and associate professor of education at the University of Virginia, where he coordinates the School Psychology Program.

David Shaffer, M.D., Irving Philips Professor of Child Psychiatry at Columbia University/NYSPI.

Robert Silverstein, director of the Center for Study and Advancement of Disability Policy at George Washington University and former staff director and chief counsel for the subcommittee on disability policy of the U.S. Senate Committee on Labor and Human Relations.

Timothy Wilens, M.D., associate professor of psychiatry at Harvard Medical School and staff member at Pediatric Psychopharmacology Clinic at Massachusetts General Hospital.

Alan Zametkin, M.D., senior staff psychiatrist of the Clinical Brain Imaging Section, National Institute of Mental Health.

Sydney Zentall, Ph.D., professor of special education and psychological sciences at Purdue University and past president of the Division for Research at the Council for Exceptional Children.

My appreciation to the following medical and mental health professionals: Gabor Barabas, M.D., Jean Bramble, R.N., Kathy Collins, M.S.W., Randy Mendelson, Ph.D., William McMahon, M.D., Richard Reutter, M.D., and Judy Welch, Ph.D., for their contributions.

Special thanks to Rivka Arotchas, founder of B'Yahad, the ADHD support group of Israel, and to her family for their friendship; to Maureen Argus for her friendship and our many discussions about educational techniques; to Richard Horne, Ed.D., senior program officer for the Academy of Professional Development Disability Studies and Services Center, and to Fran Rice, director of Advocacy Associates of Northern New England, both of whom continue to teach me about the laws governing the education of children with disabilities; and to Richard Zakreski, Ph.D., for his contributions to the text, review of my work, and continued support of our family.

I am especially grateful that ADHD brought me the added blessing of an extended family: Sandy Thomas, former president of C.H.A.D.D. and her husband, Russ, and their children Scott and Kim. Sandy, thank you for being there—always!

And to the mothers, fathers, children with ADHD, and siblings who took me into their confidence, I am forever indebted. Your stories are an important part of this book, and I thank you for your trust and honesty. Finally, love to my children for your patience and love.

Foreword

It is both a great pleasure and a great honor to have been invited by Mary Fowler to prepare this foreword for this edition of her best-selling and widely acclaimed book for parents of children with attention deficit hyperactivity disorder, or ADHD. I can think of few parents or educators better equipped than Mary to render the veritable morass of scientific research decipherable to parents of children with ADHD and to wring from that vast research literature every ounce of practical knowledge that those parents need at their disposal. Mary is among the strongest, most outspoken, and relentless advocates that children with ADHD have ever had. For that, I dedicated my own parents' book on ADHD to her. Through her writing, speaking, teaching, lobbying, and public advocacy, she has done infinite good for families with ADHD children.

As Mary knows firsthand, raising such a child successfully is a very, very tough task indeed, a task made all the more difficult by the lack of access many parents have to the reams of scientific knowledge that have accumulated on this disorder over the past century. So Mary has taken as one of her goals, once again, to use this book to break down that barrier and to let flow into the hands of parents the most accurate and most useful scientific information at our disposal for the understanding, management, and raising of a child with ADHD. Not content just to interpret the clinical and educational literature for parents, she delves further into this knowledge base by personally interviewing many of the leading researchers, clinicians, and educators working in the field of ADHD today. In doing so, she has brought forth not just a compendium of knowledge for parents but one of wisdom as well.

Better than most writers of informational books for parents, Mary understands that ADHD is more than a problem with attention or overactivity and impulsivity. She knows, as I do now, that ADHD is a developmental disorder of self-control. It is a condition that disrupts the maturation of the child's natural abilities to regulate, guide, and otherwise manage his or her own behavior. By delaying and otherwise impairing the child's faculties that would grant him or her the powers of self-governance, ADHD has left the child more at the mercy of the immediate environment and of the moment than other children of their age.

One of the most important faculties for self-regulation is the sense of past and future, and of time, more generally. Psychologists have called this faculty autonoetic awareness, the knowledge of one's self across time. My own term for this is TimeSight, the power to see through time that progressively develops from preschool until our early thirties. This ability to see through time is highly limited by the condition we call ADHD. As Mary explains here, ADHD leaves the child in a dislocated present—a condition of absolute immediacy in which the past has little or no influence over the child and the future is out of sight and out of mind. Such children are stuck in the temporal now, and the now is all that seems to govern them. All children with ADHD share a blindness to time, a syndrome of temporal neglect or nearsightedness in which only events close at hand in time are attended to, while those that lie in the more distant future go unnoticed, unanticipated, and unheeded.

Such limitations leave children with ADHD without an anchor on the seas of life and rudderless in the currents that pass by during each wave of time that washes over them. Adrift in time, they live a life of chaos. It is a life of crisis to crisis, yet they receive little sympathy from others, because others see through time, anticipate the future, and are ready for its arrival. They cannot understand why the child with ADHD fails to do so. They interpret this condition, wrongly, as a choice—a willful, wanton disregard for the consequences of one's actions. And so, those others say, children with ADHD deserve what they get. Mary knows better, and now through this book so do we.

ADHD is no choice. It is through no fault of their own that those having this condition find themselves less self-regulated than others. It is largely a neurogenetic disorder that robs the child of normal executive abilities, inhibition, and self-governance. Therefore others must step in to help govern them, motivate them, structure them, and guide them along if children with ADHD are to be protected from themselves, steered toward more acceptable and successful actions, and aimed at the future.

Richly detailed and usefully rendered in this book are countless recommendations for parents to employ in the successful raising of their ADHD child. Also included are many facts and figures, as well as information on the hard-won rights and accommodations available to children with ADHD. All this material is virtually indispensable to the executive parents who must advocate for their child in the community, in the schools, and even in their own extended families.

For make no mistake about it, despite several thousand research papers and numerous books on the subject, ADHD remains a disorder grossly misunderstood by many in the public and the popular media. It is a myth to some; to others, a side effect of our dietary evils; to still others, an outgrowth of our fast-paced, television-focused, technology-driven culture; to yet others, the outcome of a decline in our family values. None of this is true.

Still, such ignorance pervades the thinking of many in society with whom the parents of children with ADHD must deal. It cannot be overcome simply by admonishing others: "My child really cannot help behaving that way!" Yet these parents know in their hearts that they are right, that children with ADHD cannot help doing many of the things that others so easily disparage.

If there is one message that rings loud and clear at the end of this book, it is that compassion and accommodation are what children with ADHD really need, not denigration, not humiliation, and not the sneering moral judgments of others. After conducting one of the longest follow-up studies of children with ADHD ever done, lasting well over twenty-five years, Drs. Gabrielle Weiss and Lily Hechtman observed something profound in their interviews with their subjects: those with the best outcomes attributed much of their success to the fact that someone believed in them as children, buffered them from the slings and arrows of others, and defended them when they were most in need of an advocate. This book should make every parent who reads it the supporter, protector, and advocate for his or her child with ADHD.

Russell A. Barkley, Ph.D.
Professor of Psychology
and Neurology, the University
of Massachusetts Medical Center

Preface

Ten years ago, I had a mission. After five hard years of parenting a child who had a disorder which was not recognized or treated, my family—whom I love more than I could possibly express in words—had practically disintegrated. I knew that something was wrong. I feared I might be the cause. I searched for answers from many doctors, educators, elders, and other mothers. I got lots of advice, a great deal of "constructive" criticism, some helpful and some downright harmful tips. I took all to heart because I had no idea what ailed our family. I just wanted all to be well.

Back then, barely anyone outside the research community had ever heard about attention deficit hyperactivity disorder (ADHD). Most people who knew of the problem, including practitioners, did not understand its ramifications. People talked about "hyper" kids, a description which fit my son. I heard so many myths about this problem: "sugar," "diet," "needs exercise," "intolerant parent," or "he'll grow out of it." These misconceptions did not help me help my child. They confused me and added to my sense of guilt over not raising a "well-behaved" child. Possibly, the misunderstanding which did the greatest disservice to me, and perhaps to the other families and children who suffer from this disorder, was the almost nonchalant dismissal of ADHD as being "no big deal."

I knew differently from having lived with ADHD. Once I learned about the actual nature of this disorder and about what it does to families, I set out to educate as many people as I could so that no other mother, child, father, or sibling would have to bare the brunt of this problem alone, in the dark, without help. I began my efforts by starting a parent support group with a die-hard group of parents and Richard Zakreski, the psychologist who had diagnosed our children. Every day I answered numerous phone calls from parents, many distraught over their situations, some on the verge of physically abusing their children. I tried to help them find the right answers and to dispel myths. I steered them in directions that might make a difference. This work has been the most gratifying work I have ever done. In starting the support group, I hoped that parents would reach out to other parents and that the day would come when no one misunderstood ADHD.

I wrote the first edition of this book with the best of intentions but fueled by anger after I happened to hear a talk show host use the power of the media to take potshots at Ritalin, a brand-name drug from the class of medications considered most effective for the treatment of the disorder. This irresponsible individual had the nerve to ignore a vast body of scientific information about these medications and to use the power of his widely viewed broadcast to influence public opinion through lies of omission and sensationalist journalism. Had he kept his attack to the medication issue, I might have ignored him. But he went on to criticize and blame parents. After hearing him minimize the seriousness of the problems created by ADHD, I decided to write a book and tell the truths I knew about what actually happens to the children and their families. Make no mistake. This disorder can be devastating. With the right help, it does not have to be.

After the book's first publication, my anger somewhat quelled, I went to Washington, D.C. with another mother, Sandra Thomas, who was then the president of the national ADD parent support group, CHADD. I was the vice president of Government Relations. We had the privilege to serve as volunteer representatives for parents and children all across our country in an effort to fulfill their mission: improving the education of children with ADHD in America's public schools. Need I say, I became angry again. Neither Sandy nor I could believe that many national organizations of great importance and concerned with education outwardly, aggressively lobbied members of Congress to prevent any changes in the text of special education law to address the needs of children with ADHD. But parents across America stood up to these well established organizations and made their voices heard on behalf of their children. The result was a U.S. Department of Education Policy Clarification affirming the entitlement of children with ADHD to the full rights and protections afforded all children with disabilities in America's public schools. That policy clarification occurred in 1991.

Now, almost ten years have passed since the first edition of this book. A lot has changed. Today, public awareness of ADHD exists widely—not just in America, but throughout the world. Yet despite all the efforts to give people accurate information, ADHD suffers from another malady. Once unknown, the disorder has become almost notorious. Perhaps it's the old adage: familiarity breeds contempt. Or perhaps the field itself is to blame. ADHD has become commercialized to an extent. The disorder still has its critics and naysayers who are only too happy to suggest that ADHD is over-diagnosed and trendy. And easily dismissed. If you are just learning about ADHD and concerned for yourself or your child, ignore these critics and get accurate information.

I also see another form of dismissal of ADHD. Where ten or fifteen years ago no one knew enough to talk about the significant adversity ADHD can cause, today that adversity is almost hidden underneath a barrage of feel-good fanfare. In an effort to improve self-esteem and make the best out of it, many people talk about ADHD as if it were an asset. It's a lifelong struggle with ups, downs, and in-betweens. While I agree that we need to accentuate the positive, I worry that we do injustice to the recognition and acknowledgement of the significant hardships this disorder places on the people who suffer from it and their families in an effort to make it feel okay It's not okay.

I am in the classroom these days. I see what children go through as they struggle to survive and flourish in our schools. Tell the ADHD kids who get yelled at fifteen times a day, who are criticized by peers, called names, kicked off the bus, and given yet another low or failing grade, that ADHD is an asset. It's not. And they know it. What they don't know is why many of them feel that they are somehow at fault, inferior, inadequate, losers.

Recently, a young student who I suspect has ADHD was caught misbehaving and told me, "I'm not good at anything." Imagine being in seventh grade and thinking that. As it turns out, he's a good poet. But he still has poor self-control and meets with significant failure. I hope he will build on his talent. Nonetheless, as educators we need to do a lot to help him succeed in an environment where he has great difficulty.

I don't know if this boy has ADHD, although he shows a lot of the signs. Only a proper diagnostic evaluation will make that determination. The trend toward labeling oneself or one's child as having ADHD without following the recommended diagnostic procedure also adds to the thinking that ADHD need not be taken seriously. In fact, skeptics claim that everyone has a "touch of it." Shame on them for making light of a very troublesome disorder.

Regarding education, I have learned throughout the past six years of teaching in four different schools and in speaking with many parents, that most schools still do not have a clue about what ADHD really is or what to do about it. Many schools do not honor their legal responsibility to identify and accommodate children with ADHD in need of special education. Children who might have ADHD continue to go unrecognized, undiagnosed, untreated. And, in the cases where parents have had the child diagnosed by outside professionals, too frequently the schools still do not aggressively attempt to meet the child's needs. Even in cases where schools respond to ADHD in their students, they tend to minimize its seriousness.

Parents must tell Congress that where special education is concerned, schools are ignoring its intentions, not following its laws, and violating its procedures and protections of parental and child rights. Sadly, this trend applies to all areas of disability, not just cases of ADHD, although here there is flagrant disregard.

In closing, I must address one other trend I have seen since I first became involved with ADHD education and advocacy. In numerous places, even in other countries, I hear people refer to themselves as ADHD people or to their children as ADHD children. When we refer to someone by the name of his or her disability, we actually take away the person. He or she becomes the disability. My son David has taught me that I am not the mother of an ADHD child. I am the mother of a child who has dark hair, blue eyes, a quick wit, a lot of charm, an engaging smile, a silver tongue, an ability to see through things, a lot of energy, and who also has all the characteristics of and struggles with a disability named ADHD. He is not a disabled person. He is a person with a disability.

January 1999

Maybe You Know
My Kid

CHAPTER ONE

An Overview of Attention Deficit Hyperactivity Disorder

Maybe you know my kid. He's the one who acts before he thinks. It's usually upon some rash impulse that scares the living daylights out of me, like seeing how fast he can ride a Big Wheel down a long, steep, curvy hill. He's the one who says the first thing that comes to his mind. It's usually with a loud voice in a quiet crowd, and it makes me wish I could evaporate into thin air.

And he cannot remember a simple request. So I long for a trained parrot that can tell him ten times in five minutes 365 days a year to go upstairs, brush your teeth, get dressed, and make your bed. He's the kid who scrapes his knee and screams so loud and long that I worry the neighbors think I am beating him. Then, when I'm about to call the doctor, he eyes a monarch butterfly and chases it through the trees until it disappears, just like his hysterics of seconds before. He's the kid in school with ants in his pants who could do the work if he really tried. Or so we have been told over and over.

Maybe you know my kid really well. Maybe he reminds you of your own or someone else's. But maybe you didn't know that children like this are not really pain-in-the-neck kids with lousy mothers. They are the children with attention deficit hyperactivity disorder, commonly called ADHD. This syndrome, characterized by disinhibited, inattentive, impulsive, and/or hyperactive behavior, affects an estimated 3 to 7 percent of the child population. Many adults also suffer from it.

Different Names, Same Children

ADHD is not a new phenomenon. Physicians have studied children and adults with restless, inattentive, impulsive types of behavior for over one hundred years. The first patients they observed suffered from brain injury or illnesses affecting the central nervous system. As scientists looked further, they discovered similar patterns of behavior in children without any brain injury. Over the years, numerous investigators delved into the causes of such behavior in children who otherwise appeared perfectly normal.

As a result of these investigations, the disorder that we now call attention deficit hyperactivity disorder has had a series of names. As a parent you will want to know this history—but not because you need any of it to help your child; you will do what your child needs based on the types of problems he or she experiences. The reason I am providing this background information has to do with naysayers. Despite years of research and documentation, many people still hold on to the notion that ADHD is an excuse parents use to explain the poor behavior of a badly parented child! In defense of this position, skeptics cite the various names by which ADHD has been known as proof that the disorder does not exist. Knowledge is power.

Until the 1960s, the syndrome had been known as minimal brain damage. Since no brain damage could be found, the name was changed to minimal brain dysfunction, or MBD. Around 1970, excessive motor activity, the most visible symptom, gained a lot of interest. The children came to be called hyperactive or hyperkinetic, as did the disorder. Since hyperactivity lessened considerably around puberty, many practitioners believed the child's problems ended then. Thus we got the myth, "He will grow out of it."

By 1980, inattention appeared to be the primary problem of most affected children, so the name became attention deficit disorder (ADD). But not all children who showed attention difficulties behaved in a hyperactive, "always on the go" fashion. So researchers divided the disorder into three subgroups: ADD with hyperactivity (ADD-H), ADD without hyperactivity (ADDnoH), and ADD-RT (residual type), meaning symptoms carried into adolescence and adulthood. People frequently described the ADDnoH children as the "spacey" or "absentminded professor" types. Often their inability to focus and sustain attention did not seem problematic until schooling demanded concentration. The ideas that a person with the disorder did not have to be hyperactive and that symptoms could persist beyond puberty proved to be a breakthrough in the understanding of the disorder, and thus in its diagnosis and treatment.

In 1988, the name changed again to reflect agreement among researchers that inattention, impulsivity, and hyperactivity were all central characteristics of the disorder. In view of this belief, the disorder came to be called attention deficit hyperactivity disorder (ADHD), and a single list of fourteen criteria began to be used to make the diagnosis. A separate category called undifferentiated attention deficit disorder was created to diagnose individuals who had attention difficulties but little problem with hyperactivity and impulsivity. At the time, many researchers and practitioners did not think this single list accurately reflected the variations which exist within the disorder called ADHD. Thus the American Psychiatric Association (APA), which has the responsibility of creating diagnostic guidelines for the entire mental health field, responded to the concerns by establishing a workgroup to make recommendations about what ADHD should be called and by what criteria it should be diagnosed.

Based on the workgroup's findings, in 1994 when the APA published the fourth edition of the *Diagnostic and Statistical Manual of Mental Disorders* (*DSM-IV*), the following changes regarding ADHD were made. Although the name stayed the same, attention deficit hyperactivity disorder, the disorder was divided into three subgroups: ADHD predominantly inattentive type; ADHD predominantly hyperactive-impulsive type; and ADHD combined type.

I find it helpful to think about the name changes like a kaleidoscope. As scientists advance their knowledge and understanding of the disorder, they refine the name and the diagnostic criteria just as you or I turn the kaleidoscope to sharpen the image. Certainly, as explained by noted ADD researcher Keith Conners, the disorder has not changed. The children studied forty years ago had the same symptoms the children studied today have. Today, however, much more is known about ADHD.

When it comes to ADHD, what you see is what you get. Generally, you see someone who doesn't sustain attention unless the activity is highly interesting, who doesn't like to wait, who may act first and think later—if at all—and who may be fidgety, restless, or downright "hyper." The person may be quite disorganized and require extraordinary effort to get through a day without missing some vital information or breaking a rule. Someone with ADHD may also appear to have a skewed sense of time. There always seems to be plenty of time until it's too late. So much does not get done in a timely manner. And too much happens when the person is supposed to be doing something else.

ADHD and Self-Control Theory

My description leads me to discuss a new theory about ADHD put forth by Russell Barkley, one of the world's leading experts. Even though his ideas are still in the theoretical stage, for me they answer many questions and clear up confusions I've had for a number of years. I think of my son as the "typical" child with ADHD, yet I don't think of him as inattentive or not goal-directed. When he's running a race, he never loses focus on the finish line and beating his personal best time. When he's watching a hockey game, nothing gets by him, and nothing can unglue him from the action on the ice.

Boy, does he freeze when he has to read a novel! And getting his schoolwork in on time—well, what can I say. You know. Maybe your child, spouse, or you have poor self-control. That's the idea that Dr. Barkley raises in his new work: ADHD is primarily a problem with self-control, not attention. Following is a brief explanation of his theory. Take what you can use and what makes sense. Also, keep in mind that any new theory needs to be studied, validated, and found reliable. As a scientist, Dr. Barkley knows that his ideas must undergo the scrutiny of careful tests, refinements, redefinition, and change. As he said, "It's certainly going to be a temporary theory, because like all theories it's simply an effort to build a ship so someone else can build a better ship." In the meantime, this ship floats.

This new model is discussed in detail in his new book, *ADHD and the Nature of Self-Control* (Guilford Publications, 1997). The information I provide comes from my reading of that book and a personal interview with Dr. Barkley regarding his work. I have mixed both our languages to create a unified, explanatory piece. To make sure we all are working within the same frame of reference, I'm beginning with a discussion of "will," then move on to Dr. Barkley's thoughts about his self-control theory.

The dictionary defines "self-control" as the control of one's emotions, actions, and desires by one's own will. Here's where a problem begins. Will. What is it? We think of it as something we have to varying degrees. We're supposed to use it when needed. But just where does "will" come from? Could our biology actually be in charge of it? As the field of neuropsychology advances, we may find that will and self-control have a biological basis and are not a morality issue.

For the present I will offer Dr. Barkley's definition of self-control: in brief, having the ability to behave in a way that is in our long-term best interests. Sounds easy enough! Unless you happen to have biologically based deficits in the areas that allow for the altering of behavior in exchange for the long-term good—in other words, unless a primary problem of disinhibition is present.

People with ADHD typically do not do well at delaying responses or gratification or at planning for the future. They opt for the moment, Dr. Barkley observes. When making decisions about what to do or not do, we have to allow the future to get a foothold in our decision-making by delaying responses to allow the past to influence the present and the decision about to be made—which then becomes our future. People with ADHD have a biologically based disruption that keeps them on fast-forward. They have difficulty waiting, postponing, thinking first.

That interval between thinking first and taking action, as Dr. Barkley sees it, is a crucial part of how processes in the human brain guide our behavior. It allows us to think about what's going to happen if we do what we do.

Dr. Barkley refers to the processes that go on between doing and not doing as "private actions." It is engaging in these actions that makes for self-control. Before I discuss the four processes he explains, take a minute and think: What is your mind doing? Are you seeing images? Talking to yourself? Feeling anxious? Doing all three and wondering why you are reading this book? It occurs to me that we have these incredibly private lives going on inside our minds at all times. Mindfulness, or the fine art of meditation, teaches us to pay attention to what is going on when we are "doing." Those of us lucky enough to have strong inhibition (in brief, the ability to be able to "think before we act") might actually be able to identify what's happening behind the scenes.

Dr. Barkley believes that people with ADHD are prevented from participating in their private lives, which results in poor self-control. Let's look at each of these private components in detail.

Sensory Imaging

Very young children start "seeing the future" by using sensory images, particularly visual imagery. Of course, this process continues throughout life, but it takes hold at this important developmental stage, which begins between the ages of three and six months and ends between ages two and four.

Basically, Dr. Barkley maintains, "visual imaging, the sensory imaging, is using the mind's eye to use hindsight, which is looking back over what has happened to us, to create forethought, which is looking ahead to see what might happen next." Vision and hearing happen to be the two most important senses for humans. We can "see" to ourselves and "hear" to ourselves. That translates to non-verbal working memory. Nonverbal working memory allows us to keep ideas in mind, to relate past events to what might happen before making future actions.

Internalized language

Within a few years, between ages three and five, we begin to develop the second part of the private life of self-control: internalized language. In case no one has told you, you do talk to yourself, and it's a good thing! Dr. Barkley describes this element as the ability to have a private conversation with yourself in which you think, reflect, describe, and then tell yourself what to do.

We can eavesdrop on young children's private talks, because they have them out loud. With age, usually between nine and twelve, we acquire the abilty to talk to ourselves privately. However, when ADHD is present, very often such talking remains out loud. That's one reason why people with ADHD are known to "say the wrong thing." Actually, often they are saying out loud what another person is saying to him or herself. At other times, though, people with ADHD do not talk to themselves at all, out loud or silently. Consequently, they miss the important solutions to problems and guides to action that come from mentally talking through a situation. By the way, Dr. Barkley notes that adults faced with a difficult problem quite often resort to talking out loud to themselves, which we sometimes call muttering. He estimates that the internalization-of-language process takes about eight years before it becomes fully private.

Internalization of Emotion

In psychology, emotions are defined as temporary motivational states. They seem to be two-dimensional: one dimension is level of arousal; the other, reward and punishment. People with ADHD, Dr. Barkley notes, do not have altered emotional states; theirs are the same as anyone else's. Instead they appear to have trouble keeping those states private and moderating them. Internalizing of emotion seems to happen between the ages of eight and eleven. "This component is probably the least understood of the four parts of self-control," Dr. Barkley says.

Apparently, once emotions are internalized we continue to feel them, and can even create some of the emotional states we may have, but do not automatically display our emotions publicly. We may choose to work on them privately to alter them. For example, Dr. Barkley talked about anger.

Something might anger us, but we can work on our anger privately to moderate it. Perhaps we talk to ourselves or see things from a different perspective. Maybe we chant or count to ten or visualize something desirable. All these techniques alter emotions, so that someone on the outside may never know we were angry at all. Because people with ADHD do not postpone action and tend to react quickly, they may "let it all hang out" before they have had a chance to launder their feelings. Thus the outside world sees the dirty laundry. In the classroom, the child who doesn't moderate his or her anger may wind up in the principal's office. In the workplace, an adult may be shown the door.

Simulation

The last component of self-control is what Dr. Barkley calls simulation. "It's the ability to play with the information in your mind," he says. We can take information apart, recombine what we have with new ideas, thoughts, and words, and come up with good problem-solving. We allow simulation to generate different scenarios, then select those that seem to be in our best interests for the future. The ability to simulate, which usually begins to develop between the ages of nine and fourteen, is an ability to be flexible, fluid, and creative—basically, a good problem-solver.

Putting the Four Together

"Put all the above together and you've got a very powerful engine for self-control," Dr. Barkley believes. Behavioral scientists define self-control quite differently than the dictionary does. As explained by Dr. Barkley, it is "what you do to yourself to change your behavior to make a future consequence increase or decrease, which in turn alters the future."

The ultimate purpose of the four functions described above is to guide and control behavior. Now, we need to add one more factor to this equation—age. As we mature, we become increasingly governed by mentally represented information and much less by immediate surroundings, Dr. Barkley explains. People with ADHD appear to be immature because their biological problem with being able to wait and postpone today for a better tomorrow is childlike. However, it is not their fault or a matter of choice. Instead, being unable to use these four executive functions efficiently is like having an absentee boss who sometimes phones in to direct activity. It's the old problem of "Who's watching the store?"

Time

People often describe those with ADHD as "missing the boat." Their sense of time does seem to be impaired, particularly to those of us who measure time in terms of appointments kept and deadlines met—or missed. However, people with ADHD do not literally have a problem with time, which Dr. Barkley defines as a sequence of moments, or "just one damn thing after another." Instead, Dr. Barkley notes, their problem is with looking backward at things in the past, along with their consequences, and using these as the basis for predictions. People without ADHD can have a poor sense of time, too, if they have an impairment in any one of the executive functions described above. What distinguishes those with ADHD is the key feature of their impairment—disinhibition, which means not adequately regulating behavior by rules or consequences, and therefore not being able to wait before acting.

Treatment Implications

As discussed in chapter 6, stimulant medications have been shown to be quite effective for the management of ADHD. According to

Dr. Barkley, they do not directly improve our behind-the-scenes executive acts. They do, however, improve inhibition. By helping someone to wait before doing, "you not only get improvement in inhibition. You get improvement in executive control and therefore self-control," he says.

When seeing the type of behaviors associated with ADHD, people tend to draw the obvious conclusion: that training the person with ADHD to use the elements of self-control will solve the problem. Unfortunately, *this conclusion is built on the wrong premise.* Dr. Barkley has been a strong voice in telling people that "ADHD is not a problem of knowing what to do. It is a problem of doing what you know. You can't do what you know," he says, "if at the point of performance, you don't stop and let your past—your knowledge, learning, and wisdom—come forward to guide and control your actions."

So what can be done? Dr. Barkley notes that his theory is the first theory of ADHD that has treatment implications. In general, the absence of using internal processes to guide external behavior suggests that we should alter the world around people with ADHD by making it more external. In short, if you can't get the unwritten information, then put the handwriting on the wall. In Dr. Barkley's words, "Make external anything you need to control you." That includes lists, timers, coaches, posted rules, reward systems—anything that will make physical the mental part of the information required to have self-control.

I'm hoping to broaden your thinking by giving you some information about Dr. Barkley's new theory. In the meantime, you should be knowledgeable about the current diagnostic criteria in use.

DSM-IV Diagnostic Guidelines

ADHD is not a disease, but rather a medical syndrome. As with all medical syndromes, the diagnostician must decide if a given constellation of symptoms characteristic of a specific disorder is present in an individual before making a diagnosis. To complicate matters, an individual with a medical syndrome will not necessarily show all the characteristics associated with the syndrome. Thus determining if an individual has ADHD is not a cut-and-dried matter.

The *DSM* is used by medical and mental health professionals to identify child, adolescent, and adult psychiatric, learning, and emotional disorders. Following are the *DSM-IV* criteria.

Attention Deficit and Disruptive Behavior Disorders*

■ Attention Deficit Hyperactivity Disorder

A. Either (1) or (2):

   (1)   six (or more) of the following symptoms of **inattention** have persisted for at least six months to a degree that is maladaptive and inconsistent with developmental level:

Inattention
  (a) often fails to give close attention to details or makes careless mistakes in schoolwork, work, or other activities
  (b) often has difficulty sustaining attention in tasks or play activities
  (c) often does not seem to listen when spoken to directly
  (d) often does not follow through on instructions and fails to finish schoolwork, chores, or duties in the workplace (not due to oppositional behavior or failure to understand instructions)
  (e) often has difficulty organizing tasks and activities
  (f) often avoids, dislikes, or is reluctant to engage in tasks that require sustained mental effort (such as schoolwork or homework)
  (g) often loses things necessary for tasks or activities (for example, toys, school assignments, pencils, books, or tools)
  (h) is often easily distracted by extraneous stimuli
  (i) is often forgetful in daily activities

   (2)   six (or more) of the following symptoms of **hyperactivity-impulsivity** have persisted for at least six months to a degree that is maladaptive and inconsistent with developmental level:

Hyperactivity
  (a) often fidgets with hands or feet or squirms in seat
  (b) often leaves seat in classroom or in other situations in which remaining seated is expected

---

Reprinted with permission from the DSM-IV. Copyright ©1994. American Psychiatric Association.

(c) often runs about or climbs excessively in situations in which it is inappropriate (in adolescents or adults, may be limited to subjective feelings of restlessness)
(d) often has difficulty playing or engaging in leisure activities quietly
(e) is often "on the go" or often acts as if "driven by a motor"
(f) often talks excessively

Impulsivity
(g) often blurts out answers before questions have been completed
(h) often has difficulty awaiting turn
(i) often interrupts or intrudes on others (for example, butts into conversations or games)
B. Some hyperactive-impulsive or inattentive symptoms that caused impairment were present before age seven years.
C. Some impairment from the symptoms is present in two or more settings (for example, at school [or work] and at home).
D. There must be clear evidence of clinically significant impairment in social, academic, or occupational functioning.
E. The symptoms do not occur exclusively during the course of a Pervasive Developmental disorder, Schizophrenia, or other Psychotic Disorder and are not better accounted for by another mental disorder (for example, Mood Disorder, Anxiety Disorder, Dissociative Disorder, or a Personality Disorder).

Code *based on type:*

314.01 Attention Deficit Hyperactivity Disorder, Combined Type: if both Criteria A1 and A2 are met for the past six months

314.00 Attention Deficit Hyperactivity Disorder, Predominantly Inattentive Type: if Criterion A1 is met but Criterion A2 is not met for the past six months

314.01 Attention Deficit Hyperactivity Disorder, Predominantly Hyperactive-Impulsive Type: if Criterion A2 is met but Criterion A1 is not met for the past six months

Coding note: For individuals (especially adolescents and adults) who currently have symptoms that no longer meet full criteria, "In Partial Remission" should be specified.

■ **314.9 Attention Deficit Hyperactivity Disorder Not Otherwise Specified**

This category is for disorders with prominent symptoms of inattention or hyperactivity-impulsivity that do not meet criteria for Attention Deficit Hyperactivity Disorder.

According to Dr. David Shaffer, chairman of the *DSM-IV* Work Group for Child and Adolescent Disorders, there was concern that the previous criteria, which emphasized childhood behaviors at play and in school, were not appropriate for adults. Consequently, the criteria were rewritten to make them less age-specific; they now include references to work and recreation.

Dr. Shaffer commented that each subtype seems to be associated with a different degree of functional impairment. The predominantly inattentive subtype appears to be the least impaired. "It is also the group that has the largest proportion of girls," he added. As might be expected, the combined subtype (that is, inattention, hyperactivity, and impulsivity) likely has the greatest degree of impairment, including a higher incidence of social rejection.

Because attention is not a skill developmentally expected of young children, this group may be more likely to be categorized as the predominantly hyperactive-impulsive subtype. As school-related demands for sustained attention increase with age, children given this initial subtype may have their diagnosis changed to combined type, reflecting their problems with inattention.

Dr. Barkley advises clinicians to be especially careful when diagnosing adolescents and adults. He notes that current criteria list six symptoms of hyperactivity. However, hyperactivity diminishes with age. So adolescents or adults who fall just one or two symptoms short of being considered the combined or hyperactive-impulsive type may be given a diagnosis of predominantly inattentive type even though their overall behavior would be better characterized with the impulsive-hyperactive or combined pattern. "What I teach my classes," Dr. Barkley explains, "is that the *DSM* is a set of guidelines which need to be taken as rules of thumb."

Causes

No one knows the exact cause or causes of ADHD. We do know that it does not come from diet, allergy, or bad parents. Strong scientific evidence suggests the disorder is genetically transmitted in many cases. That does not mean, however, that ADHD can be directly linked, for example, from a father to a son, or a mother to a daughter. According to Dr. Paul Wender, "on occasion, it skips generations, and it blurs so that if you look at siblings in a family, they come in all shapes and colors. One sibling may have ADHD and be poorly coordinated. Another might have ADHD, good coordination, and possibly some other disorder." Of course, some siblings will not have ADHD.

ADHD is a neurobiologically based disorder. According to Dr. Bennett Shaywitz, the director of pediatric neurology at Yale University Medical School, most children with ADHD are believed to have the disorder because of "inherited disturbances in certain chemicals in the brain's neurotransmitter systems." Neurotransmitters are chemicals that regulate brain-cell functions; thus they help the brain regulate behavior. Studies to date point toward dopamine as the neurotransmitter involved.

The hot topic in research presently is the genetic work. Scientists expect to know which genes are involved with ADHD within three to five years. Meanwhile, they have located a "novelty-seeking" gene. As explained by Russell Barkley, this gene, which exists in roughly 12 to 30 percent of people with ADHD, is not the major gene, but it will help scientists in identifying subtypes of ADHD. The identified gene is DRD4, and it is in a class of genes called repeator genes. "We know it lines the interior membrane of dopamine nerve cells. Having this gene diminishes the sensitivity of the dopamine neuron, so the nerve cells don't fire the way they should," Dr. Barkley reports.

Facts About ADHD

What causes ADHD, or even what name it has, does not change what is known about this condition. Though it was once considered mainly a childhood disorder, we now know that ADHD continues to cause problems into adulthood in approximately two-thirds of cases. Children with ADHD come in all shapes and sizes. Some have very severe cases and have all the symptoms. Many areas of their lives are affected. Others have symptoms so minor that the condition almost goes unnoticed. Some have associated disorders as well.

Most clinicians and researchers agree that certain symptoms make up the disorder. However, an individual need not have all the symptoms to have the disorder—a point clarified in *DSM-IV* by the addition of subtypes.

We know that at different ages, different features of the disorder are more problematic. For example, impulsive behavior is a danger for a toddler, but sustained attention is not a skill required or expected at this stage. The symptoms can create problems in all areas of a person's environment or in just one area. For instance, the child with ADHD who has moderate attention difficulties may have trouble in school but not at home, where there are fewer tasks that require concentration and persistence. Further, the adolescent with ADHD may have done reasonably well in school and at home during earlier years. Perhaps problems only became evident after demands for self-responsibility increased. We know that in half the cases, children evidence signs of the disorder prior to age four. But we also know these signs often go unrecognized until the child goes to school.

ADHD exists in varying degrees of intensity in approximately 3 to 7 percent of the population. The estimate of prevalence in adolescents and adults is 4 percent. Boys tend to get diagnosed more than girls, but we now know females can also have the condition. Dr. Barkley notes that the disorder is prevalent in boys by a three-to-one ratio and that boys with ADHD tend to be more aggressive. Aside from the aggression, little difference in the manifestations of ADHD is noted between males and females.

These children come from all socioeconomic, racial, and cultural backgrounds. They are united by underachievement, which appears in the majority of cases. Outcome studies paint a picture of serious academic failure. These children's underachievement is not a function of their capability. Children with ADHD span the range of intelligence levels. However, Dr. Barkley has noted that a significant discrepancy may exist between overall IQ (ability) and effective adaptive performance (functioning to that capability) in a child with ADHD.

Wrong Conclusions

Despite all that is known about this disorder, many children who have it go undiagnosed. Instead, they are misunderstood. Some are even blamed for behaviors that are the very features of this disorder. Children with ADHD behave in a way that comes naturally to them. Thus they are at the mercy of their disorder and its symptoms. They are children *in trouble, not the cause of trouble.*

As the fellow parent of a "difficult" child, you probably know that I hurt, too, and have felt alone and scared, frustrated and angry, helpless and hopeless. Maybe you also suffered from the looks flashed by people who did not know your kid couldn't help it. Maybe you didn't know this either. Maybe you cried and hollered when you sent your child to school hopeful that he would succeed, and he returned home angry. Maybe you were scared when you realized the system understood him less than you did. And maybe you saw what little self-esteem your child had begin to disappear.

Presently there is no cure for ADHD. But our children and families do not have to be stressed to a breaking point. Some of the qualities associated with ADHD can be assets for the child and adult who learn how to channel them. A positive outcome is best accomplished through diagnosis and proper management of the symptoms of this disorder.

Treatment Guidelines

ADHD is a condition more managed than treated. The recommended approach is multidimensional. It begins with education of the parent, child, and child's teachers, parent training in behavior-management techniques, an appropriate educational program for the child designed to address the ADHD-related difficulties, and medication when indicated. Family and/or individual psychotherapy to address self-esteem and peer-relationship problems may be suggested at times.

About This Book

I am one of the lucky mothers. I now understand why my son behaves the way he does. I know what to expect from him and how to manage his ADHD. I know when and where to go for help. I know now that the disturbing behaviors that appeared at the various stages of his development were not of his doing or my fault. I also know now that, above all else, my child needs to feel competent. If you are the parent of a child with ADHD, I want you to know this too.

This book is intended to serve as your guide. The following chapters present a picture of what attention deficit hyperactivity disorder is and what to do about it. The information is up to date, practical, and responsible. Chapters are organized developmentally from infancy through adulthood. Each chapter describes the patterns and characteristics of ADHD at a specific stage of child development and, where possible, outlines the recommended management approaches.

Chapters are divided into two sections. At the beginning of the first section, signs and symptoms of the disorder are discussed and illustrated using anecdotes from my family's personal experience. The second section is the "what you can do about what you see" section. For this edition, I have reformatted the material so that you can find information for your particular area of concern or need under a heading or subheading. I do recommend reading the entire book from beginning to end once, as it will give you a great overview of the heart, soul, and substance of the disorder. Then you can use the clinical sections as a ready reference for particular problems that appear or reappear.

Because no two children with ADHD are alike, and because there are various subtypes of ADHD, in the second section of each chapter I have also included the experiences of other children affected by ADHD and of their mothers, fathers, and siblings. In order to observe their right to privacy, these other people have been given pseudonyms.

That this disorder appears differently from child to child is a point to be emphasized. As you read, try to identify with patterns of the disorder and how they may pertain to your situation. Try not to compare your situation to those experienced by others, for, as we know, many factors contribute to a child's development whether or not he or she has a disorder. No two children are the same.

Section two of each chapter also provides a clinical point of view based on interviews I had with practitioners nationally and internationally recognized for their work with this disorder. For the sake of readability, their credentials are described in the acknowledgments rather than throughout the text. These sections also contain information from professionals in private practice. The effects ADHD has on those who interact with the child are discussed throughout. Each chapter ends with a summary highlighting its main points.

I offer this book with the hope that it will broaden the general knowledge of ADHD. Its information is well documented and its treatment recommendations proven. You may recognize your child or someone else's within these pages. If so, you are on the road to getting help. But again, I caution against self-diagnosis and self-treatment. Just as you would seek the expertise of an eye doctor for a problem with your vision, find a practitioner who is reputed to be knowledgeable about attention deficit hyperactivity disorder.

Facts About ADHD

- Estimated to affect 3 to 7 percent of childhood population in varying degrees of severity
- More prevalent in males, but also occurs in females
- Affects individuals of all socioeconomic, racial, and ethnic backgrounds and intelligence levels
- Often continues through adolescence and adulthood
- Is neurobiologically based
- Characterized by symptoms of inattention and/or impulsivity and hyperactivity
- Possibly an overall problem with self-control, or disinhibiting behavior
- Is comprised of three subtypes:
  — inattentive type
  — hyperactive-impulsive type
  — combined type (inattentive and hyperactive-impulsive)
- Diagnosed through criteria set forth by the American Psychiatric Association *Diagnostic and Statistical Manual*
- Symptoms must be maladaptive, developmentally inappropriate, and present in two or more situations
- Self-diagnosis and self-treatment are not advised
- Often results in underachievement in school and career
- Usually causes very low self-esteem
- Managed through multiple treatment approaches including:
  — parent education and training in behavior-management techniques
  — appropriate educational program
  — medication, when indicated
  — individual or family psychotherapy

CHAPTER TWO

The Infant

I had always believed that when it came to the birth process, mother and child worked together. But David, my firstborn, is and always has been his own person. His birth came on his terms in the form of a swift, hard kick that ruptured the amniotic sac and left me in a puddle of water alone and wondering at 1:00 A.M. if this was the long-awaited moment. The doctor's examination just hours before revealed that I was nowhere near ready for birth. Yet at 2:00 A.M., without having so much as one single contraction, I was admitted to labor and delivery. My egg had decided to hatch.

Nineteen hours later, my son was born on his due date, September 25, 1979, the United Nations Year of the Child—a good omen for a superstitious mother like his. David was 7 pounds 7 ounces, 19½ inches, and beautiful. There was a fetal monitor tangled in his long, black hair, but his voyage into the world of the newborn didn't leave a mark on his body. His face was perfectly rounded, and though he was slightly blue at birth, his color improved within minutes.

As I lay on the delivery table watching the nurses wrap him in the garments of the outer world, I was struck with a sense of astonishment. Here was this little tiny body, having just emerged into our world after what had turned out to be a very long day, alert, moving his limbs, full of life, while I, his mother, could barely move a muscle. I've always tried to make sense of what seems contradictory, so I rationalized that this was as it should be. After all, I had done the work.

Six hours later, when the nurses brought the babies to the room for feeding, I had my first taste of motherhood. No more dress rehearsal. Though physically I felt like a dishrag, my sense of excitement became so great that it didn't take more than a second before I was fully awake and holding my baby, who was sound asleep. He looked and smelled like all babies do, so innocent and pure, though to me he was not like any other baby. I felt a sense of pride and joy and bewilderment that within so short a period of time I could go from taking care of my own needs to suddenly having the responsibility of someone else's. For a brief second, I acknowledged that I felt unsure about the kind of job I would do. Then I quickly dismissed this thought and went back to feeling elated.

From the very beginning, David seemed to have a profound effect on everyone. Visitors to the hospital would go to the nursery first and then report to me. "Oh, Mary," my sister said, "he's a beautiful baby, and what an active soul!"

My sister-in-law exclaimed, "He's really strong. The little guy bucked himself to the top of the bassinet. He lifted his head and looked straight at me! I can't believe how he looks all over the place. The other babies just seem to sleep."

Well, being a proud mother, what could I think? That he performed feats of strength could only mean that he was naturally a super athlete. Being highly stimulated by his environment must mean that he was exceptionally bright. Both his father and I felt this child was a gift we would have to manage very carefully.

With this attitude, it is not surprising that I grew furious at the events of his second day of life. At 4:00 P.M., the nursery staff buzzed my room to inform me that David had fussed and gotten himself into such an out-of-control state, they could not comfort him after two hours of trying. "So, Mrs. Fowler, would you please come get your baby?" What was wrong with those baby nurses that it took them two hours to realize that this newborn needed his mother?

I brought David to my room, gave him my undivided attention, fed him, and changed him, and off to sleep he went. Simple. Until day three. Then I had trouble quieting my child. He screamed so uncontrollably I thought certainly something must be terribly wrong. Rocking made him squirm so hard, I feared dropping him. I put him in the bassinet and held a water bottle to his lips. Gradually he went to sleep. I couldn't understand why my roommate could hold her baby all day long while I would have to put mine down after ten minutes. A seemingly logical answer came to mind. Her baby was a girl and girls cuddle; mine was a boy and boys do not.

By the end of day three, I realized I was off to a bad start with parenting. I became very high-strung. To make matters worse, some minor complications restricted my activity, and David developed jaundice, which is quite common in newborns, but nonetheless upsetting. Then he added a new twist to his repertoire—choking! Every time I tried to feed him, be it breast or bottle, he gagged. Even my roommate, the picture of serenity, suggested I call the nurse.

Congestion. That was all. "Nothing for you to worry about," said the nurse as she stuck a long rubber tube down his throat and sucked through the other end. After removing the worst of the mucus, she gave me the baby, and for the first time in two and a half days he once again slept peacefully in my arms. Congestion. No wonder this little fellow had been so disagreeable. I became calm.

That was a big mistake! The pressure I felt in the hospital could not compare to the stress in store when I had the full responsibility for the baby at home. His dad expected me to know what I was doing. I expected him to know what he was doing. God only knows what the infant expected. Whatever he figured on, I did not meet his needs. The baby cried every twenty minutes from eight at night to six in the morning. His high-pitched voice pierced my ears and ran through my body, jangling every nerve ending. No sooner would I fall asleep than "screech" and up I would get. First I tried feeding, then changing, then rocking, then I let him cry himself to sleep. After three weeks I was beating my pillows, screaming into them, feeling furious that I had ever conceived this kid, ashamed that I could feel this way about my son.

I tried to tell his dad that I felt strung out. He acted as though David's behavior was normal, that all babies keep their mothers awake round the clock. Since he had a son by a previous marriage, I figured he knew what he was talking about. Yet I desperately wanted reassurance that I was not just one of those women reputed to be "not cut out for motherhood," so I turned to friends and family for guidance and backing.

Some, like my sister-in-law, were sympathetic and assured me that eventually baby David would establish a routine. My mother seemed very empathetic, but above all she was a mother and thus needed to share the wisdom of the ages, which is "That's what babies are like." Since she had five, she could recall numerous incidents to verify her point. And she happily reminded me that at least my husband helped with the baby when he wasn't away on his weekly business trips.

That certainly was true during the daylight hours. But David Sr. and I agreed he needed sleep to be alert for his very demanding job. So during the night, our son fell entirely into my care. After all, I could grab a nap with the baby during the day. That is, if the baby napped, which he did not. Deep inside I felt abandoned.

Fortunately, we lived near many relatives who pitched in. My first good night's sleep came when my sister-in-law spent the night to care for the baby, as I was ill and David Sr. was away on an overnight business trip. The next morning I felt reborn and forever grateful for that night. My sister-in-law was exhausted but seemed to have developed a new respect for me. This was no easy kid.

Yet I could not help feeling that somehow David was special, different from other children. He just seemed so alert, so active, so advanced. When I reported that he rolled over at two weeks another sister-in-law, the mother of three, told me in no uncertain terms, "It's not possible, Mary. Babies can't do that." When I insisted that I put him facedown and found him faceup, she quoted from Dr. Spock and concluded that this was no doubt a freak incident that would not happen again. I began to question myself. I knew I saw what I saw, but it was not clear how David had performed this feat. I surmised that through crying and screaming, David rolled over by accident.

I called the pediatrician, not so much to say that he had rolled over, but to ask if maybe the baby had colic. Could that explain why he screamed so much? The doctor said it was possible but improbable, since the baby would scream round the clock if he were colicky. He then suggested that maybe David was one of those hungry babies "who need solid food in addition to breast milk." At four weeks he had solids. And he loved them. Though I had made the commitment to breast-feeding, I did not in the least mind the compromise. At this point I would have killed for a good night's sleep.

The solid food seemed to do the trick, and once again I thought we were bound for smooth sailing. David only woke periodically, and though he still did not sleep much during the day, I at least had more energy to deal with the constant attention he demanded. Despite his wealth of toys, little seemed to keep him interested very long. He hated the playpen and the crib. By two months, he perched himself on his hands and knees and rolled across the floor from one place to another. Our son's every move thrilled us. Friends and relatives marveled at his stamina and persistence. My sister Margaret affectionately nicknamed him "wiggle worm."

It has always been my nature to make light of situations when I am scared. So when David came down with bronchitis at two and a half months and was placed on a bronchodilator medicine, I assured myself that this was perfectly normal. But a few hours later David had a reaction to the medicine. He behaved like Superboy until he lost all control. His body flailed so wildly that I could not restrain him. The pediatrician told me to keep him safe and ride it out. A few hours later he crashed into a sound sleep. I spent the night on the floor next to his crib, terrified. From then on it didn't take much for me to call the doctor, who within the first ten months of David's life saw him twenty-six times. Some of those visits were for normal checkups. Most were for upper-respiratory and ear infections.

Did he ever have ear infections! But he never simply cried or screamed in pain. Instead he would "dolphinize," a term I coined to describe his high-pitched wail. Friends who telephoned hung up because it drove them crazy. David's dolphinizing was like a rising barometer. As the shrill increased, he became more difficult to manage. When I tried to hold and quiet him, the sound would grow louder. Distracting him worked only momentarily. After hours of hearing him cry, my ears would start to hurt. The more I tried to soothe my son, the more disturbed he became and the more frustrated I felt until eventually I was totally distraught, screaming at him to stop. When I reached the point where I wanted to jump out a window (again), I knew it was time to call the pediatrician (again).

"Why don't you bring him in, Mrs. Fowler," he would say. Then, after he examined him, "Mrs. Fowler, his ears are infected. Look at this." I peered in the scope and saw a blister the size of a pea. No wonder the poor child screamed. "What are we going to do with this kid, Mrs. Fowler?"

I simply did not know what I was going to do with this boy. Only a few things seemed to work. Humor became a coping tool I used. For the first six months of David's life, I would joke with the pediatrician and ask if he knew where to find a band of roving gypsies who might want to add a beautiful blue-eyed boy to their troop. Once I suggested that what I really needed wasn't a pediatrician but an exorcist who could drive out the evil demons that made David behave horrendously instead of crying like normal babies when he was ill. Though the doctor understood my attitude and laughed along with me, others found me disrespectful. I could not imagine why. After all, not much in our house smacked of calico and apple pie.

By the time David turned six months, our house had become a crazy place. I remember one night when a business associate of my husband's stopped by unexpectedly. We still functioned under the misconception that infants do not really interfere with a routine, so we invited this traveling salesman for some good company and a home-cooked meal. The child seemed to have radar. Though he was usually dead to the world from 6:00 to 10:00 P.M., on this particular night he awoke at 8:00, dolphinizing. Realizing that I would be pre-occupied, Dad offered to barbecue the chicken.

Hank, our guest, watched in amazement as little David crawled up my leg, down my arm, over my head, across the back of the chair, and up his leg. Though a bit astonished at the energy level of this little baby, Hank found a ready explanation: "He's just like his dad, isn't he!" We all laughed, but it wasn't a belly laugh. It was more like the laugh that signals you're not sure what behavior is appropriate.

The chicken came in from the grill black. No one had to worry about the risk of infection from this bird. We sat down to dinner with little screaming David lying on his stomach across my knees, my elbow pinning him while I tried to sway him into sleep. I decided not to mention the spider dangling from a long strand directly over Hank's rice. Fortunately, the insect retreated from the grating sound made by our guest's knife as he sawed through his chicken. Our companion thanked us profusely for a very nice evening but declined in no uncertain terms our invitation to stay the night. Hank was the first in a long line of guests who didn't overstay their welcome.

Gradually, my husband and I became separated from our friends with grown kids and our friends with no kids who preferred the more civilized pleasures. Our home was quite simply chaotic and not at all soothing to the nerves. Only on rare occasions did we function as a team. Since my husband traveled on business at least three full days each week, I saw his evenings at home as an oppor-tunity to break away from what was fast becoming a prison. When I returned to find that the baby had given his dad a hard time, instead of offering sympathy, I seized the opportunity to complain.

David Sr. would acknowledge that managing the baby could be difficult, but not that it was any reason for me to lose my temper. That statement sent me into orbit, which only proved his point. I knew I had to do something to get myself on an even keel.

I soon developed a group of friends, all of whom were young mothers, figuring that maybe if I had a social life during the daytime I would feel more satisfied and might even speak in sentences again. Most afternoons we would gather at my house, because David was the only baby who would not nap if the daily routine changed in any way. Unlike my friends and relatives with grown children, who thought I was ridiculous to remove all perishables from harm's way, the other mothers liked the security my home offered. It was not just childproof. It was a veritable fortress.

But even these seasoned mothers found David's antics to be phenomenal for a six-month-old. When they observed me change him, one asked if I had developed a unique technique for diapering boys, who are prone to hose down whoever leans over them. As you know, most babies are placed on their backs while the old diaper is removed. But David had to be placed on his stomach with my elbow pinning his chest to the table. Otherwise, I was apt to have to catch him in midair—as I did more than once—when he catapulted off the table. Had it not been for the modern-science wonder of stickum diaper tabs, I would have been unable to change him. While the other women thought my solution clever, some relatives thought I bent over backward for this kid. "You should make him stay still," I heard them say more than once. It seemed to me they thought that I took some perverse pleasure in complicating matters, that I liked the sensationalism and encouraged David's behavior.

After spending a lot of hours with me, the gals began to tell me how exhausted they became just watching me keep up with my daredevil who knew no fear. At seven months he stood and climbed, and soon the floor no longer sufficed as his playpen. He found the view from on top of the tables to be far more inviting. The stairs gave him absolute delight. When we gathered at the kitchen table, he discovered he could join the party if he climbed up the rungs of the ladder-back chairs.

This stunt proved relatively harmless until the time I didn't know where he had gone. Seeing my baby sprawled on the floor with a chair on top of him while he screamed at the top of his lungs scared me to death. I thought for sure he had been crushed. The more I tried to comfort him, the louder he hollered. I lost patience and finally out of sheer frustration plopped him into the playpen, where he soon found a suitable distraction and stopped crying. My friends stood by with looks of horror on their faces. I felt like a total failure.

I believed that a mother's gentle touch was the best curative, but my touch only made David scream louder.

On days such as these, when Dad came home from a hard day's work or a week on the road, I would recite a litany of antics David had pulled during his absence. Proud Papa loved having a rough-and-tumble boy and never thought his behavior abnormal. Instead, he thought my response to our son was overstated. He said I lacked patience. That attitude stung! My emotions became totally confused. I realized I had trouble coping with my son. Still I loved him. I simply did not know what I was supposed to do to please him.

With David the rewards were few. As long as I watched from afar or provided a myriad of stimuli to keep him constantly occupied, peace reigned. But the minute I tried to have a peaceful moment with my baby, there was no rest. I eventually learned that holding David meant bouncing him on my knee or throwing him in the air. Though he still breast-fed, he never concentrated on suckling. His eyes flitted all over the room while his hands tangled my hair or tore at the hoop in my ear. With the least little distraction he interrupted his feeding entirely. I couldn't understand why this baby was unreachable. Again I concluded that boys will be boys, and mine seemed so alert he must be destined for great things.

After eight months, a pattern began to emerge in David's behavior. While he was always very active and inquisitive, sometimes his behavior crossed the line from being overly stimulated to frenetic, which reminded me of our cat, O.B. O'Brien. One day, when O.B. was barely ten weeks old, we left him outside while we went off to shop. Upon our return, we found O.B. wildly racing in circles around the yard. At first my husband and I laughed, but as O.B. persisted, we realized that he was in a pathetic way. I picked him up and discovered his eyes were swollen shut and his fur was coated with a mass of bee stingers. It seemed that poor O.B. got tangled up with a hive and had been driven crazy. Though he eventually calmed down, O.B. remained somewhat neurotic after that.

Whenever David reached that frenetic state in which nothing I could do would calm him, I began to feel that I too might start behaving like O.B. O'Brien and do something rash if I had to spend one more second with this baby, even though I loved him. This reaction supported my suspicion that I lacked the nurturing abilities that make for a good mother.

I covered these painful feelings with a veneer of bravado and entered what I call the black-humor stage of motherhood. Some people thought it funny that I nicknamed the baby Rasputin. Others found me irreverent. Naturally I spent most of my time with the gang that liked to laugh, which included my sister-in-law and her fifteen-month-old. Every day we met at the beach. This was no simple feat. First, we had to carry the boys across the hot sand and find some unsuspecting stranger or friend to watch them for a few minutes while we ran back to the car to get the diaper bag, the toy bag, the wooden corral, which easily weighed ten pounds, the blanket, the towels, the umbrella, and the cooler. Then we set up all this paraphernalia for a relaxing day of sun and surf.

My nephew Johnny, an industrious toddler, entertained himself for hours. When he fussed, he was generally hungry or ready to nap under the shade of the umbrella. Not David! He hated that corral and alternated between throwing the toys outside, dolphinizing, and taking the toys from Johnny. I jumped up and down like a yo-yo, and after an hour I'd had about all I could take. Yet getting there always turned out to be such a major production, I could not bear to leave early. Rasputin was simply going to do things my way.

David proved so disruptive, he became the center of attention by default. The women who sat with us would remark about his escapades and his activity, but they always ended by saying, "He's such a good-looking boy!" or "Look at those blue eyes," or "He's really beautiful."

My reply was "He needs to be." Some were nice enough to tell me to ignore him and enjoy myself. People not sitting with us just glared at me with that look: "Why doesn't she do something about that kid!" If only they knew.

After two weeks of his pick-me-up/put-me-down routine, David realized he could wedge his big toe into the parts of the corral that formed a V-shape and pull himself up. I dubbed him Spiderman and watched with the others in awe as he climbed to the top and then out. "There goes the neighborhood" was my comment. There went any chance of sitting peacefully.

David quickly discovered the ocean. Since he hated the feel of the sand on his knees, he improvised by walking on hands and feet, and like a little crab headed straight for the sea. I expected that the pounding surf and cold water smacking him in the face would dissuade him, but this lemming kept to his march. So I learned to tie a long rope around his middle.

At ten and a half months he walked. It didn't take long for me to realize that once again we would do things his way.

That August David had yet another ear infection. The ear specialist told me that a very minor surgical procedure called a myringotomy was indicated. Panic set in. Though I knew older children who had had this procedure, this was my child the surgeon would operate on, my little fellow he would put under anesthesia. When I told his dad the news, he reacted with as much panic as I.

Unlike me, however, on the day of the operation David's father appeared totally composed. He even calmed me when the nurse told me hospital policy did not allow parents to accompany their child to surgery. The nurse suggested we put his favorite stuffed animal in the bed with him. But my baby had no favorite toy, no special animal he would fall asleep with night after night, no blanket he would cuddle for comfort. Dad handed the nurse his pacifier. I felt so helpless when on the way to the operating room young David saw me sitting in the hall and jumped to his feet, almost falling off the gurney. "Boy, he's an active fellow. I've never had one do this before," the nurse commented. His fragile and frightened look tore me apart. This was the first time I realized just how much my son and I depended on each other. While he slept off the sedation, I held him close. I felt like a mother who knew how to care for her baby.

Once again I saw David as being special. Because his first birthday was fast approaching, I no longer expected him to be a cuddly teddy bear. Junior Frolic, a nickname given by his dad, seemed more than appropriate. Weaning him from the breast was not traumatic. I knew it was time, and besides, I was pregnant again and ready to part with his infancy stage. The day before his twelve-month checkup, David ran full speed through the hall, stopping abruptly when he crashed into the bathtub. He now sported his first shiner. It was a mark of his passage into the world of the toddler.

I am given to sentimentality and thought I would mark my son's first birthday and each subsequent birthday by writing him a letter. In that letter I intended to write about all the milestones he had achieved during the year. I began, "Dear Junior Frolic, your dad gave you this name because you were so active, so full of life." But as I went on I found it increasingly difficult to report just what exactly had occurred during the year. Much that I had to say was uncomplimentary. Much that I had to say seemed unmotherly. So we gave him the usual toys: a little Big Wheel, a set of building blocks, and puzzles.

At-Risk Infants

David was not the only family member to receive puzzles that first year. His behavior frequently confused his dad and me. On the surface, most of the things he did seemed ordinary. At times all babies fuss and cry, refuse certain foods, have difficulty establishing routines. But these behaviors are not ordinary when they are consistently excessive. Though David could be charming, engaging, and interesting, "difficult" is a more accurate overall description of him then.

At this stage there was practically no way for anyone to know that David had attention deficit hyperactivity disorder. ADHD is a hidden disability. Determining whether it is present or not requires a careful analysis of behavioral patterns over time. Furthermore, difficult, demanding behavior in infancy is not even considered a marker for the disorder. Most children with ADHD do not happen to be difficult infants. Thus obtaining this diagnosis often proves to be a matter of trial and error.

It used to be that age eight was the average age of diagnosis. With increased environmental demands, these children could not meet the age-appropriate expectations for self-control and attention. By third grade, the developmental gaps widened to the extent that the child's age-inappropriate behavior could no longer be excused as a simple problem of immaturity. Thanks to greater public awareness of this hidden disability, more children with ADHD are being identified and diagnosed at around age five. That does not mean, however, that schools are doing what they need to do—but more about that in chapter 8.

Unlike the core symptoms of impulsivity and lack of stick-to-it-iveness, the symptom of excessive motor activity is visible early in life. But a "hyper" infant cannot be diagnosed as having ADHD. Hyperactivity is only one of the core symptoms that comprise the disorder. (In fact, a child can have all the other symptoms of the disorder and still have a normal activity level, that is, not be hyperactive at all. Some children with ADHD are even underactive and may appear lazy or lethargic.) As explained by Dr. Paul Wender: "Hyperactivity is a red flag. It is analogous to a fever or temperature in medicine. A fever tells you somebody is ill, but it does not indicate which illness the patient has."

Certainly David was more active than the typical baby. When I described his behavior to the pediatrician, even though the doctor acted sympathetic, I got the distinct impression he thought I was the nervous and overreactive type. I accepted that kind of response back then. I do not today. Then, having only limited information, I guessed that I was a big part of the problem.

So did most of the fifteen mothers I spoke with who had children eventually diagnosed with ADHD. Most of these mothers typically described their babies as colicky, given to frequent and persistent crying, not easily soothed. Some of these babies, but not all, had a high energy level as well. Many of these infants were poor sleepers and fussy eaters. At the very least, you would think that difficult, demanding, overactive infants could be earmarked as children who will eventually be diagnosed with ADHD. Yet research indicates that these traits in infants do not predict the disorder. Such traits, however, do identify the infants as "at risk."

Dr. Richard Reutter, a neurodevelopmental pediatrician and director of the Child Evaluation Unit at Monmouth Medical Center in New Jersey, believes some infants are difficult because they have a hard time regulating their state of being. They are the babies who, for instance, cannot calm themselves after a frenzied crying. Rather than respond to parental attempts to settle them, Dr. Reutter notes, these infants tend to continue crying until they wear themselves completely down.

Throughout the course of a day, infants pass through many different states of being. As described by Dr. Reutter, they may go from quiet and alert to quiet and sleepy, or from awake and irritable to full crying. The ideal state for a baby is quiet and alert, because that is when the baby is able to respond to and learn from stimuli in the environment. Dr. Reutter thinks at-risk babies (babies who may in later years be diagnosed with the disorder) have a hard time getting to the quiet-and-alert state. Once there, they often are not able to maintain that condition. Thus these infants are deprived of the good interactions with the environment that are a natural by-product of being in the quiet-and-alert state.

About Guilt

Like myself, the mothers of the difficult infants I interviewed thought they were bad mothers, some because they could not seem to please the baby no matter what they tried, others because they found it difficult to cope with the constant effort the baby required.

We assumed we must be doing something wrong. Most of us felt ashamed of and responsible for the negative responses provoked by the baby's difficult and demanding behavior. We believed "good mothers" would never respond to an innocent little baby with anger and frustration. Though we may have suspected that the baby could not be held accountable for his or her behavior, we felt uncertain about our role in causing the baby's distress.

Lynn White felt particularly guilty. The pregnancy that produced her daughter Susie was unplanned. The only way she could explain such an active and aggressive little nine-month-old girl was to surmise that her baby daughter acted out because she somehow sensed her mother's reluctance to have another child. As it happened, Susie had to be sent in midyear from second grade back to first before her symptoms were identified as ADHD. Yet Lynn White characterized Susie's overall behavior as problematic dating back to the first months of her life.

In addition to the guilt many mothers place upon themselves, Dr. Reutter has noted that quite often others reinforce the mothers' guilt feelings. The classic example is the irritable breast-fed baby. Dr. Reutter says mothers of such babies often get advice from the baby's grandparents, aunts, or uncles that she is not feeding the baby enough, or the baby needs food, or her milk is no good. As a result, many of these mothers switch from nursing to bottle-feeding. Similarly, mothers who are bottle-feeding may switch from one formula to another in an attempt to satisfy the baby. Dr. Reutter explained that the baby cannot be satisfied, of course, because the problem is not a food problem but rather a problem regulating state of being.

Besides feeling guilty, Dr. Reutter has observed, parents of difficult and demanding infants often feel cheated. Their expectations of what the interaction with their babies should be and what actually occurs are quite different. They tend to feel angry, frustrated, and embarrassed. Dr. Reutter notes that relatives and other people are often too quick to make derogatory remarks to the parents of difficult, demanding babies, such as "You don't punish the child enough, and that's why he acts that way" or "You punish the child too much." Sometimes we hear both comments within seconds of each other. Such comments fuel the parents' negative feelings. These negative feelings that parents, especially mothers, have about themselves and toward the child feed on each other. Unfortunately, sometimes these feelings border on or become violent. As a reminder, in my kitchen I keep a mug given to me by army personnel from Fort Sills, Oklahoma, where I gave an all-day training session to parents, teachers, and child care workers. It says, "I helped stop family violence." Children with ADHD are at risk for physical and emotional abuse.

Early Guidance

Dr. Reutter believes parents of difficult, demanding infants need some anticipatory guidance to recognize that these sorts of angry feelings are natural when a baby cries a lot and nothing they do soothes the baby. They also need support. He advises parents to acknowledge such feelings when they occur and to deal with them, for example, by calling somebody and talking about what they are experiencing. This step generally defuses the frustration so parents can handle the situation better.

Soothing the Situation

Know What to Expect

For coping with difficult and demanding infants, Dr. Reutter emphasizes the importance of parents recognizing that the problems are not the result of something they are or are not doing. He advises parents to expect babies who do not regulate their state of being easily to have trouble with transitions and changes in routine. Dr. Reutter says parents also need to recognize that, in addition to everyday transitions, "virtually anything that comes along, such as illnesses or routine immunizations, will challenge this type of baby more than others." By preparing parents for what to expect from different situations and at various times, physicians can help them avert even more difficulties. Forewarned is forearmed.

Develop Schedules

Once parents understand the whys and wherefores of their baby's behavior, Dr. Reutter says they can then work on various techniques that might help the baby, including establishing steady routines. Dr. Reutter advises parents of difficult infants to do the same things at the same times in a set manner each day and to be consistent about these routines, because these infants need that kind of order.

Avoid Overstimulation

Parents also need to avoid overstimulating the difficult baby. Dr. Reutter explains that these babies will often become overly excited by a simple, routine play activity if parents continue play interactions when the baby has gone beyond the point of being responsive to such activities. Thus parents need to learn to recognize the cues given by the baby. For instance, sometimes these babies will cry irritably or avert their gaze and withdraw from the situation to avoid the excess stimulation. If the stimulus is physical, the baby may arch or pull away. Dr. Reutter advises that parents interact with the baby when the baby is quiet and alert. But as he points out, difficult babies may only be quiet and alert for a few minutes out of each hour. Trying to push the baby beyond his or her internal limit will only result in further aggravating the situation.

A Few Tricks

The usefulness of various techniques for soothing the agitated baby, Dr. Reutter says, depends on the individual baby. Some babies respond to swaddling. Others respond to the stimulation that comes from being walked or rocked. Still other babies will only fall asleep easily when they are riding in the car. Like myself, there were nights when Claudia Kreiger resorted to drives around town to settle her baby. This technique must be somewhat common: Dr. Reutter told me that today there is a device you can attach to the crib that provides the sensation of a car traveling at 55 mph.

Self-care

Parents of difficult infants also need to take care of themselves. Dr. Reutter advises they get some type of a respite. He suggests that if one parent has been doing most of the caretaking, the other parent should assume a greater share. In cases where both parents are stressed, they can leave the baby with a relative or a friend for short periods of time while they get a break away from home.

Professional Input

Not all difficult infants will continue to have problems as they grow older. However, parents of hard-to-manage infants need support during these months whether the baby's difficulties are a temporary stage or not. Anyone who experiences parenting difficulty, regardless of the cause, should take the initiative and ask a health care professional for help. But I offer a few words of caution. Not every doctor can give what is needed. As many of us know quite well, some doctors too readily dismiss parental concerns, particularly when they are raised during routine visits. *Very difficult behavior is not a normal phenomenon of infancy.* Dr. Reutter affirms that such responses do little to help the parents, who really need guidance and instruction. Support will come from a doctor who, as Dr. Reutter outlines, treats your concerns seriously, offers information about why a baby might behave in a certain way, and has specific recommendations to help ease the distress.

Dr. Reutter advises parents who have difficult, demanding infants to set aside a special appointment to speak with their pediatrician specifically about their concerns. Once parents have made a special effort, if the doctor is unresponsive, Dr. Reutter suggests they look for someone or some place that deals with infants who have special problems. For more about finding professional help, see chapter 3.

Forget Blame

Everyone needs to realize that neither "bad parents" nor "good parents" cause ADHD. Dr. Wender says that studies he conducted on adopted children "show fairly convincingly that there is a genetic transmission." Additional studies, along with those done on twins, support Dr. Wender's conclusion.

The child's environment does not cause the disorder either, but it can have an effect on a condition that is present. Research indicates that ADHD symptoms intensify in situations that do not respond to the condition. For instance, practically every mother I interviewed said her child did well in school under the guidance of a sympathetic, understanding teacher. Conversely, with a stern, rigid teacher the child experienced a lot of misery.

Similarly, conditions at home play a part. Dr. Wender explains that while parents do not cause ADHD, they may aggravate the child's symptoms. "Kids with ADHD need a parent who is consistent, sympathetic, even-tempered, and unflappable," he says. Instead, he notes, the parents of a child with ADHD often have any number of problems themselves, such as depression or even ADHD. These parental problems often restrict the parent's ability to cope in a calm, consistent manner. Of course, living with ADHD affects family members, and it can rattle the most easygoing people.

Dr. Wender explains that because the child has ADHD, he or she may be overreactive even to ordinary family problems. We who live with this condition have firsthand knowledge. Just as the child over-reacts to ordinary family difficulties, the family's troubles become intensified by this child's behavior, which often dominates all daily interactions. The stresses the disorder creates leave little time or energy to deal with ordinary pressures, let alone complications such as financial problems or family illness. Families gradually become enmeshed in a dysfunctional pattern, which begins so subtly that family members grow accustomed to functioning in a disordered environment. What we don't often realize is that the abnormal takes on the appearance of normal. A vicious cycle results because the child with ADHD feeds on family troubles, and family troubles feed on the child's behavior.

We cannot blame the child for his or her disorder. Nor can we blame the parents for the difficulty they have coping with the situational demands. Until researchers solve the genetic puzzle, we need to know how to cope with the effects of this disorder. One such way is to maintain a sense of humor. And so I offer you Dr. Paul Wender's aside about the lesson he has learned from genetic studies to date.

Said Dr. Wender in jest, "You should breed with exquisite care, then marry whomever you choose." Since this notion is probably too revolutionary for most people, early diagnosis and treatment might be a suitable alternative. The sooner the child is diagnosed and the family is in treatment, the better the opportunity for families to break that vicious cycle.

Summary

- Average age of diagnosis between six and eight years
- ADHD is not predicted by "difficult" infant behavior
- Difficult infant behavior identifies at-risk infants
- At-risk infant behavior:
    - is evidenced by problems regulating state; for example, going from quiet to alert, awake to asleep
    - interferes with positive interactions

- does not meet parental expectations of infancy
- can result in physical/emotional abuse
- Parents of difficult infants, particularly mothers:
  - often blame themselves and think they are bad parents
  - often feel guilty, ashamed, embarrassed, angry, frustrated, resentful
  - develop a negative self-concept frequently reinforced by relatives and friends
- Parental support for coping includes:
  - talking with others about difficulties
  - getting professional guidance to recognize and antici- pate potential problem areas; for example, transitions, overstimulation
  - learning to avoid and manage problems
  - arranging respite time and shared parental duties
- Finding professional help
  - make a special appointment with physician to discuss concerns
  - avoid physicians who discount or minimize difficulties
  - utilize child evaluation unit at local hospital for referrals or help
- Changing perceptions about ADHD
  - is not the result of parenting
  - environmental factors can exacerbate difficulties
  - affects all family members

CHAPTER THREE

The Toddler Years:
Ages 1–3

Around the time David passed the six-month mark, I developed the rather elaborate theory that his embryonic body placed restraints on his attempts to explore, which stifled his curiosity, and that was why he became frustrated so easily. So I welcomed the toddler stage of development with the foolish belief that David would be more content once he came into his own realm. "Toddlers are supposed to be active," I told myself. "They are supposed to get into things. Toddlers are supposed to be somewhat independent, not like a baby monkey on its mother's back."

But I did not know what the toddler with ADHD could be like. Within a few short months, I found the monkey on my back was now loose in the house. I no longer had full control of him. David had mobility. He had strength. He had the ability to run circles around me, which he did. Being four months pregnant did not make coping with this one-year-old boy any easier. To keep a semblance of order in our house, I realized, David, unlike other toddlers I knew, needed undivided attention unless he was asleep.

And to think, once his dad and I foolishly pretended not to notice the great deal of time and energy required by this one small child. I gave up trying to restrict his activity level. Instead I became a mother–vacuum cleaner who followed him around, swept up after him, and swallowed all traces of disorder. Friends who marveled at this display of spit and polish asked in awe, "How do you keep the house so neat with a one-year-old around?" Little did they know it turned into a full-time job.

When David woke from his nap, he not only threw the toys from his crib, he also tossed out the sheet and blankets. And when he wasn't in the process of rearranging the house, David became engaged in inventing new uses for household objects. By thirteen months of age, he knew the stairs were for climbing, but found they could be turned into a slide. A banister became a jungle gym to be scaled from outside the staircase. It was not unusual to find him dangling in midair.

No matter what the activity, David gave it new meaning and purpose. Pots and pans turned into flying disks. Windows made wind chimes. (When you bang on them with a truck they make a shrill, melodic sound.) The drapes became rope swings, electric cords lassos. The dog he chased. David refused to acknowledge the word "No." Unless, of course, it spilled from his lips.

When I called friends and relatives to say, "You won't believe what he did today!" they laughed and said, "He's a piece of work." No one branded him as exceptionally wild, not even as they watched him progress to the point where he always walked one step ahead of me. Based on their responses, I assumed I overreacted to his behavior until my mother asked, "How are you ever going to manage little David and a new baby?" I knew I could barely manage my first child, and I had absolutely no answer for my mother's question. Since I was a few months pregnant, within a short time I would indeed be faced with finding a solution.

Meanwhile, David's energy level physically drained me. Yet I knew I could keep him from harm for at least another year until he developed better judgment skills. But his contrary response to my efforts to please him left me disheartened. We never got into sync, and I never knew what to expect.

On Halloween, I thought he would certainly be thrilled to give out candy to the neighborhood ghosts and goblins. But when a seven-year-old witch appeared on our porch, David screamed bloody murder until I closed the door. I figured this sinister creature had proved a little too chilling for his bones, but even with the princesses and fairy godmothers he threw a fit. When nothing I did calmed him, I surrendered the notion that mother's instinct was a guide I could rely on through his darkest nights.

By the time David's dad came home, my nerves were shot. "You should have stopped answering the door," he said. To my way of thinking this answer was no solution but rather a stopgap measure. Years later, when once again a witch swept our home into an uproar, I remembered we lived under a very strange spell.

Perhaps if we had known then that our son's extreme reactions were symptomatic of an underlying problem, his dad and I might have had a chance to address the difficulties more effectively. But we did not. Instead, we took each symptom as an isolated behavior and tried to rationalize it as best we could. When illness could not be considered a factor, we blamed ourselves or each other.

Over the course of my second pregnancy, our preoccupation with David's finicky eating patterns grew in direct proportion to my girth. When I told David Sr. I felt frustrated because our son would eat nothing except cereal and milk, he responded as though I had said David would only breathe on alternate Tuesdays. "He needs green vegetables. He's probably sick all the time because of what he doesn't eat. Maybe if you had better eating habits . . ." Bang!

I knew my eating habits did not cause David to be such a fussy eater. I even knew my cooking could not be considered at fault. Maybe, I thought, the problem existed because it was I who fed him. That possibility did not make me feel good, so I decided I simply did not know what kids like to eat. My friends with small children told me what they prepared. But when I placed these tidbits in front of David, in one fell swoop he brushed them to the floor, which made Pogo the dog/vulture very happy.

Shortly before the birth of our second baby, David Sr. moved his office into our house, which gave Dad more time to spend with our son and gave me some respite. There were times, though, I felt inadequate and jealous, especially when I watched them play together. While my instincts about how to nurture this child seemed lousy, Dad's roughhousing pleased young David. While I complained about how frustrating he could be, Dad found him to be "a real kick!" But where we had hoped for a boy our first time around and had one, this time I hoped for a nice, quiet, cuddly little girl.

It was so hard for me to see that I meant anything at all to my son. Whenever I tried to share my affection, David ran in the opposite direction. At times, I felt guilty for believing that this little guy set the tone of our relationship. At times, I just felt very sad.

In order for a pleasant interaction to occur, we needed a calm place and a routine activity. Every morning I made sure we sat side by side on the floor of his room and did puzzles together before naptime. At age one and a half, this child could piece together puzzles geared for a five-year-old with very little help. Nurturing David came in quiet moments such as these.

The rest of the day, however, was spent in an effort to keep David out of trouble. This task proved much harder with each month that passed. Whenever I talked on the phone or visited with a friend, David waged an all-out assault on the house. Seasoned mothers told me, "Don't worry. David's just one of those kids who is into everything. You'd rather have him inquisitive instead of dull." True. But what concerned me was David's seeming lack of fear.

After his new brother, Jonathan, was born that May, David lost all caution. His stunts became dangerous. I lived in constant fear that one day David would move just a little too fast, do something just a little too impulsive, and not be able to stop the course of action. I worried that one day I might bring my son home in a box.

My fears about David's ability to harm himself were not unfounded. One July morning while I changed the new baby, twenty-two-month-old David quietly left the room. Seconds later, I found him standing on a second-story window sill. Both his hands were pushing the thin screen, which was fastened to its frame by only a hook and eye. Until I could find a way to distract him, I froze in the doorway, afraid that my sudden movement might propel David into a forward thrust and free-fall to the pavement below.

That day I decided to buy iron bars for the windows but soon learned even bars were not childproof. The pediatrician emphatically suggested I do whatever it took to keep David safe—"even if that means you have to tie a rope around his waist and fasten its other end to your wrist."

I had already learned to put a harness on him when we walked. David had no respect for traffic. He would run across the street without pausing a second. No matter how many times I tried to teach him to stop, to look, that the street was a dangerous place, he just never listened. But tying us together with a rope? This lifeline was an umbilical cord the likes of which I never expected. I worried he might inadvertently strangle himself. So I followed my mother's advice and watched him like a hawk instead.

Such hypervigilance came with a price. Any semblance of a warm, nurturing relationship severed. Now I was tense and irritable around my older child. My mother asked, "Why are you so uptight? Is anything wrong?"

"No, Mom. I'm just tired," I rationalized.

Her inquisition was relentless. "Are you sure? Are you and big David having trouble? Is it the new baby?" I did not want to admit how petrified David's impulsive actions made me. However, I could definitely state that Jonathan in no way contributed to my anxiety.

Unlike his older brother, Jonathan was a peaceful baby, easy to manage, a happy soul. As he progressed through the early years, he took his time and studied a move before he made it. He left his environment intact. He loved to be held. Around him, I felt like a good mother. I could not understand how two boys born of the same parents could be so entirely different. Only years later did I learn that Jonathan had not inherited the ADHD disorder as his brother had, and therein lay the difference between my two sons. Where Jonathan proved the essence of joy, David remained an enigma until his dad and I learned the nature of our older son's problem.

Meanwhile, the stress created by a child who constantly seemed to be testing his limits and ours took its toll. Now my husband and I argued, blamed, and pointed the finger at who did what to cause David to do whatever. Even when we agreed that David behaved in thus and such a way, we argued about the reasons why.

My husband's explanations vacillated between "There's something wrong with him" and "We must be doing something wrong." Afraid the something wrong might be me, I immediately assumed a defensive stance and dismissed these comments by saying, "Quit making such a big deal out of everything. That's just how kids are."

But I didn't know too many kids as testy as David. My mother said, "He doesn't respect you. He's allowed to get away with too much."

"He really loves to bust your chops," my sister observed.

Since the babysitter, Mrs. Hutchinson, never found him to be a bother, I thought the observations of my mother and sister were correct. My sister-in-law, the mother of five, suggested I "make him sit in a chair when he's naughty. That's what I do with my kids." So I tried. The only way to get David to stay seated would be to sit on top of him.

Days with David became more and more like a game of Russian roulette. I could not predict either what he would do or how he would react, nor could he predict how I would respond to his behavior. He flung himself into the "terrible twos" with a vengeance. He met with constant disapproval and increasing anger from me. "Don't do this. Don't do that. I said stop that. That's bad." Instead of soothing lullabies, he heard this daily barrage of commands. He followed very few orders.

Jonathan, on the other hand, received only positive and loving attention. As David became more his own person, his behavior became increasingly sullen and aggressive. Everyone, including me, thought he had an extreme case of sibling rivalry. In actuality, David did suffer serious blows to his self-image. Now I realize he had to watch someone else get the nurturing he could not take for himself.

Maybe that's why David stopped calling me Mommy. Who knows? When I first heard him address me as Mary, I thought my two-year-old was just going through the stage when some toddlers hear their parents refer to each other on a first-name basis and do the same. Relatives found this behavior cute, and to some degree we all encouraged him. I figured in a short time he would again call me Mom. That did not happen for a year and a half.

During this time, our family dynamics mimicked a three-ring circus. David misbehaved. I reacted generally by yelling, since reasoning never worked. Of course, yelling didn't help either. Dad criticized my reaction. Then we argued. When David created another naughty diversion, we repeated the entire scene until his father and I, the adults, eventually withdrew in angry silence. Unknowingly, I gravitated to Jonathan and my husband to young David. Neither of us could see that our reactive interactions only served to drive a wedge into our family.

Nonetheless, we all felt the tension. I complained about it frequently. One afternoon at a coffee klatch, my friend Pat suggested I call the Totline, a phone service mothers called for answers from a psychologist to questions regarding their child's behavior. In the child development books I read, David appeared only vaguely in evidence on the pages. Thus when I turned to them for information, I found more questions instead of answers. This service, I hoped would provide me with a plausible explanation.

When I mustered the courage and called the Totline, my throat tightened as soon as I spoke. In a strange way, I felt as though I had betrayed young David. A sense of relief followed after the psychologist assured me most of David's behaviors were normal for his age. "You just have to be consistent with your responses," she advised. When I asked her how to handle his refusal to eat nutritious foods, she suggested I "make a game with the food. You know. Show him how broccoli is like a little green tree." Well, I only knew about airplanes. I couldn't wait for that evening to serve broccoli. But David did not like little green trees either.

I should have predicted such a simplistic solution would not fool David. All along, people told us how bright they found this child. Some even said, "He's too bright for his own good." I wondered if he was too bright to follow the norms.

After all, this child demonstrated he could understand and conceptualize complex events. When David was eighteen months old, his dad and I watched the televised landing of the first orbiting space shuttle. Young David, who sat at my feet seemingly preoccupied with a flashlight, apparently tuned in more than we realized. After the *Columbia* rolled to a stop, he turned to us and said, "I wish I could go up there someday." Neither one of us could believe what we heard.

Mysteries began to make sense to me. I reasoned David was hard to handle because his intellectual abilities far exceeded his physiological development. We only had to wait for his mind and body to get into sync. Then, I figured, he would surely behave appropriately. Meanwhile it seemed sensible to nurture David by responding to his intellect. But in doing so, I perceived David to be older than his years. Once again, in an attempt to explain the nature of this child, I took a wrong turn. I expected David to be smart enough to have greater self-control.

He was not. There were so many days I wished he, like the *Columbia,* could go up there too. Frequently I told him in various tones of voice, "David, you are driving me nuts." I made similar comments to friends and relatives as well. It did not occur to me to question how such feedback affected this two-and-a-half-year-old boy.

But I did realize David's attention-demanding behavior was not the only aspect of life "driving me nuts." During this period, major life stresses bore down on our family. First we had to adapt to a new baby. Then my husband's father died suddenly. My father became terminally ill. When David Sr. came home from the office and announced he had been transferred to another city hours away, I exploded.

Patience has never been my strong suit, but now I had even less. When I brought both boys to the pediatrician for checkups, he asked, "How's it going, Mrs. Fowler?" We had a long history of kibitzing about the trials and tribulations of being David's mother. Generally, the doctor joked with me and shook his fist while he smiled and said, "He needs a good punch in the nose."

This particular winter's day, I was in an ill humor. Instead of making light of David's antics, I held back tears and angrily told the doctor in no uncertain terms, "This kid is driving me nuts. There has to be something wrong with him." The pediatrician quickly retorted, "Maybe there's something wrong with the mother."

That remark did everyone a great disservice because I thought to myself, "Maybe he's right." After all, I took my children to him because I respected his medical judgment. I thought David's lack of control probably was my fault. This thought prevented me from seeing any clinical reason for David's difficult nature.

And this thought also made me really angry, but instead of reacting to the doctor's remark, I took my anger out on David. I decided to declare war on his behavior. Whatever it took, this kid was going to slow down, be careful, and do whatever he was asked, or else. Fortunately, before I chained him to a radiator, the business of moving distracted me. For the time being, David had a reprieve from the iron fist of Mom, the disciplinarian.

Is This Just the "Terrible Two's"?

David was not behaving like a typical toddler. But I did not know that. Nor did most parents of a children with ADHD in those years. Granted, many of our kids stood out in a crowd. Still, we assumed they were just going through a stage. After all, there had to be a reason this time in a child's life is called the "terrible twos." Most of us shared the point of view of Brian Doyle, a father who said to me, "I thought he would grow out of it."

The "it" to which Brian referred is the classic out-of-control behavior exhibited by many children with ADHD. These kids do not grow out of "it" at an early age. If anything, the symptoms of ADHD intensify as demands from the environment for quiet, in-control, attentive behavior increase.

Dr. C. Keith Conners describes children with this condition as restless, impulsive, incapable of sticking to a task, and constantly on the go. He believes the pattern of ADHD can be recognized as early as one or two years of age if you can identify the clues, but most parents and even many practitioners do not spot the behavior so characteristic of ADHD at this age. Traditionally, the likelihood of early diagnosis remains minimal, even for children who are moderately hyperactive and thereby call attention to themselves.

According to Dr. Russell Barkley, mothers often fail to recognize the behavior of the young child with ADHD as problematic for a number of reasons. First, new mothers and mothers of only children often lack experience. They do not know what behavior to identify as abnormal. Second, some children with mild ADHD-related problems do not evidence much difficulty in the years before elementary school because their primary job is to play. As these children grow older, Dr. Barkley notes, more work is demanded; teachers assign schoolwork, which taxes children with ADHD, and their difficulties become noticeable. Third, some are exceptionally bright and do not have to study or pay attention until they are in the higher grades. They compensate for their ADHD deficits in the early school years through their brilliance.

Early Signs and Symptoms

Beyond this basic, impulsive, restless framework of behavior, parents of toddlers with ADHD generally see variations on the theme. Their children may have unstable moods, possibly exploding in outbursts over a silly little problem or for no apparent reason at all. They are persistent and not readily soothed. They frustrate easily and show very little self-control. They also may be highly curious, which might explain why so many toddlers with ADHD get lost in shopping malls or why family treasures are found lying in bits and pieces around their feet. Commonly, turbulence causes disturbances in the parent-child attachment. In fact, Dr. Barkley's research shows a higher incidence of negative mother-child interactions prior to identification and management than afterward.

These early signs and symptoms are usually misunderstood. By the time some children with ADHD reach the preschool age, they are tarred with much rejection, and their world has become a very damning place.

The toddler with ADHD often appears to behave in a willful and deliberately noncompliant way. Child psychologist Sam Goldstein reports that parents usually attribute the child's behavior to a conscious choice on his or her part. Actually, the child has little control.

To further complicate matters, on some occasions the child with ADHD does behave appropriately. Such inconsistency confuses those who do not know that the child has ADHD, and sometimes those who do know as well. The inconsistent behavior also perpetuates the myth that these children have self-control when they want to. The truth is, these children are not the children who *can't or won't*. They can and do. It's just that "can" and "do" come harder for them, particularly without extra help. The attitude that the child *could* behave if he or she wanted to do so places guilt and blame on the child.

Finding Help

Children who wreak havoc upon themselves and their families do not need rejection. They need the attention of a professional who can determine whether or not there is an underlying problem creating the distress. For the child with ADHD, early diagnosis may prevent or lessen the negative effects and complications arising from the lack of intervention.

Where to Begin

If you suspect a problem exists, regardless of the child's age, note it and seek a solution. Do not let friends and relatives talk you into believing you have conjured up this notion. That happened to Claudia Kreiger and her husband, both trained child development professionals. They were told, "You're just two professional people looking for something. Leave him alone and he'll be fine." Fortunately, they only waited until their son Jay turned two to learn he had a communication handicap and ADHD.

For those of us laypeople who lack knowledge about either childhood behavioral problems or the social service system, finding the appropriate support services takes on the magnitude of a quest. Most of us have to answer these questions:

1. Does my child really have a problem? (If this thought has crossed your mind, you should look further.)
2. What is my child's problem? (Your job is not to diagnose, but if you have a suspicion, start there.)
3. What type of help do I need? (If you don't know, just keep asking questions. You'll find the right direction.)
4. Where do I find that help? (There are lots of places. Try talking to fellow parents you know and trust or someone who has had similar difficulties.)
5. How do I know if I've found the right help? (Chances are

you are not going to be sure. Trust your instinct, which is not so easy when you are in distress or overwhelmed. Give it time and you'll get guidance.)

6. How will I afford the help? (Hopefully you have a good insurance plan or live in a state that believes in financing programs for parents and children. Without these resources or independent means, you just have to keep looking.)

Since ADHD is both a physical and a mental health problem, there are a number of roads to travel in search of answers.

Once you suspect your child has a problem, even if you are uncertain that your assessment is correct, try to identify the problem. You will probably begin with the child's doctor and, as suggested in the previous chapter, make a special appointment to discuss the problem. Ask the doctor whether the child's behavior is an indication of any specific childhood problem. (Do not ask if the behavior is normal. Too often the answer is a quick yes. Remember, if your child's behavior were normal, it would not have bothered you so much that you sought help.)

If you are told, "It is too early to tell," "I don't know," or "Your expectations are too high," seek the advice of another professional well versed in childhood behavioral problems. In this regard, I am reminded of the sage advice given by one of the fathers I interviewed. "Listen to the mother," Ben Green said. "She is with the child every day and sees the problems." The message to mothers is *trust your instincts.*

The exact nature or cause of the child's problem and the help the child will need are closely related. Often the person who determines the nature of the child's problem also manages its treatment. Parents must find a competent clinician with expertise in their child's particular problem, which in our case is ADHD. Like myself, many parents do not have the vaguest idea of where to begin to find these services.

Hospitals

A good starting point is the local hospital. If it does not have a child evaluation unit or specific programs to deal with children who have difficulties, it might have a referral system that can provide names of physicians in the area who deal with this kind of situation. If the local hospital cannot be of help, Dr. Reutter recommends parents contact either the county or state chapter of the American Academy of Pediatrics for the necessary information.

Mental Health Clinics

If you get confused or frustrated as you try to find your way through the complicated maze of health care services, don't blame yourself, advises social worker Kathy Collins, who is director of consultation and education for CPC Mental Health Services in New Jersey. When concerned about your child's behavior, Ms. Collins suggests, start with a mental health center as a place to seek answers. Though the sizes and services offered may vary, most communities have mental health centers, and most of these centers are equipped to diagnose learning and behavioral problems. You can locate mental health centers through the phone book or referrals by your child's doctor. In addition to community agencies, many universities also have mental health clinics that will assess behavioral and learning problems.

Government Programs

• *Your local school*

Parents who suspect their infant or toddler has special needs can also look to their local school districts for information about where to go for help. Thanks to a law passed by Congress in 1975 and its subsequent amendments, early intervention services now exist for infants and toddlers with special needs (ages birth up to three) and special education services for preschoolers and elementary and secondary school children with disabilities (ages three through twenty-one). This law is called the Individuals with Disabilities Education Act (IDEA).

Assessment is one of the services manadated by this law. An infant or toddler with ADHD might be found eligible to receive services because of cognitive problems such as inattention or disorganization or because of problems such as difficulty following rules, planning, or completing tasks. To learn more about laws and programs, write or call for the free pamphlet "A Parent's Guide to Accessing Programs for Infants, Toddlers, and Preschoolers with Disabilities," published by NICHCY, the National Information Center for Children and Youth with Disabilities. (Please see NICHCY listing in appendix A.)

• Head Start

Head Start programs also offer an avenue of assessment and intervention services for four- or five-year-old children with ADHD found eligible for enrollment in them. The 1993 federal Head Start regulations consider ADHD to be a chronic or acute health impairment entitling the child to special education services when the child's inattentive, hyperactive, and impulsive behavior is developmentally inappropriate, chronic, and displayed in multiple settings. It must also severely affect performance in normal developmental tasks—for example, planning and completing activities or following simple directions.

Selecting a Specialist

Just as there are many agencies available to help parents of children with special needs, professionals who diagnose and treat ADHD come from many different specialities. These professionals include clinical psychologists, pediatric neurologists, pediatricians, child psychiatrists, and clinical social workers. Exactly which of these to use depends on the individual's training, expertise, and area of interest.

Parents are likely to contact their child's pediatrician first, and most pediatricians are indeed trained in childhood behavioral problems. Often, however, they have diverse and demanding practices, which may mean they do not have the time to coordinate and manage the other areas of treatment beyond medication that ADHD requires. Parents have to determine if their child's pediatrician will be able—and willing—to devote enough time to the child's treatment.

Pediatricians often refer ADHD cases to pediatric neurologists or child psychiatrists, both of whom are physicians who can treat the disorder medically. Child psychiatrists are also trained to do therapeutic, problem-solving work with children and their families, though child psychologists or clinical social workers more often handle this part of the job.

With the exception of social workers, the types of practitioners mentioned above may choose to specialize in the treatment of neurodevelopmental problems. To do so, they must seek additional training that most social workers do not receive, although many are competent to help children and families with ADHD.

Get Referrals

Referrals for a therapist who may be well suited for your needs can come from a variety of sources. Some of these sources will have formal referral procedures; others may do word-of-mouth recommendation. According to Kathy Collins, every state and most counties have mental health associations, and these agencies generally have a referral system of mental health professionals with information about their specialities. In addition, the same sources you would contact for information and assessment, community mental health centers, university mental health clinics, hospital child study evaluation units, school-based assessment teams, and family physicians can prove beneficial for therapist referrals.

Parent support organizations are also a source of invaluable up-to-date information. Dr. Paul Wender applauds the service provided by these organizations and says, "Support groups will tell you what medical societies are unwilling to say. They will tell you that Dr. Jones is available and Dr. Smith is not, that Dr. Jones listens to you carefully and Dr. Smith does not." (Please see appendix A for a list of support organizations.)

I think parents need to be wary of practioners who only address a child's behavior in theoretical terms. Deep-seated psychological problems do not cause ADHD. Even if they did, the symptoms require treatment. We parents need practical advice. Whatever practioner you use, be sure you receive good, solid information based on their good training and expertise, and your common sense. *Trust your instincts.*

Evaluate the Professional

When you seek the services of a therapist, Ms. Collins suggests, follow these guidelines:

1. When you call to make an appointment, explain your problem and determine if this practioner can help.
2. At the first appointment, do not commit yourself to being the therapist's client. Ms. Collins explains that the first appointment is part of an assessment process and should be a mutual interview. Both parties, the therapist and the parents, must decide if the therapist can help. Then the parents need to decide if they want to work with this particular person.

3. If you know, for instance, that your child has ADHD, determine how much training the therapist has in treating the disorder. If you cannot define your child's problem, Ms. Collins advises, describe the child's behavior along with any steps you have already taken, and ask for a diagnosis and assessment based on those observations and facts.

About Fees for Services

As everyone knows, health care can often be expensive. Ms. Collins says every community mental health center receives state monies, and most of them also receive local and federal funds to provide affordable services. Getting access to these funds may prove difficult, but each agency has some mechanism to provide low-cost services. Some offer discounts; others have sliding-scale fees. Most agencies accept medical insurance; many private practitioners will also take insurance payments. Some private therapists will even discount their services or treat a small percentage of patients without financial resources for no money. In addition, university mental health clinics and hospitals also offer low-cost services. Ms. Collins advises parents not to be embarrassed or think they are asking for something unusual when discussing fees.

While on the topic of fees, I can't let the opportunity of commenting on insurance pass. ADHD is a neurobiological disorder, which makes it both a physical and mental health problem. Often needs arise that cannot be managed solely by a pediatrician or neurologist. Health insurance coverage for visits to mental health practitioners is disgraceful. Despite an enormous amount of documentation demonstrating that untreated mental health problems lead to physical ailments, reduced productivity, and other difficulties more costly to society over the long haul, I have talked to too many parents who cannot get the help they and their children need because of cost. There needs to be a consumer group working for people with neurobiological disorders to demand better mental health coverage. Also, you may want to contact your legislators and stress the importance of affordable, accessible health care for the diagnosis and treatment of neurobiological disorders. Your voice can echo loudly in the ears of an elected official, especially when teamed with the voices of others in the same situation.

Help With Home Behavior

No matter who we use to make a diagnosis or give clinical help, we, the parents, have to raise the children. Doing what comes naturally doesn't usually get the desired results when parenting a child with ADHD. Most of us need some training to oversee our children effectively and to help them manage their own behavior. Participating in parent training groups and working with a counselor in private practice are ways to learn helpful techniques.

Two mothers I spoke with, Colleen Patterson and Donna Rothman, turned to their local chapter of a national parent training organization, Parents Anonymous, when their children had behavioral difficulties that went beyond the mothers' skills. Today, parent training courses might also be offered in ADHD parent support groups or through child guidance clinics, mental health centers, local child protection services, municipalities, community colleges, or adult schools of education. Hundreds of helpful books can also be found.

Dr. Richard Zakreski, a psychologist in private practice who specializes in ADHD and learning disabilities, explains that parent training, though not highly specialized, should follow certain guidelines. He suggests the ones that follow.

About Behavior

"Behavior" is a very complicated process that scientists have studied and theorized about for years. That's why there are hundreds of books on the topic. Here, given that the purpose of this book is to help you help your child with ADHD, I will provide only some very streamlined information about behavior, chosen specifically to enable you to manage ADHD more effectively.

We do not always act with great forethought. Often we do things by going on automatic pilot. In fact, behavior is a choice we make. Sometimes that choice has become habit, like putting our car keys in the same place every day. Other times, that choice is so clear we don't even need to think about it, like putting ice cream into the freezer.

Then there are the occasions when we have to apply observation and prior knowledge before we act. For instance, most people going to a wedding or retirement dinner for the first time would carefully check out what is going on around them at such an occasion. Sure, we may want to take a giant slice of the cake, but we look around and see that others are not doing so. Perhaps we remember birthday parties and our mothers stopping us a split second before our finger made a swipe over the icing. Regardless of whether we take the cake or not, we choose.

Much of what parents have to do to help the child with ADHD behave appropriately requires making the expectations crystal clear and designing situations that encourage the use of appropriate behavior.

Structure and Rules

All children, including those with ADHD, need their parents to impose structure to guide their behavior. This structure must provide rules, limits, and parameters so that the child has a clear blueprint to follow in order to figure out what behavior is appropriate and acceptable in given situations.

Children without ADHD are quick to regulate their behavior to follow the rules inherent in the structure. For instance, they will know to stop talking when seatwork begins in class. Children with ADHD, on the other hand, often have difficulty recognizing rules that are not explicitly stated. They tend to misbehave and frequently break rules because of their impulsive, uninhibited, and disorganized nature.

Children with ADHD behave better when they have a clear picture to guide their behavior. Thus they need to be guided by a structure. That structure has to be consistent and predictable. In other words, the structure must be so clear that the child fully understands what behavior is expected and the consequences for meeting or not meeting those expectations. As Dr. Barkley notes, self-control problems require a lot of external guidance.

Feedback

These children also need a considerable amount of feedback. They must be held accountable for their choices. When managed accordingly, children with ADHD have an improved ability to adapt their behavior to external limits, with emphasis on "improved." This type of management approach is not really aimed at controlling children. Rather, the point is to provide these children with a clear picture of rules followed by consistent consequences so that they develop routine responses to everyday situations. This structure and feedback helps the child develop self-control.

To get there, though, at first parents (and teachers) might have to be very much involved. The age of the child is not the major factor that determines his or her ability to have self-control, so even though a child may seem old enough, the parents will probably have to parent as though they were guiding a younger child.

Children do not follow rules simply because they exist. If you are the parent of a child with ADHD, you probably know this fact better than most. A verbal understanding of a rule does not mean a child will automatically use or apply the rule in different situations to guide his or her behavior. For instance, ask a child to explain the rule about running inside the house after he or she has broken it— and broken a vase. In all likelihood, the child knows the rule about running indoors. Yet just talking about the rule rarely makes the child embrace it, particularly when the child is younger or a child with ADHD.

Rules work because they are applied consistently and enforced over time in ways that are meaningful to the child. If running inside the house is frequently ignored, then the child will not always follow the rule. In fact, the child may actually learn that it's okay to run inside because nothing happens unless something gets broken. With David, I really didn't have a "no running" rule; I had a "no breaking" rule.

Behavior Choices

Children with ADHD do not "choose" to misbehave. The disorder is, after all, involuntary and nondeliberate. Still, when creating a system to effectively manage the behavior of children with ADHD, therapists assume that behavior is a choice that can be influenced by using external structure and consequences. Thus they try to help parents make rules and expectations clear and to train parents to have consistent consequences for the "choices" the child makes. In so doing, the parents help the child make the appropriate choices.

Often, counselors will help parents design behavior management systems. These are specifically designed to influence the child's choices by how parents (or teachers) respond to them.

Influencing behavioral choices is basically a four-step process:

1. Tell the child what behavior is expected in a given situation. For example, at dinnertime, you might tell the child you expect him to eat all the food on his plate within twenty minutes.

2. Tell the child the consequences for doing or not doing what is expected. In the dinner example, the child is given dessert after eating the meal in the specified amount of time; otherwise there will be no dessert and no food for the rest of the night.
3. Give the child an opportunity to make a behavioral decision. The child in our dinner example has the choice to eat or not eat all the food in the specified amount of time.
4. Hold the child accountable for his or her choice by applying a consequence for the behavior. If the child decided to eat dinner and did so in the specified time, dessert is given along with praise.

As simple as these steps and the example appear, we parents can get into a lot of difficulty using this four-step process in real-life situations. We need to anticipate where problems could arise. For instance, if we expect the child to eat all his dinner in twenty minutes, we must also decide if that means the child begins eating as soon as dinner is served and does not leave the table during the meal. Does eating all the dinner mean all, or is the child allowed to skip the lima beans, which you know the child will never eat no matter what you offer in return? Does nothing to eat for the rest of the evening mean nothing to eat, or does it mean if the child keeps whining about how hungry he is and maintains that he would eat if only you would cook the meals he likes, you give in and give him a bowl of cereal, thinking you are not conceding because the cereal is normally considered breakfast food, particularly if it is not of the sugared variety?

To influence behavioral choices, parents sometimes have to be very firm and rigid. Otherwise, the child gets trained to look for loopholes. In so doing, the child actually learns to manage parental behavior more effectively than the parents manage the child's behavior.

Using Consequences

The use of consequences to shape the behavior of the child with ADHD by influencing his or her choices is extremely important. By definition, the word "consequence" means "that which follows." Usually people think of consequences as being negative. In actuality, consequences can be either positive or negative. When kids do something well, a positive consequence delivered by a significant other—for example, a parent or teacher—helps them to recognize that they made a good decision. Conversely, when the child misbehaves, then suffers a negative consequence, the child understands that a poor decision led to an unpleasant consequence.

Positive consequences come in many forms: an oral acknowledgment, such as "good going"; a kiss on the cheek; material rewards, such as food or toys; or the receipt of certain privileges, such as television time. Always give oral praise along with any other positive consequence.

Negative consequences similarly range from disapproval or an oral reprimand, such as "I do not like it when you . . . ," to a withdrawal of privileges and punishment where appropriate. Although a parent may be quite frustrated or angry about the child's misbehavior, it is important that punishment be communicated to the child in a matter-of-fact, emotionally controlled manner. However, parents of children with ADHD need to realize, as Dr. Conners says, that they themselves "are human beings under extraordinary stress." Thus if mistakes are made when delivering punishment, rather than wallow in guilt, parents need to try to do better next time. The best advice I've ever heard is *"Act, don't react."* Sometimes, to avoid reacting, you may have to leave the room or count to ten; then, when you are calmer, take action and give the child a negative consequence for inappropriate behavior.

Time-out

One consequence proven effective for use with all children is time-out. Time-out means that the child is sent to a predetermined location and deprived of rewarding activity for a specific amount of time. For example, if the child smacks a sibling, time-out becomes a reasonable consequence for that behavioral decision, because the child has violated the social contract of shared living within the household—that is, no hitting. In time-out, the child no longer has the privilege of choosing where or how he or she will spend his or her time.

The actual location of the time-out spot is chosen by the parent. Once sent to time-out, in general, the child is expected to stay there for five quiet minutes, with emphasis on quiet. For younger children, two minutes is a more appropriate time. Similarly, fifteen minutes may be more suitable for a twelve-year-old. After time-out, the child should be rewarded with an approving statement for a positive change in his or her behavior.

Sensible Consequences

Consequences can also be either logical or natural. Logical and natural consequences can be either positive or negative. Whenever possible, consequences should be logically or naturally related to the original behavioral decision made by the child. A natural consequence means the behavior and the consequence are naturally related. For example, the child who does not eat dinner will be hungry and not satisfied. The baseball glove left in the rain and not put away will be ruined. Logical consequences have a logical connection between the behavior and the consequence and are imposed by people. For example, if you do not put your toys away, you will not be allowed to play with them for x amount of time. If you stretch out your bedtime, you will have to go to bed earlier. If you come home late, you will have an earlier curfew or be grounded.

Behavior Charts

To create a clear and predictable structure in order to influence behavior effectively, we might need to use a systematic approach to behavior management. Specially designed behavioral programs for home or school use provide that structure. Such programs become more effective when both parents work together. To date, behavior charts have proven the most widely used and effective approach to systematically managing behavior. The benefit of charts is that they tell the child what behavior is expected and provide daily feedback in a consistent fashion.

The drawback of charts is that they only work when you use them. Remember Dr. Barkley's observation, "ADHD is a problem of doing what you know." If you take away the external and rely on the child's internal guidance system, then you can expect poor self-control. The charts help to shape the child's behavior, and, even more important, the child develops an inner sense of self-control. We want the child to view his behavior as a series of choices he makes and to feel that he is responsible for those choices. Because good choices are repaid with positive outcomes, the child learns to make appropriate decisions.

Behavior management systems should be instituted when children are young and kept in use into the teenage years with modifications made in the program to suit age and need. These programs prove harder to implement with the teenager who has ADHD, especially one who has not previously been exposed to behavior charts. He or she will predictably balk. Nonetheless, the program should be instituted despite any resistance.

Dr. Barkley feels that behavior charts are "nothing glitzy—just good hard work at learning to manage a disabled individual." The hard work stems from the fact that the charts require daily implementation on a long-term basis, parental organization, and regimentation. After a while, as parent Hope Clark explained, "I just want to take things as they come and live like a normal family, so I stop using the chart. Of course, Tommy's behavior deteriorates within a few short days."

Many varieties of behavior charts exist. Various examples are included in appendix C. Behavior charts, however, need to be tailored to each individual child's needs. Like many parents, I found professional guidance very helpful when starting with charts.

Dr. Zakreski suggests the following guidelines for making your child's chart, which I call:

Seven Steps to Improving Behavior

1. Select behaviors needing work. The parents, with input from the child, need to select the behaviors to be managed on the chart. The child also needs to understand exactly what is expected from him or her in terms of the behaviors. Remember the no-running example!

2. Choose a limited number of behaviors to work on at a given time. With young children, only a few behaviors should be selected at any given moment, because they do not have the developmental capacity to work on more. With older children, it is generally advisable to start with just a couple of behaviors and then add more as the child meets with success. However, no more than five behaviors should be charted at any one time so as not to overwhelm the child or parents. As the child succeeds in shaping the behavior, additional behaviors can be added one at a time.

3. Ask for the behavior you want, *not* what you don't want. Behavior management is designed to encourage appropriate behavior. Use charts to help make sure the child works to meet behavioral expectations. Phrase the desired behaviors in a positive light, to tell the child what you expect rather than what is not correct. For example, suppose you don't want the child to hit other family members. Instead of writing "no hitting" on the chart, you would write something along the lines of "treats other family members, including pets, in a polite, courteous way."

4. Chart only routinely occurring behaviors. The behaviors selected for the chart should occur every day, because the child gets plenty of opportunity to develop control over them. Examples include going to bed on time, doing homework, and getting ready for school on time.

Once you and your child have developed some expertise with this system, you can move from using daily behaviors to those that occur less frequently. Even if you do not use a chart for these occasional behaviors, they should still be responded to with natural and logical consequences.

5. Build consequences into the chart. Once you have your list of behaviors, you have to give the child the choice to behave appropriately. Then you must pay attention to the child's behavioral decisions throughout the day and give the appropriate feedback. When the child makes good behavioral choices, he or she should be rewarded with praise and either tokens, stickers, or points. Stickers and points can be put right on the chart, which helps the child to keep track.

6. Determine the daily performance. The points, stickers, or tokens earned are tallied at the end of each day. Thus the child is held accountable for overall daily performance and patterns of behavior rather than one specific act.

7. Give consequences for daily results. Use the total daily score to determine what the child has earned for behavior across the entire day. Remember, consequences need to be agreed upon ahead of time. Otherwise, you might inadvertently encourage inconsistency and negotiation. The positive and negative consequences will come in the form of getting or giving up certain privileges agreed to when the chart is first designed. Such privileges could include going to bed a half hour later, having time to play video games or watch television, inviting a friend over, or going out for pizza or ice cream. When this system is used in conjunction with natural and logical consequences for specific actions throughout the course of the day, each behavior in effect produces two reinforcing consequences (positive or negative, as the case may be).

Pitfalls

Inconsistency

As you can readily see, such behavioral management systems are indeed "good hard work." Dr. Zakreski cautions parents to stick to the program once they decide to use it. By being consistent, parents give the child the impression that the behavior is important and that they mean what they say. Dr. Zakreski points out that when you make a rule and then fail to enforce it, the child does not respect you and gets the message that he or she can turn your no into a yes. For instance, children often ask to stay up past bedtime. If you deny this request and then your child continues to get up for drinks of water or something else that he or she "needs," asks you to read another story, or comes up with another ploy to extend bedtime, including whining or crying, and you give in and allow the child to have extra time, then the child has gotten control and you have increased the likelihood that he or she will challenge you in the future. It's not the time factor here that's the problem (fifteen or twenty minutes isn't really a big deal) but rather the child's defiance of your rules. Firmness and consistency are the key words in behavior management.

The point of behavior management is for parents to get better at making the child's behavior the child's problem. Otherwise, the tables turn and the child makes his or her behavior the parents' problem. Even at those times when we are tired or involved in other things, if the child makes a poor behavioral decision, we have to enforce the consequences.

Complacency

Another common pitfall of behavior management is complacency. Dr. Zakreski knows many parents who develop a good program, put it into action, and produce positive changes. Then they get really happy and are lulled into a sense that the child is doing great, so they stop the program. Within a short period of time, the child's behavior backslides and the family is back to square one.

"In order to control the behavior successfully, children with

ADHD do not need different parenting. But they do need extra parenting," Dr. Zakreski says. Thus the skills used with children with ADHD are skills that work with all children. However, for kids with ADHD, these skills must be used in a structured, more consistent, more deliberate way because children with ADHD need that extra management, organization, and feedback from parents.

Summary

Manifestations During Toddler Years
- Symptoms intensify as environmental expectations increase
- Generally, toddlers exhibit an impulsive, restless, always-on-the-go behavior pattern
- Other behavioral difficulties include:
  — unstable mood
  — problems with sleeping or eating
  — extreme curiosity
  — intense responses to stimuli
- Disturbances in parent-child attachment often occur
- Children are viewed as choosing to be noncompliant

Guidelines for Finding Help
- Discuss difficulties with physician
- Identify assessment and treatment resources at community mental health centers, hospital child evaluation clinics, local school districts, private practitioners
- Use a practitioner knowledgeable about ADHD: clinical psychologists, pediatric neurologists, pediatricians, child psychiatrists, and clinical social workers trained in diagnosis and treatment
- Referral sources include ADHD parent support organizations, community or university mental health centers, school-based assessment teams, family physicians
- Interview practitioners
  — determine amount of ADHD training and number of cases

Help for Parents
- Training in behavior management techniques to:
  — set rules
  — give commands clearly
  — limit amount of demands made

— institute consequences
— follow through on consequences: must be consistent; can be positive or negative, logical or natural
- Act, don't react to inappropriate behavior
- Use time-out
- Use behavior charts:
  — to help structure the environment
  — to develop the child's sense of self-control
  — with consistency

CHAPTER FOUR

The Preschool Years: Ages 3–5

Once I grew accustomed to the reality of our impending move, I told myself this geographic change would be a new beginning. Without the lure of friends and relatives enticing me to escape from home activities, I planned to devote my full attention toward shaping David into a quiet, ordered little boy.

But David now approached the time when a child's horizons expand to the world beyond, the preschool period of children aged three to five years. Neighborhood children and nursery school beckoned. Soon I would have even less control of him. No longer would we conduct most of our business in the privacy of our own home. Like most parents, I hoped my son would shed the difficult skin he wore and ease into the world beyond his front door.

My husband and I left the children with their aunt the day we moved into our new home. When they arrived the following day, their rooms were ready. Childproof locks secured all cabinets; curtains laced some of the windows. However, before I unpacked his toys, David became ill. As always, I attributed this fever to an ear infection, but the new pediatrician said, "A virus, probably brought on by the stress of the move."

His diagnosis surprised me. Though I knew David overreacted to little changes, I expected him to handle the relocation with ease. After all, unlike myself and Jonathan, David, like his dad, seemed to thrive on adventure. A few days later, he perked up when we attended a welcome coffee given for me by a neighbor.

Stacy Birdwell invited all the neighborhood ladies to meet me. One of them also brought along her three-year-old son so David would have a playmate. Over the din of our voices we all heard the noise from the other room where David was trying to convince Ryan to "relinquish" a toy. The little fellow stood his ground until my son's persistence forced him to retreat into the folds of his mother's skirt. When our hostess attempted to appease David with another toy, he threw it to the floor. Totally mortified, I slunk down into my chair.

This image was not the one I wished to portray in our new neighborhood. I wanted our family to be like the one in the sitcom *Leave It to Beaver* where everyone interacted in a polite, courteous fashion, where parents asserted their control and the children aimed to please them, where all problems subsided quietly and calmly behind closed doors, always within a half hour. But from that fateful spring morning, Ryan's mom always made an excuse whenever I suggested we get the boys together.

David Sr. attributed our son's aggressive behavior at the coffee to frustration. "David probably felt ignored," he said. Over time, however, I noticed he even played roughly with our dog Pogo despite the fact he had grown old enough to know better. David never behaved nastily. He just ran at the dog with so much exuberance, the poor beast turned her tail and ran in the other direction whenever she saw him. Our neighbor commented many times about our pet's good nature.

These days, so much of David's behavior proved inappropriate and could not be ignored. Every activity became an ordeal, even simple walks through the neighborhood. Logic would dictate that after a few bad experiences, a sensible person would know when to quit and make changes. And I did cut back the number of outings. I stopped taking David to shopping malls and grocery stores, but I hungered for adult company and so persevered with our daily afternoon jaunts through the streets where we lived. People always stopped me to admire the kids. After a while, I met some of them on a regular basis.

If we happened to speak for more than a few minutes, David, ever in search of action, impatiently tried to pull me away. Failing this first attempt, he then rode his Big Wheel full throttle and, on his more impish days, headed it directly toward my legs. If this action did not achieve the desired effect, he played bumper cars with Jonathan's stroller. Jonathan accepted these jolts with good nature.

But David's actions embarrassed me, and I grew increasingly resentful that he interrupted my conversations. I assigned motives to his actions that reinforced my incorrect perception that David deliberately chose to create trouble. Before long, I found myself in the habit of making sarcastic comments about him. When people stopped to say, "He's so adorable," I would reply, "He needs to be." I invited them to stick around. Those who stayed usually saw my point.

Through no conscious effort on my part, such comments reduced the shock value of David's actions and placed them in the Peck's Bad Boy category. They prepared people to expect the worst. If the worst did not happen, all the better. My remarks also shielded me from my feelings of incompetence and allowed the observer to know that though I acknowledged David's "bad" behavior, it nonetheless remained out of my control.

While my negative comments minimized the effects of David's behaviors on others, they drove the wedge between us deeper. Today, I'm certain such feedback tore at my son's self-worth. Instead of his best fan, I appeared his worst critic. I felt ashamed of my reactions to this child. Our mother-child bond had stretched to its limit. I now depended more and more on my positive interactions with Jonathan to feel like a good mother. David, to the contrary, became increasingly resentful of his younger brother. Our family had all the trappings of a miserable mess.

When the time for nursery school arrived, David Sr. and I, despite our ambivalent feelings, decided to enroll David. He thought David too young. I worried the teachers might not understand such a loud and unruly child. But I also had concerns about his social development. With the one neighborhood child out of the picture, Jonathan remained his only playmate. David bossed his younger brother so much, Jon and I both needed a few hours' peace.

The school's director listened to my concerns about David's readiness for nursery school. She told me not to worry. "Most children need to adjust," she said. The curriculum centered around play and social interaction. Since David never balked about going, after a time I assumed nursery school agreed with him.

One winter day, his teacher, Mrs. Able, stopped my car to hand me an owl he had crafted from kidney beans. "David worked so hard on this owl, Mrs. Fowler. I just wanted you to know what an effort he made," she said. Well, I beamed with pride. His mosaic depicted a flawless owl. How sweet of her, I thought, to commend David's obvious talent in person.

When the first parent-teacher conference arrived a month later, I could not wait to hear more about my son's ability. After I sat down and Mrs. Able said, "Oh, David's coming along nicely," I scratched my head. That comment did not sound at all like the glowing report I expected to hear.

"Hasn't he been doing well?" I asked.

She hesitated and then told me the kidney-bean owl represented one of the rare days when David stayed on task. She felt pleased for him and reasoned that if she made a big fuss over his accomplishment he might repeat it. But most days, David became frustrated about his work and lost his temper quite demonstratively.

"He's not a problem," she assured me. "I just say 'David, attitude, attitude, attitude!' and he catches himself."

What a great response, I thought. But when I said them, Mrs. Able's words only made David even angrier.

At least I no longer had to worry about his physical well-being every minute. David, now three years old, seemed less fragile, his actions less rash. Sure, he ran across the field during a high school football game while a play was in progress—but he saw his dad on the other side, and the shortest distance between two points is a straight line. And he did stop cold in his tracks when the referee blew the whistle to prematurely stop the play.

He now called me Mom again. True, I had to force the word from his lips, but he gave me this courtesy. He even showed signs of affection. When I landed in the hospital with a mysterious illness, I came home to find a teddy bear David had propped on my pillow. I praised him and bragged to everyone about this loving gesture he made. For years after, though I still did not get bedtime kisses, every night I received a stuffed animal, which my son selected with the greatest care.

I'm not certain why David's behavior improved. Perhaps the change could be attributed to the fact that he had grown older. Or maybe, since I had a respite while he went to nursery school, I felt less tense and did not overreact to everything he did. Who knows? But I thought David even handled the jealous feelings toward his brother in a better fashion, since he had acquired speech for a tool. One day as I prepared to leave for an overnight trip, David said, "Jonathan goes too."

Shocked at this gesture of goodwill, I skeptically asked, "You want me to take Jonathan?"

"Yes," he replied, "take Jonathan to Granny's and leave him there." Now that young David could verbalize his feelings, I concluded, he no longer needed to act on every whim. I anticipated an improvement in life around our house, at least where David was concerned.

Even though young David's behavior seemed less problematic, tensions within our marriage flared. Most of our problems did not arise as a result of trying to manage our son. If anything, David's difficulties enabled us to avoid facing the harsh realities. My husband and I found ourselves entangled in a mess of negative interactions; he blamed me, and I, of course, blamed him, for the unhappiness. Before we could address the issues, life handed us a few major stresses within a period of two months. Our marital situation deteriorated from bad to worse.

David Sr. switched jobs, and a year to the day after we'd moved, we once again relocated. Since this change brought us back home, we didn't anticipate that it would be particularly stressful. We had not learned that new jobs and brand-new houses, even in familiar territory, automatically upset the status quo. This time I flew into orbit because of the additional stress resulting from the death of my father the day after we moved.

No one had been stamped HANDLE WITH CARE for this journey. Only our belongings arrived intact—but they didn't stay that way long after being unpacked. First, a family-room lamp smashed when three-and-a-half-year-old David clipped it with his feet while somersaulting off the couch. A teacup met its destruction next, though not by accident: when David Sr. made a critical remark, I hurled the cup at the kitchen wall. For months, until I wallpapered the room, tea stains bore witness to my loss of self-control.

Young David's reactions, however, proved impossible to cover up. He unleashed his temper with a fury that rocked the nursery school walls. In one morning, he hit a child, pushed another off the slide, and threw sand at yet a third. The teacher, totally exasperated, sat him in the corner for over an hour. Even after I arrived, she refused to allow him to leave that spot until she vented her frustration on me.

He looked so frightened. I could not believe David had behaved so aggressively without provocation. Since this teacher clearly played favorites and my little boy did not make her list, I rationalized that she might be partly to blame for his behavior by doing nothing to ease his transition to this new school. I bit my tongue so as not to scream at her, "Why don't you give him a break? Can't you see how this move affected him?"

When I recounted this incident to David Sr. he agreed with my assessment of the nursery school teacher's role. But, as always, he carried his comments a step further and insisted this new teacher did not recognize David's need of special attention. By now, I suspected young David might have some underlying problem that made his life intense. But honestly accepting the possibility that my son could have a hurt I couldn't fix threatened me, so I tried to ignore my suspicions, to bury my fears. I had no conception of what more I could do for my boy.

A few weeks after the school episode, David's outbursts at home intensified with such magnitude, his rages scared me. I confiscated the croquet set along with all sticks and blunt objects. When David got mad, he let them fly at anyone or anything in his path. Punishment had little, if any, effect. His temper could not be controlled.

With the tea from my rampage still a blot on the kitchen wall, I felt responsible, as though somehow he patterned his actions after what others now referred to as "my high-strung behavior." His father continually said to me, "You're the one having the problem." There seemed no other explanation but the obvious, his mother. My self-esteem hit an all-time low. I slipped into a depression.

Life in our home became enshrouded in unpleasantness. Young David blamed everybody and everything for his behavior. When he ran in the house and crashed into a table, he smashed that "bad table" to bits. When I said, "David, you did the running," he got angrier. If he fell off his bike, instead of crying like other children, David repeatedly threw it to the ground or into the garage door. Even when playing nicely, David managed to break all his toys. His room always looked as if a tornado had just passed through. None of the children in our new neighborhood invited him to play except one very mild-mannered young boy. Often Jonathan received the full thrust of his brother's fury. But unless he had been physically hurt, Jon took David's actions in stride, and I was thankful that at least my younger son was mellow.

David's dad coped with the turmoil by denying its existence and burying himself in work. I buried my head under the covers minutes after the boys went to bed. During the daylight hours, I felt tired all the time. A friend suggested I get out more with the boys and take them to the beach. Well, I thought, that couldn't hurt. But after a week my stomach went into severe spasms.

David refused to obey the beach club rules. Such audacity always resulted in a reprimand from the owner, who then flashed me a dirty look. Time and again I redirected young David's attention, but he did not learn to stop even when I forcefully removed him from off-limits places. He pushed and pulled until he became free and immediately returned to the scene of the crime. Eventually he wore me down, and I either gave in to his whims or left the beach in a huff. The other mothers gave us a very wide berth.

That summer ended when Jonathan was hospitalized with a mysterious virus. The week before, my mother had commented about how pale he looked, but Jonathan never fussed, so I assumed his health was fine. Years later, our child psychologist explained this incident to be a prime illustration of his favorite cliché, "The squeaky wheel gets the oil." David became the center of all that happened in our house by demanding so much of our time and energy. Everyone else's needs went unattended.

Relatives warned both David Sr. and me that our younger son did not receive enough attention. Still, everyone laughed when I referred to our boys as Charlie McCarthy the dummy and his ventriloquist Edgar Bergen. David constantly interrupted his younger brother to finish Jon's every sentence. Though I agreed with my family that David clearly usurped center stage, I quickly dismissed their comments. "But the attention Jonathan gets is always positive," I explained. "David gets nothing but negative press," his father concurred. I could not understand why these people did not see how little we, as parents, had left to give.

No one who walked through our door could avoid the tension. My husband and I reacted through shouting matches or angry silences. By fall, the hostility proved impossible to submerge. We individually sought private therapy, which led to marriage counseling.

The therapist needed time to sort out the mess of our marriage. Yet he almost immediately realized that our son's behavior, though not the cause of our problems, acted as a catalyst for our negative patterns to surface. However, why all our family outings ended in disaster and why chaos constantly surrounded us remained a mystery.

After the events of David's fourth birthday party, neither his dad nor I could continue to make excuses for our son's outrageous behavior. That day, after all the little guests arrived, David flipped into a frenzy. His mood grew so dark that he zapped all the joy from the event. The party ultimately degenerated into an ugly scene at the petting zoo when David smacked a horse in the mouth, an action that totally stunned his dad and me.

All along we figured our son's aggressive behavior to be a reaction to some provocation. Clearly, he hit the horse for no apparent reason. Initially we felt like strangling him, but after the shock subsided, we realized David had no control. Where I once viewed him as the master of his deeds, now I saw he needed help. Though his dad still didn't believe our son could have a problem, we set out to find the source of what troubled him.

That journey turned into a pathetic comedy of errors. We spent eighteen months going from one professional to another before we obtained an accurate diagnosis. Our search began at the pediatrician's office. In my initial conversation I told the doctor everything about David's behavior that puzzled me.

The pediatrician sent us to an allergist who saw David in November of 1983. The allergist observed David to be hyperactive and told me no one really understood the cause of hyperactivity. David's test indicated an allergy to house dust, for which he received shots every week.

The allergist also placed David, a finicky eater to begin with, on an elimination diet to see if specific foods exacerbated his problems. We then used the Feingold diet, which promised to alleviate hyperactivity by restricting food additives, preservatives, salicylates, and sugar. The promises of the Feingold diet proved worthless. I figured I must be doing something wrong. Though none had tried this diet personally, every mother I knew said she heard it worked miracles with other mothers' kids. A year later we learned that diet and allergy do not cause ADHD and that no miracles cure it.

In the meantime, we landed in a child psychiatrist's office. After taking a family history and observing David interact with us, the child psychiatrist said, "David is hyperactive." He told us our son would outgrow his hyperactivity around puberty and suggested we could use medication if we needed to "slow him down" until then.

The real issue of treatment, he believed, centered around David's angry and ill-mannered behavior. When I asked why our son acted so horrendous, the child psychiatrist said, "Because he has an extreme case of sibling rivalry. You introduced another sibling at the crucial individuation/separation stage of development." At ninety dollars an hour in 1984, I figured he knew his material.

This doctor suggested that I read about individuation/separation. He gave me a clinical text offering an in-depth discussion of this critical stage and other stages as well. He then made a recommendation that validated my gnawing suspicion that I was a horrible mother. The psychiatrist told David Sr. to give our son at least two hours a day of individual attention so young David could work through this stage again. When we pointed out that Dad traveled every week, the doctor said, "Hire a neighborhood teenage boy as a substitute father." Though our marriage wavered on shaky ground, neither of us believed David Sr. could be that easily replaced. A few months later, we ceased using this doctor's counsel when he recommended we gag David to stop him from releasing his ear-piercing shrieks when riding in the car. Nothing improved in our house under that professional's care.

With the school year drawing to a close, my husband and I faced the decision of whether or not to enroll our soon-to-be-five-year-old son in kindergarten. Having no confidence left in our parenting abilities, we attended a seminar on "kindergarten readiness" for direction. As usual, the norms did not fit David. The speaker, a licensed and certified school psychologist, suggested he evaluate David privately.

That evaluation lasted an hour and a half. Though David could sustain performance a full year ahead of his age, the psychologist recommended we not place him in kindergarten. In his three-page report to us, the psychologist wrote, "David is very active and has a poor attention span. He is easily distracted and will not stay with tasks for very long. He is a very intense young child and given to open displays of anger and yelling. David does not like new or different situations and cannot re-adapt even after some exposure to them." He had described a child who displayed all the behaviors that are the very hallmarks of attention deficit hyperactivity disorder.

Instead of telling us the source of David's problems or referring us to a clinician who specialized in the disorder, his report contained these recommendations: "I would prefer David to be in a very structured and controlled setting at home. If things are always organized and predicted, and quiet and arranged so as not to stimulate David, he can calm down readily and have some control. His activity is not beyond him."

How ridiculous! David's activity proved beyond him, beyond me, beyond the entire family. Unfortunately, knowledge and understanding of attention deficit hyperactivity disorder proved beyond this child development specialist, as well as the other professionals from whom we sought counsel and guidance. Today, thanks to better education about ADHD, few parents have to lose precious years looking for help.

Signs and Symptoms

Signs and symptoms of ADHD become highly visible at this preschool stage, except in very mild cases. Children between the ages of three and five with mild to moderate ADHD generally experience problems in one major setting: at home, in preschool, or with peers. Children like David, with moderate to severe degrees of the disorder, show difficulties in all three areas.

Nursery school teachers mainly notice an inability to follow directions and stay on task. Children with ADHD tend to be away from their desks more than their classmates. Frequently teachers describe them as "immature."

In nursery school, children with ADHD demonstrate problems in different degrees of severity. While only one teacher made only one serious complaint about David, Jan Lawes received such negative reports about her son Doug's behavior that she became a volunteer at his school. As she explains her rationale: "I thought if I did ever thing they could possibly want, they would tolerate my kid a little better."

Unlike Doug Lawes, Steven White, who does not have the hyperactive or impulsive symptoms of the disorder, was not at all disruptive in school. Still, his mother, Lynn, heard frequent complaints from Steven's preschool teacher because he daydreamed so much and seldom paid attention. Imagine being in this parent-teacher conference: To defend her son after hearing so much negativity, Lynn said to the teacher, "Well, you know some kids march to the beat of a different drummer." The teacher insensitively replied, "And some have no drummer at all." These words crushed Lynn. From then on, she worried herself sick about him. An evaluation in third grade revealed that Steven had the inattentive type of ADHD. (He also has petit mal epilepsy.)

Children with the inattentive type of ADHD have a very hard time. Many of them are not diagnosed or even recognized as having a problem in early years because they do not antagonize others. Instead, they stay quietly off task, do poorly in school, may have accidents due to not paying attention, and suffer in silence. Ultimately, they get labeled—usually as "lazy." They also tend to be invisible, meaning that their difficulties go unnoticed. They live lives of quiet desperation.

Social Behavior

While these children with the mainly inattentive type do not create disturbances, they do have trouble fitting in socially, usually because they don't know how to involve themselves in typical childhood activities. Their behavior, however, tends to be unlike that of hyperactive, impulsive children, who are frequently verbally or physically aggressive with their peers. Though boys tend to be more aggressive than girls with the disorder, they do not corner the market on aggressive peer interactions.

According to her mother, five-year-old Maggie Anderson did not fit the "sugar and spice" mold supposedly characteristic of young ladies. When Maggie went to a friend's house, if something did not go her way, she literally knocked her female playmate to the floor. After each incident, Maggie's mother apologized and explained that her daughter had a problem with self-control, which she and Maggie's dad were trying to correct. Nonetheless, Maggie would still be banished from the other child's home for a period of months.

The overall social behavior of these children is aptly described as immature and insensitive. Dr. Russell Barkley explains, "Children with ADHD lack self-awareness. They are mentally and developmentally immature, and so they behave like younger children. Younger children do not pay much attention to how their behavior affects other people or themselves."

In addition to immature, Dr. Keith Conners describes them as "socially insensitive." For example, he notes the frequency with which they blurt out very embarrassing comments in company. Such gaffes are made, he explains, because children with ADHD are insensitive to the demands of the situation and how their interactions might affect others.

Instead of using a rule as a guide to action, these children apply the rule in a hard-and-fast way. Since they tend to be insensitive to internal states in themselves, they often prove insensitive to how others are feeling. These children also misread feedback they receive from others about their social behavior. Dr. Conners says, "Often these kids are amazed they have had an effect on somebody."

If you consider the child with ADHD's immature and insensitive nature and factor in the impulsivity that may accompany this disorder, you can easily see why social problems become a constant thorn in his or her side. These children generally react before they make an accurate assessment of a situation to determine what behavior is appropriate. They also tend to be disorganized and so behave in a chaotic manner. Dr. Conners explains that the prerequisites for good socialization are being able to wait your turn, to share with others, and to follow the rules of the game. Since children with ADHD often cannot delay impulses, impulsivity prevents them from learning these basic rules of fairness. Dr. Conners also cites two other factors that contribute to social problems for children with ADHD. Because of their hyperactivity, these children are usually not in one place long enough to play a game or to learn the rules. Children with ADHD frequently have associated visual-motor problems, which makes playing sports somewhat harder too.

According to Dr. Conners, "Children with ADHD are different from the antisocial kid who wants to hurt other children. Children with ADHD just cannot control themselves." The inability to restrain behavior and respond appropriately to the demands of a social situation often cause children with ADHD to experience negative consequences in every arena of social interaction, be that the playground, the neighborhood, the school bus, or the classroom. These children are rejected by playmates, isolated from groups. They receive many unkind comments and are usually the last kids picked for teams if they are picked at all. Most parents know too well the sad fact that their sons and daughters often find themselves excluded from birthday parties. Dr. Conners makes the point that children with ADHD *want* to be liked and *want* to be involved, but their ADHD characteristics often prevent them from positive social interactions.

Friendship Building

Generally, children with ADHD can make friends, but they have trouble keeping the friends they make. We parents can help them by taking certain steps at home that build social bridges. These steps take time and effort, so parents need to be persistent and involved.

Dr. Zakreski, a clinical psychologist, helps parents do social bridge building in his private practice. He says this technique works better with younger children.

Find a Playmate

Steps for social bridge building may be easy, but they do require planning, organization, and time. Also, keep the goal in mind—especially in the beginning. You want your child to have a positive interaction with another child. Do not worry at this stage about bringing to your child a friend for life. Begin by finding a child who can be a playmate. A good choice would be someone with whom your child has already made a positive connection. For instance, if your son or daughter comes home from school and says, "Johnny was nice to me," Johnny becomes a good candidate. Dr. Zakreski advises the parent to make the invitation. Otherwise, the child may never get around to it or may be reluctant to ask for fear of rejection.

Design a Successful Activity

The next step becomes critical. Remember, you want to create a situation that allows positive interactions between the two children. Selecting the right activity for the right amount of time is essential. You want the kids to do something that lends itself to parental involvement and supervision—for example, baking cookies or going bowling. This way, you can control the activity; if problems arise, you can intercede. Your involvement also allows you to give your son or daughter feedback about prosocial behavior.

Do the bridge-building process as often as necessary to encourage friendship and a routine interaction between your child and the playmate. As these children gradually begin to interact positively and successfully with one another, you will increase the amount of time they spend together and decrease your direct supervision. Do not rely on the child's age to determine how much play and how much involvement you have. When ADHD is present, your involvement or lack of it is determined by the social skills of the child.

Repeat the Process

When one successful relationship has been started, begin another. Dr. Zakreski advises parents to keep interaction to a one-on-one situation, which avoids the possibility of the odd-man-out problem.

Some clinicians recommend social-skills training groups. To date, most research does not support their effectiveness. The children seem to do well while in group, but they do not often apply the skills taught in groups outside of the group setting. According to Dr. Barkley, disinhibition (not adequately regulating behavior by rules or consequences) and the lack of thinking through situations are what create the difficulty. Consequently, disinhibition cannot be trained out of a child.

Problems at Home

During the preschool years, in the absence of an effective behavior management program such as the one described in the previous chapter, most children with ADHD continue to be hard to manage. Psychologist C. Keith Conners notes that particularly during these preschool years, since the bulk of the child care falls primarily on the mother, fathers often do not see the child as the master of his or her behavior. Many fathers tend to think that the child's behavior problems are the mother's fault, that she is either too strict or too lenient. Ben Green, a father I spoke with, said he initially thought his wife somehow provoked their son's negative behavior because his son behaved fairly well for him.

In his book *Attention Deficit Hyperactivity Disorder: A Handbook for Diagnosis and Treatment,* Dr. Barkley notes that in general these children are less oppositional with their fathers, possibly for the following reasons. Since Mom usually spends more time with the child, she is more likely to be making a greater amount of demands than the father. Consequently, moms have more opportunity to be in situations of conflict. Also, moms are more likely to use reasoning and affection to encourage compliance with requests. Dads, on the other hand, use less reasoning and more punishment. Though Laurie Maxwell's husband did not find fault with her parenting style, friends often asked, "Why don't you spank your son more?" She did not spank him more because physical punishment does not make children with ADHD behave better.

Children with the disorder lack self-control. People have a hard time accepting that the ability to regulate behavior according to the rules and demands of a situation results from neurobiology and not free will. Frequently parents either hear from others or believe that they are doing something wrong. Not so. A simple reprimand will usually work with most children. ADHD happens to be a problem of behavioral inhibition. Because these children tend to be "managed by the moment," as Dr. Barkley puts it, they usually do not learn from experience. Thus the disciplinary techniques that work with most children prove ineffective when the child has the disorder.

"Children with ADHD do not respond to the softer management techniques and subtle social consequences," Dr. Barkley observes. Thus most parents of children with ADHD need to be trained (as described in chapter 2) in how to set rules, how to institute consequences, how to give commands clearly, how to follow through with appropriate consequences, and how to limit the number of demands they make upon the child.

Common Parent Pitfalls

Inconsistent Consequences

Before many of us learn appropriate ways to manage the hard-to-handle child, Dr. Barkley notes, we parents of children with ADHD tend to administer consequences in an extremely inconsistent way. The child on one day may have the roof fall on his or her head for a mildly inappropriate behavior. The next day, when he or she repeats the behavior, the parent may make little of it or perhaps even find it mildly amusing. Also seen in our families is noncontingent punishment—that is, the consequences are not contingent upon something the child does. The child with ADHD becomes the family scapegoat, and everyone's bad mood falls onto the child's shoulders.

Talk and Reason

What mother doesn't like to think of herself as a reasonable individual? That's part of the natural tendency to nurture. Often when making a request, parents—particularly mothers—accompany it with hundreds of reasons to justify it. That's a big mistake with ADHD. I have learned that reasoning only invites more opportunity for conflict, and as most of their parents eventually discover, children with ADHD make great lawyers. As Dr. Barkley explains, "For children with ADHD, reason carries no weight whatsoever." I'll take it a step further. When I try to reason with my son, who is now in late adolescence, he becomes irritated, usually because reasoning takes time, and time is something he never has, or so he thinks. He just hates to wait!

Say It Again and Again and Again

Parents often fall prey to the excessive repetition of commands. Though parents usually repeat themselves to get the child to listen and do what is asked, excessive repetition may actually train the child *not* to pay attention! Think about how you respond to a back-seat driver type, the kind of person who is always "in your face." Chances are that the minute you hear that voice, you tune out. These children are prone to do likewise.

Good Cop/Bad Cop

Increases in oppositional behavior can also result from persistent disagreements between spouses over the best way to manage the child. The seriousness of such disputes caught my attention recently when a tearful mom told me about the horrendous difficulties that befell her teenage son, including a brush with the law. Since the child's earliest years, this mom, who did all the disciplining, had been trapped in a bad-cop role because her husband constantly dismissed the child's inappropriate behavior as "no big deal." The dad's pattern was to sympathize with his son, which in turn made him the good cop. This father has continued to feel sorry for his son, who has managed to get away with some pretty serious stuff, like skipping school, without negative consequences. Thus the mother's attempts to hold the child accountable for his behavior have become virtually useless and, sadly, almost laughable to her son.

Of course, the roles played by Mom and Dad could just as easily be reversed. Nonetheless, this scenario underscores the importance of parents working as a team. While in the toddler years perhaps parents are disagreeing over seemingly minute punishments such as withholding dessert for not eating dinner, the stakes become considerably higher when the older child learns to play one parent against the other, as the example shows

Parents in Quicksand

The ineffective techniques described above often join together and form a pattern of interaction between the parent (usually the mother, but also the father) and the child with ADHD. This pattern is so significant that it even has a name: the coercive interaction pattern. It can be seen between teachers and students as well. According to Dr. Barkley, when this pattern becomes the typical way the parents and child interact, the likelihood that the child will be more hostile and oppositional in the future increases significantly.

As explained by Dr. Barkley, here's what happens. The parent demands that the child do something the child views as work and does not enjoy. At this point, the child either does or does not comply with the demand. (In families where this pattern occurs frequently, Dr. Barkley notes, reward or appreciation is seldom given when the youngster does do what is asked.) In the case where the child does not do what is asked, usually the parent repeats the command, which of course postpones any consequence the child would receive for being disobedient.

By talking and repeating, the parent becomes less effective. Why? The child sees that Mom's or Dad's word is not backed up. By the time the child receives punishment, he or she has been allowed to continue to do things his or her way. Without realizing, parents have actually reinforced the misbehavior, because the child wins at doing what he or she chooses and at waiting out the parent.

The pattern doesn't stop here. Typically, after about fifteen or twenty minutes of the child not doing what is asked, the parent makes threats. As the youngster ignores each threat, the parent becomes frustrated, then makes bigger threats, which the child knows will be modified in some way. For example, the parent might say, "You'll never see your bike again," or "I'm throwing that play station in the trash." With each threat, both parties become more out of control.

At this point, in 70 percent of the cases, Dr. Barkley says, the parent gives in, which means the demand was not met the way the parent initially requested. Either the parent steps in and does whatever is asked of the child, or the demand is simply not met at all. About 30 percent of the time the child is punished, but punishment occurs too late in the interaction to be of much value.

Another form of giving in, which does not happen very often, is the situation in which the parent actually rewards the child for not complying. Dr. Barkley says when the parent acquiesces in this manner, the likelihood the child will engage in future oppositional behavior increases by 400 percent. This type of response is seen most frequently when the child throws a loud and obnoxious temper tantrum. The parent not only stops making the demand but may hold the child or stroke the child's hair in a calming effort.

Getting Out of Quicksand

To defeat coercive interactions, Dr. Barkley suggests that parents make the following changes. First, parents should limit the amount and type of demands they make upon the child with ADHD. Before making a demand, the parents should also determine if the child is capable of meeting it. Once they do make a demand, parents must follow through on it and administer consequences.

Second, parents should provide substantially more rewards, such as those suggested in the previous chapter, when the child does comply with a request. Dr. Barkley says that not responding to appropriate behavior is perhaps the biggest mistake parents of children with ADHD can make.

The best way to *increase* good behavior is to acknowledge and reward it. The best way to *decrease* good behavior is to ignore it. Parents should also be mindful of the things they do that are pitfalls when disciplining the child with ADHD. The less these ineffective techniques are used, the better the chance of taking positive action.

Too often during the preschool period, the rewards prove few and far between for the child with ADHD. Between the ages of three and five, some of these preschoolers display temper tantrums, outbursts of rage, and aggressive and destructive tendencies, often in public places. When asked to be accountable for their behavior, children with ADHD commonly place the blame on someone or something other than themselves.

No one knows for certain what causes these aggressive and acting-out type of behaviors. They could be a part of the disorder itself, or a result of the manner in which the child and his environment interact, or both. I suspect the child with ADHD is like a tumbleweed rolling over the desert where each movement gathers a little more dust and dirt. Though David as an infant evidenced a moody and irritable disposition, certainly my reactions to his ADHD behaviors served to make his symptoms and our overall situation worse. The ultimate irony of this disorder is the child with the worst symptoms needs the greatest support, but receives instead the lion's share of negative feedback.

Family Effects

Self-esteem

Though the primary pain of ADHD falls mainly on the child's shoulders, all family members experience the disorder's negative effects. Parents frequently fall into the guilt-and-blame trap. Mothers especially become convinced they are bad parents and suffer from low self-esteem. We feel depressed, ashamed, resentful, and embarrassed because of our apparent failure as parents to raise a well-mannered and obedient child.

Dr. Conners has observed that mothers of children with ADHD will invariably cry if he says something to this effect: "I'm surprised you're still hanging in there. You must feel awful about yourself for some of the responses this child has elicited from you. But I really admire you. You must really care about your child to do as well as you have done." He commented that these mothers feel a tremendous sense of guilt because they think they have let the child down. Dr. Conners believes parents of children with ADHD need to understand that "the disorder creates a great deal of stress and that they are only human."

According to Jean Bramble, a former ADHD caseworker at Primary Children's Medical Center in Salt Lake City, adoptive parents of children with ADHD, like biological parents, also feel guilty. She has observed, however, that in some cases, adoptive parents feel an additional layer of guilt as well. This other guilt comes not only from feelings of inadequacy because of their inability to manage their adopted child, but also from their belief that perhaps they were never meant to have children. She said, "Indeed that is not the case. These parents are loving and readily seek help for their adoptive children."

Marriage

In addition to feelings of guilt and blame, marital discord often arises as a by-product of this disorder. That is not to suggest that the child causes the marital problems. As this country's staggering divorce rate reveals, many marriages are flawed and for many reasons. In the case of ADHD, the marital discord arises because, as Dr. Conners notes, "Marriages are held together by the peace and quiet of ordinary times. Those times are missing in most of these families." Particularly prior to diagnosis and intervention, as husbands and wives struggle with the child's behavioral difficulties and the seemingly constant turmoil, their interactions appear to be at cross-purposes and out of balance.

Further compounding this distress are the family histories of children with ADHD. These often reveal other stressors as well. Dr. Barkley reports that psychiatric disorders are more common among parents of children with ADHD, with the most common disorder being ADHD in the parent. Marital disputes have a higher incidence in families where ADHD is present. Divorce is twice as common. Sixty percent of the mothers suffer from low self-esteem; about one-fourth of them become clinically depressed and require professional intervention. Fifteen percent of the fathers evidence alcohol or other substance abuse problems.

Siblings

The family disruption does not stop with marital discord. Dr. Conners describes the effect this disorder has on the siblings of the child with ADHD as "profound." He notes that siblings suffer because ADHD is so disruptive to family life, adding: "Frequently, younger siblings feel terrorized by this child who does not know his limits and will actively avoid any contact with the child with ADHD. Older siblings are usually more distant and don't spend much time around the sibling with ADHD because they are embarrassed by his or her behavior."

Younger sister Heather Flood told me she often felt her parents were not fair and always gave her brother far more attention. Diana Stevenson, an older sibling I spoke with, said that whenever she had to go out to dinner with the family she worried someone would say, "Look at the looney tune and his family. They're probably all like him."

Dr. William McMahon of Primary Children's Medical Center notes that siblings of children with ADHD commonly place the blame for all their arguments and fights on the child with ADHD. Some siblings do so with such skill that they appear perfect. Dr. McMahon follows one family in which the younger sister of the child with ADHD frequently sets her brother up so that the parents do not realize that she has caused the trouble. Ordinarily, when they play, she ends up screaming and the boy gets punished for upsetting her.

Melanie Hartsgrove, the mother of Sandy, a child with ADHD, said, "Sandy became the family scapegoat. Whenever he and his sister had a fight, Sandy got blamed because I expected him to be the bad child. His sister instigated a lot of the trouble, but because Sandy is louder and can't cover up as well, he got in trouble."

Psychologist Sam Goldstein stresses that the siblings of a child with ADHD need to be part of the treatment system. In counseling, Dr. Goldstein strives to make the siblings either positive or at least neutral toward the child with ADHD. He recalled one case in which both siblings, because they had such legitimate complaints about their brother's behavior, practically convinced him that the family would be better off if the child with ADHD moved away.

In homes where great difficulties exist among siblings, therapists often deal with the problem using behavior management techniques for the siblings as well as the child with ADHD. In the case cited by Dr. Goldstein, to get the siblings to stop picking on the child with ADHD and vice versa, he used superordinate goals. For example, the entire family would be treated to a trip to the amusement park provided there were no fights or arguments among siblings.

For Peace Sake

Certainly, problems between siblings occur in most families. But when AD/HD is present, the conflicts are perhaps more frequent, more intense, and more destructive. To restore family peace, parents must acquire behavior management techniques. We must be trained to make rules clear, to set consequences, to institute those consequences properly, and to reward good behavior. A parent without these skills can usually slide by when ADHD is not present. But a child with ADHD finds every loophole a parent might leave open. Behavior management is an essential tool to order a disordered environment.

Though many parents find such rigidity a drudge, happy side effects do arise from good behavior management. Instead of losing both patience and face because the child does not obey, parents have the option to step out of the line of fire. They can apply a consequence immediately for their child's misbehavior and thereby place the responsibility for the child's actions where it belongs, on the child and not on the parent. That includes making siblings accountable for their behavior as well.

Couples also need to make extra efforts to enjoy life and each other. Husbands and wives can easily become overfocused on the child with special needs to the exclusion of nurturing their mutual interests. Of course, parents often discover that even when they make attempts to spend private, quality time with each other, their efforts are sometimes thwarted because babysitters also find children with ADHD hard to manage.

Liz Sacca once hired the daughter of a town councilman to watch her child with ADHD and his brothers. When she arrived home later that night, Liz found the sitter in a heap in the middle of the floor, crying because long after she put the children to bed, the child with ADHD managed to wake his brothers and engage them in a game of toss with Mom's precious knickknacks. Other mothers, like Betty Garver, never hired babysitters because they worried that a sitter might underestimate their daredevil child with ADHD.

Finding and keeping babysitters can be especially tricky in situations where ADHD runs the household. Through the use of behavior management, parents usually meet the challenge of getting ADHD-related difficulties under control, which results in an absence of chaos. Quiet, peaceful moments tend to reappear—as do the babysitters who in the past proved unwilling to set foot through your door a second time.

In addition to spending time nurturing the marriage, the parent who is home with the child needs some special time each day to recharge. The time alone does not have to involve an exotic activity. Some mothers renew themselves by taking walks. Others, like Laurie Maxwell, find peace in the bathtub. Whatever, we need to develop a healthy respect for the extra energy required to parent a child with special needs and not push ourselves to the max. Time out for quiet time is sage advice.

Meditation is just one way to achieve peace of mind. It doesn't require that you sit in a lotus position for hours on end. And, as appealing as it may sound, you don't even have to run off by yourself and go live in an ashram. Actually, meditation can be any quieting activity. I like to think of meditation as a way of managing my behavior. When I am calm, I can handle the distress around me with greater ease and skill, so taking care of myself has become essential. Meditation calms the mind and lifts the spirit. Bookstores have lots of books on this subject. A good one to start with is *Wherever You Go, There You Are* by Jon Kabat Zinn.

Summary

Signs and Symptoms During Preschool Stage

- Often become highly visible
- Difficulties arise at home, in school, with peers
- Preschool parents and teachers commonly report these difficulties:
  — following directions
  — staying on task
  — immaturity
  — easily frustrated
  — temper tantrums
  — aggressive and destructive behavior
  — noncompliance
  — noisiness

Social Interactions

- Social rejection often occurs
- Parental involvement in encouraging prosocial behavior advised:
  — invite a child to be a playmate
  — devise a structured play situation
  — limit the length of play period
  — pay positive attention to appropriate social behavior
  — repeat process frequently with same playmate

Ineffective Parenting Techniques

- Inconsistent consequences
- Noncontingent punishment
- Talk and reason
- Excessive repetition of commands
- Idle threats
- Good cop/bad cop

Effects of Ineffective Techniques

- Increase likelihood of oppositional behaviors
- Reinforce negative behaviors
- Develop a cyclical pattern of negative interactions

Effective Parenting Techniques

- Limit amount and types of demands
- Follow through with immediate consequences

- Provide lots of rewards—that is, *catch the child being good*
- Make the child accountable for his or her behavior

Effects on Family Members

- Parents, especially mothers, often become depressed and develop poor self-esteem
- Feelings of guilt develop
- Marital discord arises or intensifies
- Siblings become fearful or distant
- Conflicts with siblings become more frequent and more intense
- Siblings blame child with AD/HD for sibling behavior
- Finding babysitters proves difficult
- Couples must structure special time to be alone
- Parents must recharge themselves; try meditation

CHAPTER FIVE

Diagnosis

The fall David turned five, his dad and I decided not to launch his public school career. We both felt our son behaved too immaturely to succeed in that environment. Instead we placed him in the private kindergarten offered by his nursery school with the idea that he could then begin the public school's kindergarten program the following year.

Where previously David's blue eyes had caught the nursery school staff's attention, his black-and-white world now cast him in a different light. David did not see shades of gray. He related to everything and everybody in either/or, good-or-bad, yes-or-no terms. Teachers once assured me David just needed to mature. Now they asked me why he lagged behind.

By now, I realized David's nature had been extreme since day one and would more than likely remain so. Halfheartedly I joked with his teachers about the way his life would unfold. "David," I told them, "will either be a Rhodes scholar or an eighth-grade dropout, but he will never know mediocrity."

When the school's director administered some standardized tests in October, David's results bore witness to my comments. In most of the areas tested, such as listening comprehension and math concepts, David scored in the normal to above-normal ranges, but he performed quite poorly in the tests that measured simultaneous processing (the ability to distinguish parts from the whole) and visual discrimination. This score disparity led the director to believe our son had a learning disability. She suggested the school district's child study team evaluate David to find out "why this very capable child could not perform."

Though the evaluation promised some long-awaited answers, I felt threatened by the idea that David might not be able to survive on the basis of his intelligence. All along I had told myself David's intellectual capabilities would compensate for his interpersonal difficulties. Now even that idea seemed unrealistic. His father and I agreed to have our son evaluated by the child study team, though we did not have the vaguest concept of what such an evaluation entailed. Next, we learned that child study teams fell under the rubric of special education.

Talk about a week! First I had to accept that David might have a problem. Well, I had seen enough to know that something was amiss for this wonderful child who really had a good heart and mind, even if he did have a difficult manner. But then to be told he might need special education! That seemed absurd. Clearly, this child had a lot of capability. True, he had a really hard time getting that capability in sync with his performance, but why should that require anything special, I wondered. Contributing to my confusion was the perception I had, albeit from the Dark Ages, that special education was a place where children with the most severe disabilities were sent to learn life skills.

I now know that special education is the opportunity given to all children with disabilities that allows them the chance to become an integral part of society by providing them with a meaningful education. With great wisdom and compassion, Congress passed the law providing special education in 1975. Then the law was named the Education of the Handicapped Act (EHA). This law, which was renamed the Individuals with Disabilities Education Act (IDEA) in 1991, has integrity. It ensures an appropriate education for children with disabilities. The law also provides funds to states and local school districts to assist them in the provision of special education. IDEA is the educational bill of rights for children with disabilities and their parents.

Every law has a set of rules and regulations created to implement its intent. For IDEA, those rules and regulations are created by the U.S. Department of Education. They mandate the establishment of child study teams in every school district. These child study teams must evaluate any child known to have or suspected of having a disability to determine whether or not that disability adversely affects the child's educational performance. Based on the evaluation results, if warranted, the district must develop an individual educational program for that child designed to meet his or her unique and special learning needs.

Each state, in accordance with the federal law then develops its own statutes to implement IDEA's rules and regulations. Minimally, every school district in every state must have a multidisciplinary team trained to perform educational evaluations. At least one person on that team must know about the disability for which the child is being evaluated. Otherwise, these teams might miss some valuable clues about how the child's disability might interfere with education. (Please see appendix B for more information about this very important law.)

In the state where I live, the child study team is comprised of a school psychologist, a school social worker, and an LDT-C, the acronym for learning disabilities teacher consultant, which is a teacher trained in the identification of and special teaching methods for children with disabilities. Other professionals (for example, pediatric neurologist, child psychiatrist, speech/language pathologist, physical/occupational therapist) can be invited to submit reports to assist the child study team in its deliberations.

Over the course of six months, from October of 1984 through February of 1985, David's father and I learned the nuts and bolts of a child study team evaluation. The LDT-C and the school psychologist visited David's classroom to observe how he performed academically as well as how he interacted with the teacher and his peers. These team members also spoke with David's teachers to gather their comments and observations about our son that might assist the child study team in determining the nature of David's difficulties. They talked with David to determine what he thought and felt about himself. The social worker met with me for the purpose of gathering a social and medical history, as well as information about any factors I could think of that might contribute to his difficulties.

The LDT-C and the school psychologist administered a battery of educational tests to determine David's intelligence, to assess areas where he did not perform to his ability, and to identify his learning strengths and weaknesses. They also sent David to outside medical consultants.

When the team's social worker came to interview me about our family, I felt at ease. I wanted help for David, so I naively answered her every question, though I could not understand what our son's relationship with his grandfathers had to do with his academic performance. I also responded in great detail to the social worker's queries about our marriage, our family relationships, and our social

histories. By the time I finished my description, she knew everything there was to know about our family.

In January, the team leader sent us a letter in which she requested
we take David for a neurologic examination. I thought of neurologists as heavy-duty doctors who only treated people with gross illnesses or injuries. When I asked the school's director if she knew
why the team wanted this consultation, she too expressed confusion
and concern.

The fact that a hospital housed the neurologist's office added to
my fear. My imagination conjured visions of mad-professor-type
laboratories where men in white coats hooked people up to masses
of electrodes. When young David and I arrived for the exam, I soon
saw that the office contained the usual equipment found in any
doctor's examining room. But not all my fears subsided. I worried
about what conclusions David drew to explain why he had become
the subject of so much scrutiny these days.

When the doctor arrived, I grew very tense. This neurologist
made no attempt to warm up to his little patient. Instead, he got
right into the business at hand. The exam took thirty minutes. After
he took a detailed medical history of David, the doctor questioned
me about my son's personality characteristics and home behavior
and asked if I could think of any recent family stressors, such as a
divorce, that might account for his difficult behavior. But I could
unhappily report to the doctor that David, now five years old, had
showed such difficult tendencies since infancy.

After speaking with me, the doctor gave David a physical examination. He next asked David to walk, skip, and touch his finger to his
nose as fast as he could. David copied geometric designs, drew a
crude picture of a person, and attempted to complete two-step commands. He functioned poorly on all these tests and could not repeat
words in a sequence. The data gathered from these tests and exercises
allowed the neurologist to determine inferentially how David's brain
regulated his behavior. Some of these tasks, such as sequencing and
drawing, provided data about David's motor behavior. They also gave
the doctor insight into our son's ability to attend to tasks and allowed
him to determine whether impulsivity prevented David from taking a
careful and studied approach. Once all the tests were concluded, the
neurologist turned to me and said, "David has attention deficit disorder with hyperactivity." Though he explained what the term meant,
I still did not fully understand David's problem.

When the doctor then proceeded to describe David as negative, aggressive, and developing a poor self-image, I became very confused. I never viewed David as someone with a poor self-image. He always seemed so much in control, so much the master of his deeds, so selfish in his demands for everyone's attention. I felt certain David regarded himself too highly, that he thought no one else deserved as much as he.

"Not so," the doctor said. He then told me David showed some features of anhedonia, which meant he did not derive pleasure or satisfaction from things and so might not respond to the reward systems generally used with children who have ADHD. The full impact of this consultation took effect, and my head began to spin.

Once I collected my thoughts, I pushed the neurologist for the prognosis for a child like David. In a clinical, matter-of-fact voice, he said, "Your son is likely to abuse drugs or alcohol. He could become psychotic or schizophrenic. Treatment might help him." I tried to feel strong, but tears rolled down my cheeks for what seemed like a very long time.

Suddenly, I became aware of David's presence. The entire time the doctor and I spoke, David had been in the room to hear every word. Though he probably did not understand such terms as "anhedonic," "schizophrenic," and "psychotic," I'm sure he could not help but pick up the vibes. I became furious with myself and the doctor for our insensitivity and stupidity. I left the room abruptly. Once outside the office, I tried to explain to David that he need not worry, that everything would turn out fine. David yanked my arm by way of a reply.

I felt nauseated the entire ride home. So many thoughts raced through my head. Did I tell the doctor too much about David's history? Did I color his thinking? Did I exaggerate and make David's problems sound worse than they were? Did I cause David's problems? What did the doctor mean, "anhedonic"? David enjoyed himself from time to time. That evening I told David's dad about the meeting. He dismissed the neurologist's prognoses. I decided to wait for the child study team's findings.

When we met with the child study team two weeks later, each member handed us a typed report. In addition to my husband, myself, and the child study team members, all of young David's teachers and the school's director attended this meeting. The social worker presented her report first. I quickly discovered that what I understood to be our private conversation had become my own personal book of revelations. Very little of what she wrote pertained to David's school situation. I learned after the fact to reveal to school child study team personnel only the family information I wanted to see in print.

The next report came from the learning disabilities teacher consultant. Her less-than-stellar findings dashed my hopes that David did poorly in school because he found the work too mundane for his genius ability.

His teachers told the LDT-C that David was easily distracted and impulsive. With regard to social behavior he functioned on a two-to-three-year-old level. When she observed David's classroom performance, though he could follow directions, she saw how David could not remember to raise his hand or wait to be called on. He could not keep his place on a worksheet, nor could he form numerals with ease.

David approached the testing experience with the LDT-C willingly. However, when the tasks became difficult for him, David shut down and could not be redirected to complete the activity. When asked to throw a bean bag at a target, he became frustrated and wildly threw it around the room. She surmised, "In order to protect his self-image and decrease any embarrassment, David manipulates activities so that he appears successful." This sentence gave me great pause. I always thought "manipulative" implied shrewd or devious. Since David always overstated every thought and action, I never dreamed he could cast a smoke screen.

In this report I also discovered the word "perseveration." This behavior is somewhat akin to the action of a phonograph needle stuck in the groove of a record. As used in David's case, perseveration meant that during testing, he circled the first choice on an entire page of multiple-choice questions, which made an accurate appraisal of his ability impossible.

The school psychologist's report upset us the most. In general, she described David's behavior as immature for a five-and-a-half-year-old and said he repeated words, made nonsense statements, and engaged in baby talk when she asked him questions about himself. Though David behaved this way with us too, we did not know he acted similarly in school. One teacher told the psychologist that David showed no sense of humor and that he demanded perfection from himself and the other kids. The psychologist assessed David's drawings of a tree, house, and people as angular and distorted, and she also saw signs that suggested neurological impairment. Before I could absorb what any of this meant, the school psychologist drew our attention to the next page of her report.

I have no idea how my face looked when I read the part that described David's behavior during the testing. But David Sr.'s pallor turned to a putrid shade of green. We read how David lost his compliant manner and suddenly began to climb on the tester's lap. In his highest-pitched voice he made obscene comments to the examiner, who interpreted David's behavior as an attempt to avoid the work, to test his limits, and to get a reaction. I raised my eyes to check my husband's response but quickly lowered them when I noticed the blank stares on the faces of all the people in the room.

The final paragraph of this report gave me a rare glimpse into the secret world of David's mind. The psychologist wrote, "The examiner tried reading incomplete sentences to David and asked him to verbally complete them. David could not attend to this activity for very long or very well. Two sentences he did complete were 'I wish I could stop . . . being bad,' and 'I worry about . . . strangers.' His comments about what he drew also suggested angry feelings. For example, he described his male person figure as liking to shoot people because he's a bad person when people bother him."

Though others had said David had a poor self-image, until I actually read his words, I had no concept of the darkness that enveloped his world. By the age of five, David no longer possessed a child's capacity to greet each day of life as though it were a huge gift-wrapped package waiting to be opened. He had lost the joy of childhood—and so had I.

With the reports finished, the team leader wanted David's dad and me to sign a form that would make David eligible for special education services. We were stunned to discover on the consent form a label that characterized David as "neurologically impaired." My husband and I jumped to the conclusion that this implied our son had brain damage. His teachers were so alarmed they advised us not to sign the consent form. In fact, we all had been mistaken.

The team leader corrected our misconception when she explained that this label meant a child had a neurologically based problem that impaired learning. Since the services for David at this stage proved to be minimal, we decided not to accept them. Besides, David Sr. still had reservations about the entire process.

The school psychologist made attempts to bolster our spirits. She seemed to understand that when parents first learn that their child is less than perfect, that their child has a disability, the experience proves saddening, scary, disappointing, discouraging, humiliating, and guilt-provoking. She suggested we seek private counseling and recommended a psychologist whose practice mainly dealt with children who had attention deficit hyperactivity disorder. Finally, we had met someone who could help us.

Making the Diagnosis

The diagnosis of ADHD is made on the basis of the child's observable behavioral difficulties. Though it is a hidden disability, the problems caused by the disorder are quite visible. Children with ADHD will evidence academic, social, and emotional difficulties. Usually what draws attention to the child's problems with inattention, disinhibition, impulsivity, and hyperactivity are the outcomes of these characteristics—for example, not completing tasks, losing things necessary for tasks, disorganization, poor planning, and difficulty waiting. Unfortunately, when a child has such difficulties, rather than recognizing them as arising from a neurobiological disorder, the untrained observer often blames the child.

Recent increased public awareness about ADHD has aided in the earlier identification of children who suffer with this disorder. But caution is advised. ADHD has the potential to create lifelong problems. Children should not be considered to have ADHD without undergoing a proper evaluation.

Evaluation: Should You Use the School or an Outside Practitioner or Both?

When a child experiences difficulties that suggest that ADHD may be the problem, parents can have the child evaluated either through the school or by an outside professional. I wish there were a hard and fast rule about which one to choose, but honestly, the decision depends on many variables. Personally, I prefer the outside professional route for three main reasons:

1. You can make your choice based on the practitioner's training and expertise. If you suspect ADHD, select the services of a clinician trained in the assessment and treatment of the disorder. This way, you can avoid the misinformation and wrong diagnoses that can hamper efforts to get help. Also, this practitioner may refer your

child to other specialists for any necessary assessments in their areas of expertise. For instance, a clinical psychologist may refer a child to a pediatric neurologist to rule out other neurological problems or to prescribe medication. Similarly, a pediatrician might refer to a clinical child psychologist if the child needs neuropsychiatric tests or behavior management.

2. ADHD is a medical diagnosis. Schools perform educational assessments. They are concerned with determining whether or not a child meets the eligibility requirements for special education. Thus they focus their evaluations on how the disability affects the child's educational performance, academically and socially. What happens outside the school setting is immaterial to them at the point of diagnosis.

3. Many parents have found their school districts slow to respond to requests to evaluate and offer services for the child suspected of having ADHD. Until you know the source of your child's difficulties, you and your son or daughter cannot get the help you need— which is why I suggest not waiting. Of course, some school districts do give timely and thorough evaluations. You can find out if your school district does so by contacting an ADHD parent support group and asking other parents about their experience.

Even in the best cases, school-district evaluations do not determine the extent of difficulties at home or the need for medication, although districts may choose—or be required by state law—to send the child to an outside licensed practitioner who would look at these factors as well. (Under federal law, a school district is only required to send the child for a medical examination if it believes such an evaluation is necessary to determine special education eligibility.) As mentioned in chapter 3, practitioners licensed to make medical diagnoses include clinical psychologists, neurologists, psychiatrists, pediatricians, and clinical social workers.

I don't want to cause any confusion for you. Please understand that when dealing with your school, you and your child have rights. I would never advise you to give these rights up because a district is being difficult. Instead, get what you need, and then get what you can.

Benefits of Using Both School and Private Evaluators

For children suspected of having moderate to severe degrees of ADHD, parents will most likely find getting both a private evaluation and a school evaluation to be the best course of action. This way, they obtain a medical diagnosis and a thorough educational evaluation, including the administration of special tests designed to identify ability, achievement, and performance. The educational evaluation should also assess all functional impairments your child may be experiencing. Outside practitioners can do educational evaluations, but these can be quite costly. The school does not charge. Also, the school will then determine the need for any special educational program or modification to your child's current program. In effect, the school's assessment becomes the basis for all eductional planning. (See chapter 6 and appendix B for what schools should do.)

Guidelines for a Good Evaluation

The process of diagnosis is much like solving a puzzle; the diagnostician must look at the child from many different angles. In all instances, the evaluator must make a "differential diagnosis"; in other words, determine not only whether your child has ADHD, but whether other disorders are present instead or as well. ADHD-like behaviors can result from a number of different factors including psychosocial stressors, such as parental divorce, death, or sexual abuse, and neuropsychological or physical problems. To make the correct diagnosis, the practitioner has to look at all the factors, differentiate the symptoms, rule out other reasons for the child's problems, and also consider the possibility that the child has more than one disorder.

An issue I believe to be of concern for most parents is the type of diagnostic evaluation performed. We need to be informed consumers. Though not all clinicians will assess ADHD in exactly the same way, there are guidelines that they should follow. A thorough diagnostic evaluation uses multiple sources of information about the child in home, school, and community settings. It has the following components:

1. clinical interviews with parents, child, and teachers (provides relevant information about the developmental, social, and academic history; also looks at present-day concerns)
2. medical history and examination
3. behavior rating scales
4. psychological tests

When assessing for the disorder, practitioners look to establish a pattern of off-task, inattentive, and/or uninhibited, hyperactive behaviors exhibited by the child over a period of at least six months and prior to age seven.

Clinical Interviews: The History

With regard to making a differential diagnosis, psychiatrist Paul Wender says, "A good history is always the most important aspect of any psychiatric evaluation." He suggests the child's history be obtained from the parents and other people, such as teachers or grandparents, who deal with the child on a frequent basis. In fact, Dr. Wender places great stock in the information supplied by teachers since they observe the child's performance in the major developmental tasks of the school-age child, namely, academic performance and social interactions.

The history reported by parents also provides valuable clues about the nature of the child's problems. Many parents, however, are not aware of the importance of their observations. For example, when a pediatric neurologist based a diagnosis of Tom Sacca on a half-hour examination and his mother's depiction of him, Liz Sacca felt skeptical. "I wondered how good the diagnosis could be. Everyone else thought Tommy climbed on mannequins in store windows and never listened to me because I was a bad mother." In Tommy's case, the telltale signs of ADHD proved so obvious, they might as well have been outlined with neon lights. Nonetheless, a thorough assessment would use more than one source of information.

In addition to the child's developmental history, which is obtained during the parental interview, current practice recommends the taking of a family history as well. The family histories of children with ADHD often reveal incidence of ADHD in other family members, learning disabilities, alcoholism, maternal depression, maternal feelings of low self-esteem, and the family pattern of reaction to stress. Dr. Russell Barkley notes that 50 percent of the parents of children with ADHD in his clinic need some form of therapy to treat their problems. In fact, he reports that nationally, among parents of children with ADHD, 30 percent of all fathers and 20 percent of all mothers require treatment as adults for their own ADHD. This family information proves useful for devising a treatment plan as it alerts the practitioner to potential sources of strength and conflict.

Child Interview

Another aspect of the diagnostic process is the interview with the child. This interview allows the examiner to observe your child's behavior firsthand. Caution! As Dr. Conners notes, children with ADHD will often behave like model children on the first visit to a clinician's office. He calls this exemplary behavior the "novelty effect." Dr. Conners explains, "On the third visit that same kid will dismantle my desk if I let him." I also suggest following Paula Anderson's example. When she brought her daughter to see a clinical psychologist, instead of trying to control or manage Maggie's behavior, she let Maggie do whatever she pleased. This way the examiner saw her child's typical behavior.

Parents of daughters beware. Though Maggie's out-of-control behavior caught the examiner's attention, girls generally do not exhibit this type of behavior to the extent that boys with ADHD do. Thus girls go underidentified and, consequently, underdiagnosed. As Dr. Conners notes, "One has to be a really deviant little girl for someone to take her seriously."

Dr. Sally Shaywitz of Yale University Medical School believes this might reflect a bias in referral. "ADD with hyperactivity is so widely accepted as a predominantly boy's disorder that there may be a failure to even consider the possibility of ADHD in girls and consequently a failure to identify all but the most severely affected girls," she says.

The Medical Examination

A pediatric examination is also warranted as part of the diagnostic procedure. Its purpose is to rule out the presence of other physical problems that might create ADHD-like symptoms. In some instances, vision and hearing checks may also be indicated. In all cases, a thorough and up-to-date medical history of the child should be compiled.

Often clinicians, pediatricians included, will refer children being evaluated for ADHD to a pediatric neurologist for a neurological examination. During this exam the neurologist looks for any gross neurologic problems, for instance, epilepsy. Pediatric neurologist Dr. Bennett Shaywitz reports that in 99 percent of cases, the results of these exams are normal; ADHD is considered neurobiological, but this terminology does not mean there is something wrong with the brain's structure. The pediatric neurological assessment also looks for the presence of "soft signs." Unlike paralysis, cerebral palsy, or epilepsy, which give hard evidence of neurologic dysfunction, soft signs—which include poor motor coordination—are somewhat more common in children with the disorder. Dr. Shaywitz explains that soft signs are not diagnostic criteria. In fact, many children without ADHD present soft signs as well.

Being a parent, you want to remember that an ADHD diagnosis is made on the basis of observable symptoms, not by brain anatomy and physiology. Thus, unless a doctor finds evidence of another neurological problem, Dr. Shaywitz advises against the use of sophisticated and costly medical tests such as EEGs, MRIs, and PET scans because they do not reveal the presence or absence of ADHD. Of course, these technologies provide great benefits when used for the purposes for which they were designed. They are also being employed by ADHD researchers in scientific studies. Technology is changing, however, and before long we will probably see some form of these tests put to positive use. Still, at the present moment for most of us in search of diagnosis, these tests would not be useful:

• EEG (electroencephalogram) measures the brain's electrical activity and has great value in detecting seizure activity.

• MRI (magnetic resonance imaging) uses the brain's magnetic fields to give a picture of the brain's anatomy. Since ADHD is not an anatomical problem, MRIs are not useful here.

• PET scans (positron emission tomography) have been used with excellent results for ADHD research purposes. Dr. Alan Zametkin, who conducted the groundbreaking studies of ADHD using this technology, explains, "This technique measures brain metabolism using a form of sugar or glucose that is labeled with a small amount of radioactivity." He emphasizes that PET scans are not biological tests for determining the presence of ADHD but rather one way to try to find out where the mechanisms for controlling attention are in the central nervous system. In fact, the subjects in Dr. Zametkin's study at the National Institute of Mental Health have been diagnosed with ADHD prior to being selected for his research. To date, this technology cannot be used to diagnose the ADHD disorder.

Behavior Rating Scales

Perhaps the most widely used instrument to determine the presence or absence of ADHD behaviors and the degree to which they exist are behavior rating scales. Usually parents and teachers are asked to complete these scales. There are many types, and they vary in purpose. Which one is used by the person doing your child's evaluation depends on preference and the specific information he or she is looking for. Some scales measure a number of childhood behavioral problems; others look for only ADHD-type behaviors.

With most scales, the same procedure is used. Basically, the parent rates the child in terms of frequency of occurence of certain behaviors such as these, which appear on the Conners Parent Symptom Questionnaire: cries easily or often; doesn't get along well with brothers and sisters; restless in the "squirmy" sense; problems with sleep (can't fall asleep; up too early; up in the night). Dr. Conners, the author of this questionnaire, explains that the investigator gets a good indication that a child has ADHD when the parents or teachers continually check those items that show a restless, inattentive, easily frustrated, and impulsive pattern in the child's behavior.

Psychological Tests

As part of the routine exam, many evaluators also give a battery of psychological tests. Some of these tests measure the child's social and emotional adjustment. Others determine whether the child has another disability that impairs learning. Often, children are given IQ tests. Though intelligence tests do not diagnose ADHD, they tell the evaluator whether or not the child can work to his or her potential. Dr. Conners says such tests and formal examinations also allow the diagnostician to observe the child during a structured, intellectual exercise, and thus make note of the child's degree of frustration and ability to stay on task.

Many experts believe that a complete psychoeducational battery of tests should be given routinely when diagnosing ADHD. Besides offering confirming evidence, these tests provide a valuable safeguard. As reported by Dr. Sally Shaywitz, research studies of diagnosed children reveal a significant incidence of learning disabilities that have gone undetected in these children because the appropriate in-depth educational evaluations have not been done.

When these learning problems go undetected, unfortunately, any special instructional needs your child has also go unnoticed. Dr. Shaywitz believes that the behavioral problems shown by these children, especially the hyperactivity, catch people's attention. Thinking they have identified the problem, they do not do an appropriate educational evaluation. She agrees that complete psychoeducational testing should be done as part of all routine diagnostic procedures.

ADHD and the Presence of Other Disorders

ADHD seldom exists by itself. As a case in point, a significant number of children with ADHD also have learning disabilities such as dyslexia. For example, research indicates that one third of all children with ADHD seen in clinics also have a reading disability, and a Yale University study found that 10 percent had a reading disability. (While this figure is lower, Dr. Sally Shaywitz, the study's co-investigator, explains that it came from an epidemiological sample, meaning a study of the general population. So, in fact, the 10 percent figure has added significance because the children seen in this study had ADHD in all degrees of severity ranging from mild to severe; in contrast, children seen in clinics tend to have more severe forms of ADHD and thus a higher probability of having coexisting problems such as learning disabilities.) You need to know this information because schools will often advise you that ADHD requires little, if any, special treatment.

Two other disorders that have a strong likelihood of co-occurring with ADHD are oppositional defiant disorder (ODD) and conduct disorder (CD). Symptoms of ODD include negative temperament, hostile affect, aggression toward others, and repeated intrusion on and violation of the rights of others. Children with ODD often have a negative explosive mood, combined with refusal to obey and aggression toward peers and other people. CD is a repeated pattern of violation of social rules and the rights of others. Behaviors include truancy, lying, stealing or vandalism of property, sexual promiscuity, cruelty to animals and people, and frequently starting fights.

Dr. Barkley estimates that ODD is apparent in approximately 40 to 60 percent of elementary-age children with ADHD. Of this group, between 20 and 30 percent develop CD. Dr. Wender notes, "Hyperactive kids tend to be oppositional and have a greater than ordinary risk of being conduct-disordered and learning-disabled. We can identify pure forms of each disorder. One is not the other, but there is higher probability that each will occur with the other than on a chance basis alone."

Researchers are not certain why these disorders co-occur, although environmental factors seem to play a significant role in the development of ODD and CD. In other words, although parents do not cause

ADHD, if they deal with ADHD-related difficulties through negative emotional reactions and power struggles, they may actually contribute to the development of the negative, hostile, aggressive behaviors associated with ODD and CD. Of course, inborn personality traits are another important factor contributing to the mix.

Dr. Barkley notes that these three disorders sometimes evolve in a developmental fashion with a child evidencing ADHD first, followed by ODD, and then, in later years, CD. His clinic samples show that children who develop ODD have a very high probability of later developing CD. Both disorders also happen to be predictors of substance abuse. However, children with ADHD do not necessarily develop these disorders.

Some clinicians maintain that ODD and CD develop in children from families in which excessive punishment and coercive interactions frequently occur. With this being the case, early diagnosis of ADHD and the multifaceted treatment of its symptoms, including parent training in ways to manage behavioral troubles effectively, may prevent the onset of these other disorders in many cases.

Just as there are disorders that have a strong likelihood of co-occurring with ADHD, there are conditions that may look like ADHD but are not: for example, central auditory processing disorder, which is a disorder of perception, sound, and language; and fetal alcohol syndrome (FAS) or fetal alcohol effect (FAE). Symptoms of hyperactivity, inattentiveness, and poor impulse control are present in these disorders. By using the elements of diagnosis described previously in this chapter, the evaluator would have enough history and medical information to differentiate between ADHD and these other conditions, although similar treatments might be used to manage behavioral difficulties.

After Evaluation

Once the evaluation process is completed and the ADHD diagnosis made, education about the disorder and its manifestations proves to be the first step of treatment. By demystifying ADHD and by replacing with knowledge the myths that we often create to explain our child's difficult behavior, we parents can change our belief systems. Dr. Barkley, for instance, uses education about ADHD—its characteristics, its developmental course, and the risks associated with the disorder—to help parents come to view the child as having a disability. "We don't wish to overwhelm parents with grief," he explains. "If I had to choose from all the childhood disabilities one could have, I'd choose this one. ADHD is by far the least disabling."

Nonetheless, left unrecognized and untreated, this disability has the potential to cause considerable distress for its sufferers. Changing the way we view the child's difficult behavior is an important first step toward achieving a positive outcome. Dr. Barkley has observed that parents who change their perspective expect less from the child and so become less frustrated themselves. Therefore, they do not punish or otherwise come down hard on the child nearly as much.

This change in parenting behavior calls to mind a major principle of behavior management told to me by noted expert Jim Swanson, which is "Don't shoot the dog!" The diagnosis of ADHD helps parents to stop blaming the victim for ADHD-related difficulties. "Don't shoot the dog" also suggests that we parents have to change the way we deal with the child if we want to see a change in the child's behavior.

While diagnosis often brings a sense of relief to parents, it also raises a question. Generally we ask, "What should I tell my child and when?" The explanation Dr. Barkley provides depends on the age of the child. For the older child, he will spend up to an hour on the matter. However, with younger children he suggests a brief explanation. He tells them, "Some kids are good at bike riding, others are not good at art. You have a hard time concentrating on things that are boring, and we understand you can't help that."

After the ADHD diagnosis, the clouds of confusion that surround the whys and wherefores of a child's behavior lift for both parents and child. With the knowledge that neither the parent nor the child caused the problems, guilt and blame are replaced by hope and help.

Summary

Special Education and Child Evaluation

- Under federal law, local school districts must have multidisciplinary assessment teams to evaluate children
- Federal law guarantees all children with disabilities the right to a free, appropriate public education
- School systems evaluate children who may need special education services

- Under special education, school systems must develop an individual educational plan

Diagnosis

- Diagnosed on the basis of observable behavioral difficulties: not completing tasks, losing things necessary for tasks, disorganization, poor planning, difficulty waiting
- Requires a proper evaluation by a trained professional
- School districts perform assessments but may use outside medical professionals when necessary for diagnosis
- Requires a differential diagnosis to note or rule out the presence of other disorders

Elements of Diagnostic Evaluation

- Multiple sources of information
- Clinical interviews with parents, child, and teachers
- Thorough medical, social, developmental, and academic history and medical examination
- Observations of the child
- Behavior rating scales
- Psychological tests

*Medical Tests **Not** Used for Diagnosis of ADHD*

- EEG—Electroencephalogram
- MRI—Magnetic resonance imaging
- PET scans—positron emission tomography

Commonly Co-occurring Conditions

- Learning disabilities
- Oppositional defiant disorder—ODD
- Conduct disorder—CD
- ODD and CD may result from environmental factors

Results of Diagnosis

- Leads to a change in belief system
  — inappropriate behaviors viewed as result of disability rather than a willful choice made by child
- Suggests need to change parenting behavior and educational approach
- Replaces guilt and blame with hope and help

CHAPTER SIX

Management Approaches

Once we had a diagnosis for David, I hoped we would have smoother sailing. But after the first visit with Dr. Burke, our new child psychologist, both David Sr. and I learned that there is no magic cure for ADHD. In fact, a lot of counseling would be required to restore a smile to David's face. Results from a test administered by the psychologist pointed to David's excessive worry and self-criticism as an indication that our son had become depressed.

Both his dad and I made the assumption that only David would be counseled. However, Dr. Burke insisted the entire family be present at the sessions. He explained that a family is a system of reciprocal emotional relationships. Thus David's behavior affected us and ours affected him in a cyclic and ongoing way.

Before any positive changes could occur, David's dad and I needed to unlearn the ineffective parenting techniques we had fallen into using. Our inconsistency, criticism, rejection, and physical punishment proved to be the worst possible responses to the behavior of a child with ADHD. These only served to heighten David's sadness. Like most children with ADHD, he had no idea why his world had turned out to be such a capricious place.

Neither did I until after an ugly scene erupted between young David and myself. Like Pavlov's dog, David responded to the ring of a bell, only in his case, the ring of the phone sent him into action. During his toddler years, he took this cue as the time to make mischief. As a preschooler, he dropped whatever he might be involved with and demanded my undivided attention. On the occasions I chose to ignore his peskiness, David disconnected the phone plug and left me to hang in midsentence.

In his latest strategy to end my conversations, David played mummy and wrapped himself in the cord. As in the past, I ignored this obnoxious behavior, but in order to continue my conversation, I had to exert untold pounds of pressure so the phone receiver would not recoil from my ear. One day I became fed up and reacted impulsively. In an attempt to unravel David, I gave the cord a herculean tug. I not only sent him reeling to the floor, the cord left a five-inch burn mark across his neck. Whenever anyone asked him about the mark on his neck, young David, who is not prone to go into great detail, simply replied, "My mother pulled a cord around it."

With David's neck still red and raw, we could not help but bring this incident to the psychologist's attention at our next appointment. Though Dr. Burke counseled David about his inappropriate behavior with the phone cord, he made certain both young David and I understood that a neck burn could never be a natural or logical consequence. Instead he suggested time-out as an alternative. Dr. Burke explained, "When David is disruptive, time-out will interrupt him and give everyone a chance to cool down."

In earlier years, our attempts to use time-out failed. After the psychologist walked us through his method, I could see why we had been unsuccessful. He first told my husband and me to select a safe, quiet, boring place to send David when he misbehaved. We had tried to put David in a corner in the kitchen, but he never stayed. Dr. Burke explained that, in light of all the activity in that room, the kitchen proved the worst possible place for David because most children with ADHD react to the activity and do not get the essential message that time-out is a punishment for misbehavior.

David's dad and I also thought the length of time our son stayed in time-out should be in direct correlation to how ticked off he made us. But Dr. Burke told us to set a timer for no longer than five minutes. Aside from the fact that this punishment is designed to be a brief consequence for inappropriate behavior, Dr. Burke warned, "If you keep David there too long, he might forget what he did to get sent to time-out in the first place."

Even with such expert advice, I continued to have reservations about this method's success. I figured David would refuse to go to the time-out spot, or leave it before he should, or come back and continue his misbehavior. When I raised these concerns, Dr. Burke told us we might initially have to escort David to time-out and force him to stay there. If his behavior did not change, David would be sent back to time-out and told he would continue to go back until he behaved respectfully. Dr. Burke included David in the time-out discussions, and when situations at home warranted this procedure, he did not resist us. However, in the beginning, his dad and I frequently forgot to use time-out as the first resort.

After our third session, the child psychologist requested that David's dad and I note the times our son behaved inappropriately. Our next meeting revealed this startling fact about our assessment of our son's behavior: both his dad and I did not always know when behavior was inappropriate. For example, though we agreed disrespect should never be tolerated, we sometimes interpreted a disrespectful comment as okay when David couched his remark in truth or humor. Where young David's world proved to be black and white, ours proved to be excessively gray. We did not take his actions at face value.

The behavior modification charts Dr. Burke taught us to design and implement soon improved our inconsistent approach to managing our son's behavior. As a starting point, he asked us to select the three behaviors that bothered us most from our rather extensive list. We settled on David's horrible behavior during mealtimes, his refusal to obey us, and his nasty treatment of his brother. When the psychologist asked what behavior we would like David to have, I found the question simplistic. Of course, I answered, "I want him to be nice and to behave well."

"Does David know what 'behave well' means?" he replied.

I always said to young David, "You'd better behave." I assumed he understood what I wanted perfectly well. But Dr. Burke explained that behaviors need to be specifically stated because such broad terms as "behave well" are not clear to the child. That made sense, so I suggested that on David's chart we put, "Does not hit brother."

Dr. Burke agreed this sort of behavior should be discouraged. However, he explained, since we really wanted to encourage David's use of appropriate behavior, these behaviors should be phrased in positive terms. He suggested we write, "Treats other family members in a polite, respectful, gentle fashion, that is, no hitting, yelling, or running away." Also, because of the pervasive daylong nature of this behavior, he suggested we pick a manageable time period to focus on initially, such as two hours in the afternoon.

"This time limit is not to say that polite, respectful behavior is not important at the other times too. As we get positive results, we'll gradually extend the time period to require such behavior all day,"

Dr. Burke explained. The other two behaviors we targeted for reward were "Cooperates with the morning routine: washes and dresses self, eats neatly, ready on time, no yelling" and "Is well-mannered at evening dinner table: comes on time, sits and eats meals without complaint or hassle."

Ever mindful that I had two children close in age, I wondered how David would react to Jonathan's free-agent status. Until Dr. Burke suggested we also use a chart for Jonathan, the thought had not occurred to me that a child need not have a problem to benefit from good parenting techniques. After all, my husband and I wanted to encourage these behaviors in both children.

With our list of target behaviors complete, Dr. Burke showed us how to construct the chart. He drew a rectangle on a piece of paper and then divided the rectangle horizontally into one large section and seven smaller but equal-sized sections, then vertically into four equal-sized sections so that the rectangle ultimately resembled a grid. In the first and largest horizontal section, Dr. Burke listed the target behaviors separately one below the other. At the top of each of the next seven sections, he wrote the days of the week, Sunday through Saturday, one after the other. In the remaining bottom section below the list of behaviors, he wrote "total daily score." (Appendix C has a sample of this type of chart.)

When children are young—preschool through kindergarten—it is often best to use a "star" or "sticker" chart. One star is given if the behavior is done spontaneously by the child or immediately upon first request. No stars are given for noncompliance or if constant or repetitive commands are given.

Later, when the boys were older, Dr. Burke rated each behavior on a numerical scale of three (excellent), two (good), one (needs improvement), and zero (poor). Throughout a given day, David received feedback about his behavior by earning or losing points toward the total daily score. This way, appropriate behavior was reinforced immediately. On the other hand, when David behaved inappropriately in one of the three target areas, he lost a point in conjunction with being sent to time-out. At the end of each day, we sat down with David and watched while he tallied the score for each behavior and then the total daily score. Thus the chart let David literally see where he met with success or failure.

Dr. Burke had also established score ranges to denote excellent, good, and poor behavior days, with consequences—positive and negative—set ahead of time for each outcome. The positive consequences came in the form of rewards. In selecting rewards, Dr. Burke made sure we understood one of the cornerstones of behavior modification, specifically, "A reward is only successful if it has meaning for the child." Since both boys bargained for additional time before they went to bed, we made extended bedtime something they could earn. Normally, they went to bed at 7:30, so we decided that for a good behavior day, they earned this regular privilege. For an excellent behavior day, the child was allowed to stay downstairs with us until 8:00 P.M. Similarly, on a poor behavior day, the child went to bed a half hour before the regular time as a predictable consequence for lack of cooperation and effort during the day.

Beyond that we sweetened the pie with a daily monetary reward of twenty-five cents for an excellent day, ten cents for a good day, and nothing for a poor day. In addition, at the end of a good week, each boy could receive a bonus such as a pack of baseball cards or a trip to Dairy Queen, and for an excellent week a video rental or special time with Mom or Dad.

Dr. Burke began each counseling session by studying the weekly charts. Rather than criticize David for the bad days, he offered his condolences and said, "Gee, Chief, sorry you had a problem here." With our child psychologist as the overseer of this system, David soon saw we took both the charts and time-out seriously. Eventually David learned not to blame us for his low scores and accepted the responsibility for his behavior. We learned that David often behaved quite well. Throughout the months we added new behavior patterns and dropped others that no longer proved problematic. We never concentrated on more than five types of behavior at a time.

Over the course of the summer of 1985, life in our home improved measurably. David was nearing six years of age, and Jonathan had just turned four. I attributed this change to the home management techniques we now employed and the child care program both boys attended for six hours a day. Initially I opposed the idea of sending the boys to a summer program, but Dr. Burke emphasized the importance of structure in David's day and advised us not to expect him to make good, orderly use of free time.

When fall arrived, we moved again. After I enrolled David in the public school kindergarten in this new town, I agonized about whether to tell his teacher he had ADHD. Even though David had had problems in nursery school, I still viewed his behavior difficulties as primarily a home management problem and conned myself into believing he would not meet difficulty in school. Besides, I worried that David might be stigmatized as "that pain-in-the-neck kid" if I drew attention to his problems. Despite the child psychologist's recommendation, I decided this situation could be best handled in the privacy of our home.

By mid-October, David's dad and I noticed a change for the worse in our older son's behavior. His frustration level lowered, and he quickly became angry whenever any task presented a slight challenge. He had difficulty keeping himself in control. He talked incessantly, dolphinized, screamed, and hollered. When he began to clear his throat constantly, we rationalized that his change in behavior had been prompted by some form of allergy.

Though we still went to the child psychologist and used the behavior charts, nothing could stop the course of his behavior or the chain reaction that ensued. Since I no longer worked outside the home, I spent every afternoon with David. By evening, after a full five hours of his argumentative, negative, angry, nasty ways, my nerves rattled. I too slipped back to the argue, yell, holler, and scream mode.

Dr. Burke felt certain David's frustration grew out of the demands the school made on him. But I could not understand how a mere two-and-a-half-hour program could create this much distress. Besides, whenever I casually asked his teacher how he was doing, she never gave a negative report.

However, when the long-awaited first report card arrived home, our six-year-old son's performance seemed totally lackluster. David earned "satisfactory" as a mark in most areas, but "work habits" and "social development" had been checked "needs improvement." Under "comments" the teacher wrote, "David must work on following directions given once. Criticism of peers continues to be a problem. Good knowledge of beginning sounds." At the parent-teacher conference, I learned David seldom participated in class activities and apparently "tuned out." During free play, he stayed by himself.

Not all the teacher's comments proved negative. She drew my attention to David's picture of a house. Though I saw a crude structure, the kindergarten teacher said that in all her years of teaching five-and-six-year-old children, David was the first student to include a basement on the house drawing, which she thought indicated he was a divergent thinker. She assured me David was a bright child who would do well when he "clicked in."

By mid-November our quasi-docile home environment deteriorated into a bad dream. The child psychologist suggested David needed medication to help treat his ADHD symptoms. The pediatric neurologist, who a few months earlier had assessed David's symptoms to be mild, now witnessed the change in behavior at firsthand. David could not contain himself during any part of the examination. The doctor rated our son's ADHD as severe.

In addition, the neurologist said David's constant lip licking and throat clearing represented involuntary motor actions called tics. This information surprised David's father and me. We assumed scarlet, cracked lips to be a sign of cold weather. Because of the tics, the doctor, following common practice in those years, did not prescribe the medication usually used to treat ADHD. The neurologist informed us about alternative medications, and though he did not want to prescribe them at this point in time, he suggested we consider their eventual use if needed.

Three weeks later, the neurologist placed David on one of these medications. Unfortunately, it did not produce the desired results, and within a couple of months, from a medication-intervention standpoint, we were back to square one.

During this entire time, we continued to use behavior modification and went as a family to the sessions with the child psychologist. He continued to teach us about the disorder. How we came to understand the extent to which the disorder affected David and the family proved much like the process of peeling an onion. We needed to get through layer upon layer to reach the center.

We first had to learn that children with ADHD need a calm, quiet, predictable atmosphere. Changes in the routine prompt changes in behavior. As a family, we continually went on spur-of-the-moment outings or undertook major home projects. We seldom thought to keep these things to a minimum or to prepare David for any necessary changes.

We constantly subjected David to large-group activities despite the fact that such situations sent him into a frenzy. We thought, "The more the merrier," but for David too many people meant an unhappy time. We missed this point over and over again in our desire for normalcy. We wanted David to be like all the other children. When he balked at playing soccer or going to birthday parties, we forced him to participate, until the child psychologist raised our level of awareness. He advised us: "Avoid large-group activities as much as possible. David will do better in one-to-one situations that are short in duration, structured, and well organized."

During the course of these sessions, David's dad frequently identified similarities between young David's behaviors and his own. When Dr. Burke said things like, "David prefers to play with younger children because he may be a more desirable playmate to them and can be more in control of events," David Sr. responded, "So did I." Eventually Dad realized he had been very much like his son—not a problem child, but rather a child with a problem.

By the end of January 1986, David's classroom difficulties escalated. The kindergarten teacher said that he tried on many occasions to take charge of the class and became verbally aggressive with peers. When he did not meet with instant success in a task, he became extremely upset. During playtime he wandered around the room and withdrew from all social involvement.

The child psychologist spoke with the teacher and observed David in class. He instituted a behavior modification program. A month later, the teacher reported an improvement in David's attitude and effort. At home, his behavior seemed to deteriorate.

Lately, the thought had crossed my mind that David would be better off if I left home. When Dr. Burke asked, "Why do you think he behaves his worst with you?" I could only surmise that something about me brought the worst out in my son. But the psychologist offered another possibility. He thought David stored all his frustration until he came home from school because he trusted my commitment to him and felt safe enough to act on his feelings. Though intellectually his explanation made sense, emotionally I felt no better.

The child psychologist, who still hoped that David could benefit from medication, prodded us to see another pediatric neurologist highly regarded for his work with ADHD. Though this doctor charged $350 for an evaluation, David Sr. and I had grown accustomed to the fact that answers for David were an expensive proposition, and we made the appointment.

The waiting room of the specialist's office contained a jungle gym, a slide, and a slew of toys. Six-and-a-half-year-old David became so excited at these prospects, his voice level went beyond dolphinizing. As he attacked each new toy he yelled to his five-year-old brother to come and play, but these days Jonathan withdrew from that kind of heavy-handed activity. Instead of joining his brother, he sat next to his dad and quietly read a book. When the time finally arrived for David to be examined, his activity level had reached the fevered pitch we knew so well.

As the nurse ushered us into the doctor's office, she looked rather tentative. The doctor introduced himself and told us that as long as David could be controlled, he would prefer to examine him without us. Before we were halfway back to the waiting room we heard young David make a pronouncement. "I'm the boss of this office," he said. I thought a summons would certainly follow, but we did not see either David or the doctor for over an hour.

Much to our surprise, when the neurologist finally delivered our son, he remarked about the good manner in which David behaved. Before he brought us into the office, he said to David, "Please wait here while I talk to your mom and dad."

David quietly replied, "Oh yes, I'll wait here."

I often joked that a lobotomy might do David some good; now I wondered what the doctor had done!

Once inside the office, the doctor told us David's waiting-room behavior had been the worst his nurse ever observed. Thus the doctor thought he would have a difficult time with David's exam. Though initially David had been highly distractible, his ability to concentrate "improved remarkably during the individualized attention." This evaluation did not reveal any new information, but at this physician's urging, we tried David on another medication primarily used to control tics.

In early May, the doctor saw him in a follow-up examination. Though his vocal tics had stopped, David's hyperactivity and impulsivity showed no improvement. The doctor increased the medication, but no positive result occurred, so he stopped the medication in June. David ended the school year with improvement noted in that environment. The teacher commented on the final report card, "David's effort in reading, although sporadic, is much improved. His interaction with peers has improved but continues to be difficult for David. I look forward to hearing of his continued success in the first grade." We headed into the summer with David's behavior somewhat under control.

Recommended by Experts

Currently, ADHD has no known cure, no quick fix, no magic treatment. Don't be discouraged. Much can be done to lessen the effects of the disorder on the child's life and on the entire family. When I think of managing ADHD, I get an image of trying to harness the wind. We can't stop the wind. But we can harness the wind, channel its force for good use. We can ride it and use it to power the sails. With the exception of medication, most of what we do to treat ADHD is external management. As parents and teachers, we need to manipulate the environment so the child experiences competence and success.

The Multimodal Approach

Typically, the most successful management of ADHD is achieved with what health care professionals call the multimodal treatment approach, which consists of four major parts: education about the disorder, parent training in behavioral management, educational planning, and medication (where indicated). On occasion, individual or family counseling may be necessary.

Since most aspects of the multimodal approach have been or will be explained in other chapters, this chapter focuses mostly on the complicated issues of medication and unproven treatments. First, however, I will provide a short description of how the multimodal approach works.

• *Education* helps parents, family members, the child with ADHD and outside caregivers understand the precise nature of the disorder. A major goal of ADHD education has to do with changing the way we view the child's behavior. Often by the time diagnosis occurs, our children are seen as little brats with indulgent parents. Blame and shame fly everywhere. Of course, nothing kills the spirit more than to be misunderstood and to receive constant criticism.

• *Parent training* helps us help our children to better manage their behavior. We add structure, routine, consequences, and consistency. Training takes the guesswork out of what to do and how to do it, so we can stop grasping at straws. (Earlier chapters have described these techniques.)

• *Educational planning,* which may result in a modified school program, is usually needed by students with ADHD. Getting schools to make changes to fit the special needs of students with ADHD often proves difficult. In fact, most parents have the greatest complaints about the mismanagement of their children in the educational arena. (See chapters 8 and 9 for in-depth discussion.)

• *Medication* may be necessary. Sometimes the wind can't be harnessed without changing what causes the wind. Some children, no matter what we do, need medication to help their biology. In fact, results of a multisite, federally funded study show management with medication to be the most effective means of combatting ADHD.

Which of these strategies to use and to what extent depends on the severity of your child's symptoms. Jim Hopkins, for instance, evidenced difficulty mainly in school, so his treatment primarily addressed that problem. Maggie Anderson needed both home and school management but no medication, whereas my son needed all three treatments.

Dr. Keith Conners underscores the wisdom of using multiple treatment approaches. "One aspect of the treatment is not enough. The parenting behavior is not going to diminish the vigor of the abnormal biological system in the child. On the other hand, diminishing the vigor of the abnormal biology with medication is not going to teach the kid the rules of the game or his ABC's," he explains.

Recent Findings

In 1998, the National Institute of Mental Health (NIMH) reported results of its five-year, multisite study about which treatments, and in what combinations, proved most effective for ADHD management. Children in the study were given a variety of treatment approaches. One group was given medication only. Another group received psychosocial intervention which included behavior-modification, parent training, social-skill building and summer programs. A third group received a combination of both medication and psychosocial intervention. The study produced a lot of data which has not yet been analyzed, but by far the biggest result was the finding that, on the areas measured by researchers, the group of children who received medication only did just as well as the group that received the combination treatment of psychosocial intervention and medication. Of interest though, is the finding that children with ADHD and the co-morbid condition of anxiety did better on the combined treatment.

The group that received only psychosocial interventions did not have an effect nearly as large as the other groups.

In fact, they did not show much improvement over the group of children assessed for ADHD and given no interventions. Finally, a percentage of the cases studied no longer met criteria for ADHD after the medication only or combined intervention program. However, we cannot assume the disorder has been "cured." Not known is whether they will again meet the criteria for ADHD once the treatments are pulled away. For now, parents can feel confident that medication seems to produce the best results, and that psychosocial interventions including behavior management systems with medication can be very helpful for certain children. Of course, using a knowledgeable practitioner to design the interventions your child needs is advisable.

Work With a Team

ADHD management requires a wide network of caregivers all working as a team. Parents, significant others, educators, and medical and mental health professionals have to join forces. As the child matures, he or she should also be part of this treatment partnership. In fact, treatment efforts have greater success when the child buys into the treatment program instead of viewing interventions as something being done to them.

Along these lines, I also suggest that parents become part of an active support group—especially in the beginning. A good group provides ongoing and up-to-date education about the disorder from reputable sources. It helps with the feelings that accompany living with and having ADHD. We parents can easily lose sight of the fact that the child is *in* trouble, not *the cause* of trouble. When well run, support groups often direct our thinking to problem-solving approaches.

Use a Case Manager

Given all the approaches needed, when a treatment program begins, it generally requires a professional to act as case manager. This professional will most likely be a child psychologist or clinical social worker since their practices are designed to give them the time it takes to manage multiple sources of information. Pediatricians, child psychiatrists, and neurologists can and sometimes do serve as case managers, but generally their practices do not allow for much time, so you need to confirm your doctor's availability if you are considering using him or her in this way.

Of course, once we acquire some knowledge and training, we parents generally take on this role. No matter how you feel right now, remember, you know your child better than anyone else, and you are the one who will possess all the pieces that need to be fit together. You will also have your child's best interests at heart. The job can be tiring, frustrating, and time-consuming, but it is necessary and ultimately rewarding. Even if your child does not "turn out" exactly the way you want, great satisfaction comes in knowing you did all you could!

Medication

Of all the management approaches for this disorder, medication continues to capture the most attention and to be the most controversial. Let's address the controversy first. Most of it comes from misinformation and the judgmental attitudes of people who don't accept ADHD as a serious problem that can cause lifelong difficulty and significant distress. Critics say medication is prescribed too liberally or used as a "silver bullet" by parents and teachers who desire calmer, quieter children. The truth about medication is that it has produced significant and positive results for many children. As with any medication therapy that requires long-term use, guidelines must be followed before prescribing and during use.

Many parents find the decision to give their child medication a hard one to make. Unlike an antibiotic for an ear infection, the medication used with ADHD must be taken on a long-term basis. There's a logical reason why: medication does not cure ADHD; instead, it makes the child's symptoms more manageable.

Only a physician can prescribe medication. However, often a non-physician with primary responsibility for the child's treatment program, such as a psychologist, will advise the use of medication. When making a determination about if and when to use medication as a form of treatment, psychologist Sam Goldstein says, most practitioners follow this basic guideline: medical treatment is recommended when other interventions do not produce the hoped-for results.

However, in cases where the child's behavior is out of control, medication may be started before any other treatment. Dr. Russell Barkley reports that at least 60 percent of children with ADHD need medication in addition to other interventions. Parents must thoroughly discuss the pros and cons of medication with their child's doctor before deciding for or against its use.

Not for Diagnostic Purposes

Children should not be placed on medication unless they have a diagnosis. The reason this point needs to be made is that some doctors have recommended to their patient's parents that the child be given medication as a way of determining if ADHD is present—the logic being, if behavior improves, then ADHD is the problem.

Dr. Timothy Wilens, of Massachusetts General Hospital and Harvard Medical School who is also the author of *Straight Talk About Psychiatric Medications for Kids,* emphatically says you don't prescribe medication to diagnose. He gives two reasons. First, "stimulant medications are nonspecific," he explains. "Most people who take stimulant-class agents will experience changes in attention and motor activity." While these responses may seem similar, they are not entirely the same. Whereas a person with ADHD might have a wide attentional focus narrowed to a somewhat normal state, a person without a wide attention span may actually become overfocused. Second, about 30 percent of children with ADHD do not respond to stimulants, so relying on a response as proof of the problem's existence could lead to a missed diagnosis. The previous chapter outlined the recommended diagnostic procedure, and this method is not on the list.

Not as the Only Treatment

Furthermore, medication should never be used as the sole course of treatment. In fact, Dr. Bennett Shaywitz will not prescribe medication unless a child has an optimal educational program and the parents also understand the implications of the ADHD diagnosis. He explains, "ADHD is a chronic problem which the child will have throughout life. You don't just write a prescription for medication without making changes in the child's school and home situations. Besides, without the right kind of support, the medication probably won't work."

Is Medication Right for My Child?

No predictive tests exist to determine if a child will benefit from medication. Dr. Paul Wender compares prescribing trial medication for children with ADHD to prescribing medication for a patient with hypertension. In advance, the doctor cannot be sure that a specific blood pressure medication will lower this patient's blood pressure, but the physician knows the drug has been researched extensively and has proven safe and effective for this purpose, and therefore recommends that the patient try it to see if it helps. If it doesn't, another may be substituted, and so on. However, Dr. Wender cautions that, as with all prescription drugs, physicians must determine if the advantages of treatment outweigh the disadvantages.

Medications, particularly the most commonly used stimulant medications, get better results when compared to behavior management. According to Dr. Barkley, even when combined with behavior modification systems, the positive effects from the combined treatment are not significant. To date, medication appears to be the best the clinical community can offer.

This is not to say that we should forget other management techniques. When you think about ADHD as a disorder of disinhibition and recall Dr. Barkley's notion that self-control is affected by sensory imaging and self-talk, then you realize that to assist people with this disability, you have to change the environment by making the structure externally clear. So you want to provide rules, regulations, and assistive devices such as timers and charts, as described in other chapters. Should medication be used, you also want to know about it in detail.

Having decided that medication would be worth trying for a particular patient, the physician must choose which medicine, in what dose, and when and how often the child should take it. Presently, three classes of medications are given to treat ADHD: stimulants, tricyclic antidepressants, and antihypertensives. Of course, some people with ADHD may have other problems, such as depression, and thus physicians should prescribe accordingly. So it is possible to be taking a medication that alleviates ADHD problems and, in the case of depression, a selective serotonin reuptake inhibitor (SSRI) such as Prozac, Paxil, Zoloft, or Nuvox. New medications specifically for ADHD are being researched all the time, and Dr. Wilens notes that some look very promising. For now, let's look at the currently used preparations.

Stimulants

Medicines that belong to the class of drugs known as stimulants most often prove to be the first choice—for good reason: to date, stimulants have been the most effective. The most commonly used stimulant medications are Ritalin, Adderall, Dexedrine, and Cylert.

On deciding which stimulant to use, Dr. Wender says: "The rule is anybody might get better on anything, and with that as a given, the only way to tell whether methylphenidate (Ritalin) or d-amphetamine (Dexedrine) is better for a child is to try both. However, if the child responds to the first medicine tried, then that's great." In some cases, after the child has been on a medication for a while, it appears to be less effective. In that case, physicians will often try another of the stimulants or combine the medication with another class of drugs to get desired results.

According to Charles Popper, M.D., former editor of the *Journal of Child and Adolescent Psychopharmacology,* medications also have positive effects on aggression, oppositionality, frustration tolerance, endurance in working on boring tasks, and increased sociability. "They have also been demonstrated to improve the behavior of peers and parents," he adds with humor. This statement reflects the positive effect the medications have on the child's ability to inhibit "pain-in-the-neck" behaviors that irritate others.

Side Effects

Of course, all medications have side effects. Those produced by stimulants are generally mild. The most commonly reported side effects are loss of appetite, stomachaches, difficulty falling asleep, increased irritability, and perhaps teariness.

You may have heard that stimulants will inhibit growth. This is unlikely; as reported by Dr. Wilens, new data suggest that these medications do not affect height. He cites a study comparing children with ADHD treated with stimulant medication and children with ADHD not treated with this medication. The comparison showed that ADHD itself, not medication, seems to slow the rate of growth, because the prepubescent children in both groups appeared a bit delayed. The good news for concerned parents is "they catch up," Dr. Wilens adds.

Rebound is another concern with stimulant use. As the medication wears off, some children experience a worsening of symptoms. As explained by Dr. Wilens, in rebound the medication wears off too fast, so to minimize this effect, the physician can either prescribe a very small dose of the medication about an hour before the previous dose wears off or can switch from a short-acting preparation to a longer-acting one. Either way, this side effect can be eliminated.

Safety and Effectiveness

According to Dr. Wilens, there have been well over two hundred controlled trials of stimulant medications. In fact, they are the best studied of all medications used in any child or adolescent psychiatric disorder. The stimulants that have been in use the longest are methylphenidate (Ritalin), d-amphetamine (Dexedrine), magnesium pemoline (Cylert), and Adderall (a combination of amphetamine salts).

With the exception of Cylert, these medications can have the side effects described on the previous page. Dr. Wilens points out that in a very few cases there has been some liver toxicity associated with Cylert; early detection seems to avoid a serious problem.

Ritalin, the medication most used for the treatment of ADHD, has been prescribed for over fifty years. In a 1988 report to Congress, the Food and Drug Administration wrote: "We continue to believe that Ritalin is a safe and effective drug if used as recommended in the approval labeling suggested by the FDA in the treatment of ADHD."

These medications provide a substantial return at relatively low cost. Dollar cost aside, the lack of side effects compared to the beneficial effects on ADHD difficulties continues to make them an effective treatment. Most studies show that these medications consistently improve academic performance, reduce behavioral disruption, and thus aid in improving self-esteem. As Dr. Wilens says, "I still find it hard to beat the stimulant medications for across-the-board efficacy for hyperactivity, impulsivity, and aggressiveness."

How Stimulants Work

People sometimes question the wisdom of giving a "stimulant" to a "hyper" person. Of course, we seldom think of "hyper" as a consequence of too little and instead consider it as being the result of too much. Dr. Popper notes that in ADHD "there have been abnormalities in the three major neurotransmitter systems that have been theorized to be associated with hyperactivity and impulsivity."

Neurotransmitters are natural chemicals that help the brain regulate behavior. The three major neurotransmitter systems suspected to be involved in ADHD are dopamine, norepinephrine, and serotonin. Dopamine appears to be the most involved.

As Dr. Wilens explains, the stimulants make more dopamine available. "In some kids there's enough dopamine," he explains, "but when it goes across the receiving neuron receptor [called the d4 dopamine receptor], the 'glove' to catch the dopamine may be improper or not work efficiently." As a result, when a stimulant is taken, the abnormal biology is altered to a more normal state, so the child with ADHD is better able to inhibit behavior.

Parents also need to be aware that sometimes a medication works great—and then the response changes. Because each of the medications works slightly differently from the others, should this problem occur doctors will often switch preparations, for example from Ritalin to Adderall or Dexedrine, or perhaps to a combination of a stimulant and a tricyclic antidepressant or an antihypertensive.

Finding the Right Dose

When a patient begins taking stimulant medication, the physician starts with the smallest dose possible. The dose is then titrated, meaning it is raised in small increments until the desired result is achieved. Doctors also follow this practice with the other kinds of medication used to treat ADHD.

The prescribing physician, with input from the parents, must determine when during the day the child needs to take the medicine. Ritalin happens to be a short-acting medication; thus its therapeutic effects wear off in a matter of hours. The child's ADHD symptoms then reappear like clockwork. Since Ritalin is usually in and out of the body within three to four hours, children will often take a morning and afternoon dose. Some will even require a late-afternoon or early-evening dose.

Ritalin also comes in a longer-lasting, sustained-release form, which works for about six to eight hours. The same is true for Dexedrine. Adderall lasts about four to six hours. Dr. Wilens notes that within the next couple of years, new medications, new delivery systems, and old medications with new delivery systems will be available, so dosing information is bound to change. Of course, any time medication is prescribed, discuss it fully with your child's doctor.

When to Take Medication

Most physicians agree that children who need medication will require it during school hours. Why? School is the environment that places the greatest demands for performance in the areas where children with ADHD have the greatest difficulty: paying attention to things that may be uninteresting, thinking before acting, sitting still, and otherwise controlling motor activity.

Some practitioners also believe all children should have drug holidays. Therefore, they do not prescribe medication for after school, weekends, or summers. Yet children with ADHD can have the same difficulties in the home and with friends that they do in school. Many do benefit significantly from continuous treatment. The doctor should decide when and how often your child takes medication on the basis of his or her individual symptoms and not, as Dr. Goldstein points out, in an arbitrary fashion, "based on old wives' tales."

About Abusing Stimulants

I almost hate to raise this subject out of concern that children who can benefit from medication may not be given that opportunity for fear that use of stimulants might lead to their abuse. It seems that these days, any and all substances have this potential, from the whipped cream in the can in your refrigerator to the butane in lighters. Still, I would be remiss not to at least touch on the subject.

According to Dr. Wilens, "Stimulant abuse is not a common form of (substance) abuse in ADHD kids." Results of studies done by his group of researchers at Harvard indicate no difference between ADHD and non-ADHD kids, adolescents, and adults in terms of what substances they abuse. He notes that the stimulants do not appear even to "kindle" abuse. In fact, data exist suggesting that children who have been treated successfully with medication— meaning they had a reduction in symptoms—actually had lower trends toward substance abuse or misuse and toward arrests because of substance abuse.

Conversely, Dr. Wilens notes that youngsters with ADHD and conduct disorder or ADHD and bipolar disorder are at a much greater risk for substance abuse. The CD group may show problems between the ages of twelve and fifteen. When substance abuse appears in kids with ADHD alone, it develops somewhere between approximately age nineteen and age twenty-two.

Because there is some risk for some kids, parents are advised to be vigilant. And while children with ADHD do not tend to abuse their medication, stimulants do get abused by others. Dr. Wilens suggests that this medication, like any medication that can be mood-altering, should be kept locked up, and parents need to be aware of how much they have on hand. Of course, we have to be mindful and observant, nevertheless.

Tricyclic Antidepressants

These medications are given to people who either do not respond to stimulants or who need them in combination with stimulants. The most commonly used are desipramine (Norpramin), imipramine (Tofranil), and noretryptolene (Pamelor). They are not to be confused with selective serotonin reuptake inhibitors (SSRIs), such as Prozac or Zoloft, which Dr.Wilens says "do not work for ADHD." However, Dr. Wilens also points out that these medications do work well for some coexisting disorders—for example, depression, anxicty, and obsessive-compulsive behavior.

The tricyclics have been around for a while. Dr. Wilens notes that they are relatively easy to use, although they do require monitoring and more attention to following prescription directions. The most common side effects are dry mouth, irritability, mild constipation, sedation, and sometimes increased excitability. Cardiovascular effects have been reported with some tricyclics, particularly desipramine. Cardiovascular risks, reports Dr. Wilens, did not appear to be measurable when studied by a group of cardiologists.

His group just completed a study with Pamelor that found it very useful for kids with ADHD and oppositional behavior, as well as those with ADHD and anxiety. "It was well tolerated, easy to use, parents loved it, and it actually put a little weight on the kids, but didn't make them fat," he noted.

Antihypertensives

The antihypertensive medications most commonly used for treatment of ADHD are catapres (Clonidine) and guanfacine (Tenex). According to Dr. Wilens, these medications "probably have less effect on attention and cognition but seem to have efficacy for hyperactivity, impulsivity, and aggressiveness." These medications are being tried with more frequency to help combat some of the ADHD symptoms, particularly as adjuncts to the other categories of medication. They appear to be helpful for very young children who have hyperactivity, impulsivity, and aggression, but do not have signs of inattention, as well as for children with Tourette's syndrome or other tic disorders and ADHD.

Dr. Wilens also notes that many clinicians prescribe them to help kids sleep better. Finally, they may work for children who cannot tolerate other medications. According to Dr. Popper, the most common side effect is drowsiness; some people also experience what he calls the "nuisance" effects of headaches and stomachaches. Blood pressure must be checked periodically.

Follow-up

Children on medication should receive regular follow-up. When the child begins taking medication, the prescribing physician will often monitor the child's response. Parents should be asked to get reports from teachers, coaches, camp counselors, or other caregivers. That responsibility is given to parents in Dr. Wilens's practice because, he says, they are in the best position to collect the information. "We also do it because then the parents know exactly what's going on," he adds.

Once the medication seems to be working smoothly, the doctor usually examines the child once or twice a year, although many doctors have phone contact with parents prior to renewing monthly prescriptions. Such practice ensures safety and efficacy. Of course, some medications, like Clonidine, require more frequent follow-up. If questions or concerns arise, don't wait for a periodic follow-up appointment. Call your doctor right away. Side effects should also be noted and reported. Don't be shy about seeking second opinions either.

The "Why Are You Drugging Your Kid?" Guilt Trip

When faced with the decision to use medication, particularly Ritalin, many parents receive input from "well-intentioned" friends, relatives, neighbors, and, in some cases, virtual strangers. Some of these people misguidedly wonder why medication is given to children "who obviously just need more discipline." Others are misinformed and think the medication has dangerous side effects.

Either before the child goes on medication or even afterward, most parents hear comments similar to these:

"Do you really think your child needs drugs?"

"Gee, he doesn't seem that bad."

"If you give your child drugs, won't she become a drug abuser?"

"Couldn't you provide more activity and just tire him out instead?"

Some parents have even been accused of giving their child medication to make the family's life easier. Many parents wrestle with the notion that if they were better parents, they could control their child's behavior.

Such misguidance and misinformation does little to help the child with ADHD or the parent. As parents of children with a disorder that can have significant and devastating effects, I believe, we need to be aware of all the treatment options available. We also must have correct information about those options so we can make intelligent and informed choices. We all need to know that medication is not given to make a bad child into a good child or a poor student into a better student. ADHD is biologically based. Consequently, the medication used in its treatment is given because it effectively alters the abnormal biology into a more normal state.

In fact, for the child in need of medical intervention, such therapy is often the kindest help. Nineteen-year-old John Brett told me that when he began taking medication in sixth grade, his life turned around. The years he spent off medication between eighth and tenth grade he called "a living hell." John was taken off medication for those years because of two common misconceptions: people thought that ADHD symptoms disappeared with puberty and that the medication no longer would work once the child reached puberty.

Current research demonstrates that medication is effective treatment for ADHD in both adolescents and adults. At the age of fifteen, John Brett went back on medication after home circumstances and his ADHD symptoms proved so intolerable that he entertained thoughts of suicide. When I spoke with him at age nineteen, John had an optimistic attitude and asked me to tell every person with ADHD, "If you put your effort into something, you can get what you want out of it."

What to Tell Your Child

Stimulant medications tend to be more effective for children with ADHD when parents and the child understand the basis for the treatment. With consideration given to the age and sophistication of the child, Dr. Paul Wender will frequently explain the ADHD medical treatment in these terms: "Not being able to sit still and concentrate happens because there are chemicals in the brain. Some people make too much of them, and some people make too little. Maybe you make too little."

Dr. Wender then tells how the medicine can help the patient to compensate for the lack of chemicals. However, he emphasizes that although the medicine might be very helpful to the child, it is not a mind-controlling drug. The patient still has free will and must exercise his or her autonomy. For instance, the medication will improve the child's ability to focus attention while studying for a test, but the child must choose to study. The medicine will help the child control his or her temper, but only if the child wants to. *The medicine does not control the child.*

Determining Response

Many children are not even aware of the manner in which medication has helped them. According to Dr. Wender, because children with ADHD characteristically lack insight into their behavior, they will frequently report that medication has had no effect even when he and the child's parents note a big therapeutic change. When Dr. Wender asks the child to account for why he or she has not been to the principal's office in three weeks, or why sleepover and birthday party invitations are pouring in, the child will respond, "Just lucky, I guess."

Assessing the positive effects of medication by using behavior rating scales and clinical observation often gives an accurate appraisal of the treatment benefit. In fact, many physicians use behavior rating scales to get a before-medication and after-medication measure to determine the extent to which the drug is working.

Dr. Swanson cautions parents and teachers not to judge how well medication is working according to the changes it makes in their lives: "We want to be sure that the child is performing better, not just sitting quiet and still."

Resistance to Taking Medication

Some children resist taking medication. When this situation arises, each parent, child, and physician must deal with it on a case-by-case basis. Dr. Keith Conners finds that children commonly resist this treatment because of social disapproval, demonstrated by the derogatory names other children assign to Ritalin such as "stupid pills," "smart pills," and "spaz pills." For the child with ADHD, these unfortunate labels produce guilt by association. Thus the child equates not taking the medicine with not having a problem. Also, as Dr. Wilens conjectures, "Some kids hear in school that drugs cause kids to become addicts, and they are afraid of that."

Blatant resistance to taking medication is more apt to arise in adolescence as teens struggle with the developmental task of becoming independent. Perhaps they view medication as a form of dependence rather than as a therapeutic measure taken to address a biological condition. Or maybe they just don't want to be different, to do anything to call attention to themselves as "not normal."

Regardless of the reasons a child is resistant to taking medication, if the child needs medication, Dr. Wilens has this advice: "I think you have to have repeated conversations about what it means to have ADHD. You have to keep the kid engaged in what's going on."

Other Considerations

We parents, and also the child's teachers, may inadvertently cultivate the notion that medication is a means to control the child or adolescent. We must avoid making statements or asking questions that give the medication too much credit or blame for the child's behavior. For example: "You're acting hyper. Did you take your pill today?" "Gee, you're really having a good day. Those pills must be working."

Parents and teachers are advised to consider these guidelines when their child or student must take medication:

1. Handle the situation sensitively and discreetly. Don't give too much credit or blame to the medication or call public attention to its use.
2. Dispense the medication as prescribed.
3. Monitor side effects.
4. All caregivers, including parents, teachers, and physicians, should communicate frequently with each other.

We also need to think about overreliance on medication as a long-term treatment, especially in light of the results of research done by Dr. Swanson at the University of California, Irvine, which was funded by the U.S. Department of Education. He found that within one year of drug intervention, 30 percent of the children no longer took medication, and approximately 60 percent ceased using it after two years. Reasons why remain speculative. Yet, these statistics strongly caution us against thinking of medication as the be-all, end-all treatment for ADHD. Perhaps this therapy is best viewed as a window of opportunity to work with the child to develop skills to help him or herself cope with ADHD problems.

Common Treatment Misconceptions

ADHD is one of the most widely studied and publicized disorders. It's also one that seems to be wide open for anybody to come along and offer new cures and treatments claimed "to work." I'm not at all amazed that many parents, myself included, have been seduced by these claims. After all, the idea of a "drug-free" answer can be so comforting. Perhaps even more soothing is the notion that if we just do the right thing, find the right method, eliminate some food or give the right supplement, our children will no longer be plagued by difficulties. Unfortunately, these answers—as wonderful as they sound—do not hold water. In fact, Dr. Barkley suggests parents first try the proven treatments, which offer the greatest results. He cautions against a number of purported remedies because they have no validity in the treatment of the disorder: high doses of vitamins; scalp massages—which he notes may have some associated risks; visual perceptual and ocular motor training; biofeedback, allergy treatments; and dietary treatments.

The following information highlights some of the more widely talked-about treatments that have not been proven effective. Correct information is your best ally.

Sugar

Time and again we hear that sugar causes ADHD, specifically hyperactivity. Take away the sugar and the child is fine. Numerous scientists have tried in careful studies to prove this theory. Each time, they prove the opposite. *Sugar does not cause hyperactivity.* The most recent report of a study with this finding was published in the *New England Journal of Medicine* by noted Harvard researcher Marcel Kinsbourne, M.D. As laypeople, we might be inclined to say, "So what!" As informed consumers and parents, we need to know that where a study is published and by whom means a lot. The *New England Journal* is one of the most highly regarded medical journals. You can count on a study that it publishes as being good science and on the validity of its results.

Feingold Diet

Another common misconception about diet has to do with the widely known Feingold diet. In fact, a number of mothers told me they tried this diet with their children. I tried it too. Supposedly, it eliminates hyperactivity by restricting additives, preservatives, salicylates, and sugar. The only effect this diet produced turned out to be the placebo effect, an improvement in response to the fact that a treatment is being tried rather than to the nature of the treatment itself. Liz Sacca's experience is typical. Initially, Liz thought the diet had some positive result because she made a huge effort trying to do something to help her son. This diet happened to be the first thing she tried. Later, she realized her feelings about herself as a mother improved, but her little boy's symptoms did not get better. As Dr. McMahon notes, "Any treatment carries a tremendous placebo effect, but generally this effect does not last over time."

With regard to dietary treatment, certainly no ADHD expert suggests that children be given a lot of additives, sugar, or preservatives. However, we need to realize that these elements do not cause ADHD and keeping them out of the body does not cure the disorder. In addition, Dr. Keith Conners, author of *Feeding the Brain: The Effects of Food on Children,* cautions against diets that are unreasonable and exclude essential elements of children's nutrition. He explained, "We found on the Feingold diet, kids developed vitamin C deficiencies because they missed all the vitamins that come in fruits."

Allergy

According to Dr. Conners, about 25 percent of all children have some form of allergy; the incidence of allergy is slightly higher among children with ADHD. However, he says, "it is very unlikely that allergy causes the disorder." Dr. Barkley goes a step further and warns parents against "the visit to the clinical ecologist who does the huge three-day workup of allergies." Though allergy treatment may help a child's allergies, no evidence exists to show that it helps a child's ADHD.

I knew one mother who flew two thousand miles with her son to have one of these huge workups done. She returned from the experience energized and hopeful. In following recommendations, she made all sorts of adjustments to meal preparation, recipe ingredients, and the materials found in their home. Despite her enthusiasm, hard work, and diligence, the promises offered did not come true. Meanwhile, she had wasted many dollars and much time.

Biofeedback

This technique for the treatment of ADHD has sparked a lot of controversy. Logic would say it makes a great deal of sense. According to Dr. Barkley, brain studies of children and adults with the disorder indicate that their frontal lobe areas seem to be underactive or underreactive. Biofeedback proponents believe that people with ADHD can be trained to increase electrical activity in these brain areas and thereby decrease the symptoms of ADHD. Unfortunately, no studies have been done on a large number of people with the disorder over a long period of time to support the claims made by biofeedback backers. Dr. Barkley also notes that even in the few small studies published, the positive effects that can be linked solely to the technique remain unclear. Though this approach seems harmless, it costs a lot of money. Experts advise parents to spend their resources on accepted treatments.

Blue-green Algae

No ADHD expert recommends this "alternative," which I first heard of a few years ago when I came across a leaflet at a public gathering. In it, a man claimed his son's ADHD had been cured by blue-green algae. As explained to me by a local health food store, this substance is a protein that oxygenates the blood and is mostly sold for the purpose of boosting energy by cleansing the body of "sludge." There are numerous suppliers, and some blue-green algae is prepared with other supplements. It can be bought in a health food store or through multilevel marketing. The latter is a kind of business venture in which one seller introduces the product to a client, who in turn can purchase a kit and become a distributor of the product and can also sign up new people to become distributors. Anyone who has a hand in any sale gets a commission. Thus, sales of this product are based primarily on word-of-mouth recommendations.

I recently met a very savvy mother of an eight-year-old suspected of having ADHD. Her report about what happened when she went to a pediatrician's office shocked me. During a routine annual checkup, Iris mentioned her son's school problems and the possibility that they were caused by ADHD.

"The doctor jumped right on it," Iris said. "I've had fabulous success with ADHD when I've changed the diet and given them blue-green algae," the doctor told her.

With that, the physician gave Iris a two-month supply of the supplement in pill form and another enzyme that had to be taken with a hot meal. The cost—$75.32. On top of that, the doctor told Iris about the multimarketing approach, gave her a sign-up form to become a distributor, and told her to come back in a month.

"I'm embarrassed to admit I bought it," Iris explained somewhat sheepishly, "but you get desperate. I thought it could be a magic pill."

Her son did take the supplements for two months. She also changed his diet considerably. Although she described him as calmer, when asked if the blue-green algae could be the reason why, Iris exclaimed, "Definitely not."

From a scientific viewpoint, a problem with substances like blue-green algae and St. John's wort is that they have not undergone clinical trials. Not to discount anecdotal reports, but how do we know what works if it isn't offered for study? Also, as Dr. Wilens observes, these compounds "get very expensive over time. They're also untested [for] all drug interactions, and as potent as any of the drugs we're using [in mainstream medicine]."

What's a Parent to Do?

Given the popularity of ADHD and society's desire to find medical alternatives, not surprisingly, ADHD is at risk for "cures" of all kinds. A lot of what you hear may sound good, but we have to be careful when treatment approaches sound "too good to be true." Maybe you don't remember the turn of the last century (I don't either), but I have heard about the traveling salesman with his valise full of Lydia Pinkham's elixir and snake oil to cure everything that might ail you.

So what's a consumer to do? I suggest trying common sense; when that fails, follow recommendations by experts in ADHD. Gut reactions also play a part. Most of us know when something doesn't sound right. In this case, we have to investigate. Good questions to ask are: Who says so? What are his or her credentials? What controlled scientific studies exist to back up this claim? Where can I go for more information?

Take Heart

Understandably, we hope for an end to the difficulties experienced by both our children and the whole family. With luck and continued medical advances, this hope will become reality. In the meantime, wishful thinking and quick fixes should not replace the courage needed to face ADHD problems responsibly by using multimodal intervention. ADHD difficulties respond to treatment—especially when a number of people are involved in helping the child. That includes Mom and Dad and other concerned adults such as grandparents, coaches, teachers, clergy, and scoutmasters, as well as siblings.

In my situation, our family therapist proved to be an extremely important part of the treatment team. We saw him regularly when Dave was first diagnosed and then made appointments on an as-needed basis. As parent Paula Anderson said, "I'm comforted by the fact that I can call him whenever a problem comes up that I don't know how to handle." The more you know about ADHD and the more you do to handle its effects, the fewer circumstances arise that you can't handle.

Summary

Management of ADHD
- Presently no cure exists, but symptoms can be managed
- Requires involvement of all family members
- Need to unlearn ineffective parenting techniques, such as inconsistency, criticism, rejection, physical punishment
- Requires use of behavior charts
- Major goal is to increase child's self-esteem and competence

Multimodal Management Approach

- Consists of four major components
  — education about the disorder
  — parent training in behavior management techniques
  — appropriate educational program
  — medication, when indicated
    also:
  — possibly individual/family counseling
- Requires a wide network of caregivers, including parents, educators, medical and mental health professionals; the child must also be involved

Medical Management

- Generally recommended when other interventions do not produce hoped-for results
- Should *never* be sole course of treatment
- No test exists to predict which patients will benefit from its use
- Benefits must outweigh disadvantages
- Discuss thoroughly with physician

Commonly Used Medications

- Stimulants (Ritalin, Dexedrine, Adderall, Cylert)
  — usually first choice of physicians
  — effective for attention problems, impulsivity, and hyperactivity
  — positive effects on aggression, endurance in tasks
  — mild side effects *may* occur, which include decreased appetite, stomachaches, difficulty falling asleep, rebound
- Tricyclic antidepressants (Norpramin, Tofranil, Pamelor)
  — usually second choice when stimulants contraindicated
  — effective on all three core symptoms
  — mild side effects include dry mouth, constipation, sedation, sometimes increased excitability
  — cardiovascular effects have been reported (usually mild)
- Antihypertensives
  — usually second or third choice
  — positive effects on impulsivity and hyperactivity
  — milk side effects, most commonly drowsiness
  — blood pressure must be monitored

Stimulants/Ritalin

- Used for over fifty years; most widely studied medicine given to children
- Seldom results in serious side effects
- Short-acting; symptoms reappear when dose wears off
- Usually administered two or three times a day
- Effective in children, adolescents, and adults

Considerations

- Avoid giving too much credit or blame for behavior to medicine
- Handle sensitively and discreetly
- Dispense as prescribed
- Monitor side effects
- Communicate with physician frequently

Therapies Not Proven to Be of Use

- Megavitamins
- Scalp massages
- Visual perceptual and ocular motor training
- Biofeedback
- Allergy treatments
- Dietary management, including Feingold
- Blue-green algae

CHAPTER SEVEN

Self-esteem

An odd occurrence happened in our home for the second summer in a row: life improved. Without the stress of the school environment, David's symptoms became reasonably manageable. Sure, for both his dad and me, the effort required to keep David within limits often felt like pedaling a bike uphill, but we coped fairly well, as did Jonathan. Though David constantly lorded it over his younger brother, fortunately Jonathan had a very calm, quiet disposition and seldom balked when David insisted on running our younger son's life. Provided Jon did not get hurt, we ignored most of David's actions.

During this summer of 1986, David even developed friendships with a couple of the neighborhood children. Interestingly, Jonathan gravitated to a little boy who behaved much like his brother, while David became best friends with a little girl who proved as mellow as Jonathan. With the other children as suitable distractions, David no longer demanded my constant attention.

Even the two-week visit by David Sr.'s seventeen-year-old son, Mark, did not upset the status quo as it had in the past. Though young David adored his older brother, until this summer he could not handle the change in routine. Within a matter of hours after Mark arrived, David's voice grew intolerably loud and he became frenetic and overly emotional. As a consequence, the tension level for the entire family increased, thereby decreasing any chance of a pleasant visit for Mark. But now we knew how to keep a lid on David's behavior, and Mark finally enjoyed a happier atmosphere along with the constant attention enthusiastically showered on him by his younger brothers.

When September rolled around, I felt ambivalent about the arrival of school. For years, I anxiously anticipated the peace and quiet I would have once David attended a full-day program. Now I wondered if the school pressures might once again mean a change for the worse in my son's behavior. Over the summer, the child psychologist tried to alert both David's dad and me to the potential risks for David in the primary grades. Until the final hour drew close, we both chose to bask in the sunlight of David's improved disposition. When our son charged through the door at the end of the first day of first grade with a smile stretched from ear to ear, both the psychologist's concerns and my own seemed foolish. David had a wonderful teacher who wrote "I love you" on every paper. In turn, he fell in love too.

During these happy days, David nicknamed me "Kitten." Though I prefer dogs, David loves felines of any type. When he called me Kitten I accepted this name as a demonstration of his love, a sign I had gotten my seven-year-old son back. This nickname and the stuffed animals he brought to my pillow each night served as booster shots to help me through the bad days.

In mid-September when I brought David for a follow-up visit to the pediatric neurologist, he proved to be a mere shadow of the wild fellow this doctor had seen a few months before. While we sat in the waiting room, David picked up a copy of *Marvin K. Mooney Will You Please Go Now!* and began to read aloud. He finished the story while the neurologist and I stood by in total amazement. David had never read an entire book nor sat still in a doctor's office. In a report to the child psychologist, the doctor wrote, "David is neurologically stable at this time. He is doing well in school and I noted a significant improvement in his attentional problems from previous examinations."

I should not have been fooled by David's apparently reformed behavior. Just as the return of the swallows to Capistrano heralded the spring season and the promise of happier days in our home, the arrival of David's birthday at the beginning of fall meant a change for the worse in his behavior. This year, when he turned seven, the only difference was that the change caught me off guard. Our son's dark side subtly crept into our lives.

I first noticed that David's mood had become transformed into a negative frame of mind when he began to take issue with my driving. He insisted I tell him where we were going, what roads I planned to take. Heaven help me on the occasions I made a last-minute decision to take a different route without first informing him. David would carry on as though I had violated a sacred oath.

To make matters worse, my car had a speedometer like a digital clock, which showed the exact speed in brightly illuminated numbers. Whenever we drove anywhere, David eagle-eyed the speedometer and yelled at me if the number exceeded the posted speed limit. I had no idea why this child turned out to be so inflexible. To David, driving at 37 mph in a 35 mph zone meant speeding. No matter how many times I tried to explain that a slight variation could be acceptable, this boy would not listen to my explanation, and I in turn caught his full wrath and fury.

One day, I gave up trying to explain myself to him and yelled, "I am the boss, not you." I then warned my son about the terrible fate he would meet if he did not learn to mind his own business. I didn't hear a peep about my driving until a week later when David arrived home after school. With a shaky voice but nonetheless firm resolve, he announced, "Now you're in trouble. I stopped the police car and told him that you speed all the time." I could not believe he turned his own mother in to the authorities.

Here stood proof that once David set his mind to an idea, he never let up. The child psychologist, Dr. Burke, explained to us how our son's propensity to get stuck on a topic, his inability to adjust easily to change, his short attention span, his impulsive behavior, and his poor social skills could really create a miserable existence for him in school. Again Dr. Burke urged us to ask David's teacher to initiate a child study team evaluation so an appropriate school program could be developed for him.

After our first experience with this procedure, I felt reluctant to go through an evaluation again. Besides, both my husband and I now felt fearful of "the system" and worried about the repercussions of having David labeled. When we voiced these concerns to the psychologist, he explained that unless the school recognized David's disorder and appropriately modified his program, David could very likely be tagged as the "kid with the ability who refuses to do the work." He said teachers might come to view David's failure to perform as either his voluntary choice or the result of some underlying emotional difficulties.

Dr. Burke then bluntly added that children with ADHD label themselves as bad kids with behavior problems. "Which label would you rather David have?" Dr. Burke asked. Well, we knew we would rather have our son understood as a child with special needs that made certain aspects of learning and socialization difficult for him. In mid-October I spoke with David's teacher.

When the conference began, I told the first-grade teacher about our home situation and the tremendously hard time David had been through as a result of this disorder. The teacher listened intently to this information and to my concerns that David meet with success in school. Since all of David's papers came home with stickers that read, "Super," "Good Going," or "I Love You," I was surprised that she had already recommended David for the school's basic skills program, which did not require an evaluation.

Still, this program did not address my son's other problems. As in kindergarten, David had difficulty paying attention and could not seem to follow directions. Because he rushed, most of his work looked very sloppy. She kindly assured me that David tried very hard and that many first-graders have similar difficulty, but when I looked around the room at the other children's drawings and papers, I could not help but see that David's work did not measure up to theirs.

Nor were his work habits the only problem. Just as in kindergarten, David bossed his classmates and reprimanded them whenever they made a mistake. The first-grade teacher told me David tended to be a very serious little boy; she felt his intensity interfered with his ability to make and keep friends. "David's a nice little boy. He's just very hard on himself and his classmates," she said.

We ended the conference in agreement that a child study team evaluation for David would be warranted. I knew my son had a chronic problem. But now that I realized that parental determination could not alleviate his problem and that the results of the child study team evaluation might offer him more help, I found the evaluation process palatable.

Meanwhile, after eighteen months of going to the child psychologist, some of the finer points of home management became a part of my repertoire. For instance, David needed to be prepared for all changes in routine, so when Halloween arrived, this seven-year-old had been well rehearsed for the events of the day. In the afternoon, David and his five-year-old brother would participate in a Halloween parade and play at school, which parents and grandparents attended. That evening, the entire family along with two friends would go trick-or-treating.

This first-grade year, David opted to be a witch. Jonathan, now in kindergarten, had grown so accustomed to being David's shadow, he chose entirely of his own accord to be the witch's black cat. For Jon's costume, I found a black sweat suit, whiskers, a tail, and cat's ears. David would don a black robe, a cape, a witch's hat and broom, a ratty brown wig, a wart-covered nose, and green face makeup. I felt so good about their costumes that I could hardly wait for the boys to come home at lunchtime to get ready for the school parade.

At the stroke of twelve noon, David flew through the door and screamed in horror, "Witches are girls. Get me another costume. I'm not being a witch." I felt panic. We did not stock a cache of costumes ready for any whim. David began to lose control and started to yell, scream, and call me names for "being a stupid mother." Even time-out could not get him calmed down.

He did, however, stop his tantrum the moment the idea dawned on him that his little brother could be the witch. "I'll be the cat," he proclaimed. Jonathan, who had been subservient to his big brother's spell for so long, picked this day to take a stand. He would not hear of a change in costume, and I supported his decision. Recognizing defeat, David slipped back into his nasty temper.

I felt like a genius when the obvious solution came to my mind about twenty minutes later. I told David he could be a warlock. "What's that?" he yelled. "A male witch," I replied. But David did not buy this brilliant idea and continued his tirade. Only ten minutes remained of the lunch hour, and David, who had not even begun to get dressed, started to criticize Jon's costume, at which point I almost sent him to school as the fabled headless horseman.

Fortunately, my mother arrived on the scene and convinced him that Halloween costumes knew no gender. David put on his costume. I applied the final red blotches on his green face and took him to school, where all his classmates already sat at their desks. When we opened the door, the entire class cackled and shrieked, "Look at the witch." He did look great.

David ran out of the room and ripped the wig off his head and the warty nose from his face. "They're laughing at me," he screamed. Though his teacher and I tried to explain that the kids just thought his costume looked so real, this seven-year-old witch could not make the distinction. He only agreed to rejoin the festivities after I wiped every smudge of green paint from his face.

As I sat in the audience and watched all the little children, including my son Jonathan, enjoy themselves and revel in their costumes, I became overwhelmed with sadness. This celebration proved to be anything but a party for my son. David's disorder still prevented him from being like all the other kids. I fled the scene because I could not stop crying.

David came home from school that afternoon no longer dressed in his costume but relatively calm. I, on the other hand, felt stretched to my limit. When the time arrived to get ready for trick-or-treating, I soon discovered this evil spell would not quit. David acted up again, and when I snapped and screamed unmercifully at him, Jonathan joined forces with his brother and began to yell about his costume. By the time my friend and her two children arrived to go out trick-or-treating, I felt like a basket case. I had no idea what could have possessed mild-mannered Jonathan to act up that Halloween day. Normally, Jonathan played a very passive role. At times, I could even fool myself into thinking that my younger son took all the family stress in stride. This horrible scene proved to be the precursor of many bad days to follow.

At our next appointment with the child psychologist, I recounted the horrors of Halloween. He explained that the holiday had all the makings for a blowup: too much stimulation, too much change in the routine, too much excitement, and, for David in particular, too little self-esteem. The constant negative feedback from his parents and peers, the frustration he felt from not being able to perform up to his ability in the classroom, and his socialization problems commanded a high price. David could in no way handle being the center of all that attention. The psychologist reminded me that scenes like Halloween would become exacerbated if I responded less than matter-of-factly to my son's behavior. As a result of this nightmare, David had experienced yet another blow to his already damaged self-esteem, and I again felt like a terrible mother.

For the next couple of months both his dad and I searched for ways to help David feel better about himself. We tried sports like swimming, gymnastics, and basketball at the YMCA, but David balked at these activities. He put a great deal of pressure on himself and could not tolerate the fact that he did not do these sports perfectly. Eventually, we did not force him to go. At least three days a week, I encouraged David to have a friend over to our house after school. David bossed these children so much that I felt embarrassed for my son and uncomfortable for them. Back then, I did not know how to help David build friendships. After a couple of months, only one little boy who never challenged David remained on the social scene.

By December, the school workload increased. Now that homework had been introduced, David had spelling words to study and sheets of math problems to do. He could barely control himself long enough to sit still and do this work. The moment a task presented the slightest challenge he fell apart. He would scream for my help, then he would complain about my input. The child psychologist suggested we add to David's chart, "Completes homework on time without argument." Though the chart helped, I began to feel that the load we had to carry to keep David on track had grown too heavy.

Despite all the behavior management both his dad and I used, we could not get a semblance of normalcy in our home. Our efforts proved to be only a partial solution. In January 1987, both young David and I crashed and burned as a result of the stresses this disorder placed upon us.

The actual circumstance that brought us to our knees began quite innocently. David had a story to write for homework, and I tried to help him. He behaved so nastily that I threw up my hands in disgust, which made him extremely angry. The more he mouthed off, the angrier I became. Pretty soon the scene approached near-Halloween proportions. I had the presence of mind to pull out of the fight. However, the next day I insisted he take a note to his teacher in regard to the problems we had with the assignment.

Throughout the entire school year, David's teacher and I communicated by note, so when no reply came home that day or the next, I questioned David. He developed a guilty posture and avoided answering any of my five hundred questions until I grabbed his face, looked him straight in the eyes, and demanded to know what he did with my note to the teacher. By the time he admitted he never delivered it to her, I was in a fury. I ranted and raved so much that David probably thought he had committed a violent crime.

I could not get control of myself. Practically every ounce of frustration I had stored up over the past seven and a half years gushed out. Later that evening, as David changed for bed, I continued to obsess about the note until I ultimately threatened him. I hollered, "Tomorrow you will take another note, and that note will tell the teacher what the first note said and that you did not give it to her."

All the color drained from my little boy's face. David covered his ears and began to scream, "I hate myself. I'm going to climb up a tree and touch an electric wire and die." I felt terrible. I lifted him off the floor and rocked him back and forth while I told him over and over again, "Mommy was wrong to yell at you, David. You're a good boy. I love you very much. You didn't do anything so bad. Forget the note. It's not important. Your teacher always tells me what a good boy you are."

After a while his sobs stopped and he went to bed. Then I fell apart. My son, though still a small child, felt so much misery he wanted to die. I knew he fought hard to fit in, to belong, to feel loved. Yet he stood alone, a ringmaster forced to keep the lions of the world at bay lest they swallow him up. Maybe this night, when the lion became his mother, the effort proved too much.

The next day, we had an emergency appointment with the child psychologist. Even though David's emotional state had stabilized that evening, guilt, shame, and fear overwhelmed me. I thought I must be the worst mother ever, but Dr. Burke said I too had become a victim of this disorder. He explained that I had reached the point of emotional overload and suggested I go away for the weekend to calm down and recharge my batteries, which I did. When I returned, I felt better, though still unsettled.

A few days later, we also saw the pediatric neurologist. After I described our family situation of the past few months and the ultimate crisis, the doctor said the time had now arrived to try stimulant medication, specifically Ritalin.

Though the medication did not promise to be a magic cure, for our son, this treatment provided the missing puzzle piece. The medication enabled David to regulate his own behavior, emotions, and impulsive decision-making. His hyperactivity diminished. His attention span and ability to concentrate increased along with an improvement in his organizational skills. Use of the medicine in conjunction with behavior management techniques, family therapy, and the school program allowed David to experience the world as a kinder place where he could be quite successful and well liked by others.

Three weeks after David began medication, we went on vacation to Mexico. These ten days we spent together turned out to be the most wonderful time we had ever experienced as a family. Mexico takes a lot of adjusting to, yet David maintained a positive attitude and, for most of the trip, acted as resident cheerleader. We came home on Valentine's Day, and that evening I found this note on my pillow: "To cat meow. I live you kitty cat. The best cat in the world." How the tide had turned in one short month. Even Jonathan now sought out his older brother as a playmate.

As a family we continued to work in therapy for the rest of this year. David's behavior grew consistently better, so we now addressed some of the bad patterns our family had fallen into over the years as we wrestled with his condition. The most difficult one for us to break proved to be using David as the family scapegoat. Jonathan had subtly become a master puppeteer who knew precisely how to pull his brother's strings. Whenever any disturbance erupted, David got so much blame that he confessed to sins he never committed. We also concentrated our efforts on raising our little boy's self-esteem.

Dr. Burke told us what we had to do to make this change. First, David's dad and I had to look and listen at all times before we reacted. We had to learn to view a situation through David's eyes. Oddly enough, when we did put ourselves in David's position, many of our perceptions changed. Above all, we needed to learn not to yell or say damaging things to our child. Dr. Burke told us, "Kids with ADHD really test your patience, so it's understandable that you lose your temper. But you have to understand how hard life is for them too."

We learned in therapy that David could not help himself and did not understand why we got angry with him or yelled at him. Dr. Burke said we had to step back a bit and not take the child's behavior personally. Even though he acknowledged how difficult such steps could be, he reminded us that since the child cannot stay in control of his or her emotions, the adults have to do so.

"ADHD must be managed thoughtfully, not emotionally," the child psychologist told us. Eventually we learned that the goal of any encounter is to teach the child what behavior is and is not acceptable. Years have passed since these early lessons. Some days I fall back into old patterns of response. So does David. We even go through periodic downs, but never to the extent we did during these bleak days.

The Makings of Self-esteem

The darkness of David's first-grade year occurred because his self-esteem hit rock bottom. Though not all children with ADHD experience the loss of self-esteem to the extent that they feel despair, still in all, not feeling good about oneself runs rampant in children with this disorder. Given the factors that contribute to the development of self-esteem, that our children prove to be at risk for a poor self-image is not surprising. The lack of self-control shown by children with ADHD sets them up for years of negativity.

Self-esteem develops over a lifetime. It also ebbs and flows with the changing circumstances and interactions of our lives. Our feelings of self-worth, confidence, and competence contribute to that overall sense we have about ourselves called self-esteem.

According to Judy Welch, Ph.D., young children do not know how to nourish their sense of self, so they look to others for support, acceptance, and approval. Initially, we parents provide this affectionate care and attention. Then significant others such as teachers, siblings, peers, and coaches play a role. Teachers play a very big part, as they provide feedback about individual ability and how a child compares to peers.

A child's self-image can be elevated, Dr. Welch explains, by the opinions the child holds of him or herself. The child forms these opinions in three ways: the messages the child gives him or herself, those received from others, and how the child interprets the messages from others. Positive feedback helps the child develop an inner confidence, which nourishes the sense of self and leads to a happy, well-adjusted adult.

Unfortunately, many children with ADHD often receive mostly negative input. They develop an extremely poor sense of self and eventually think even messages intended to be positive are negative. They also develop a pattern of giving themselves negative messages. Poor self-concept dogs them every step of the way.

Healthy Signs and Warning Signals

Our actions and attitudes mirror the way we feel about ourselves. As Dr. Welch notes, children with high self-esteem take pride in their accomplishments, act independently, assume responsibility easily, tolerate frustration well, approach new challenges enthusiastically, and feel capable of influencing others. They make comments like, "I can handle that job"; "I made this picture all by myself"; "Wow! I'm learning long division"; "I really like this story I wrote about dinosaurs."

A child with low self-esteem expresses a defeatist attitude a great deal of the time. He or she avoids anxiety-producing situations, puts down his or her talents, feels others don't value him or her, blames others for his or her weaknesses, is easily influenced by others, becomes defensive and easily frustrated, and feels powerless. This child might make statements like: "I'm not going to school today. There's a hard math test"; "Nothing I draw looks any good"; "I flunked the test because the teacher didn't give me enough time to study"; "I can't find the scissors. Now I'll never finish."

Susie White's mother, Lynn, recognized her daughter's lack of self-esteem when she asked all the little girls in her Brownie troop to draw a self-portrait. Susie did not draw a bold picture or use most of the paper like the other little girls. Instead, she drew her self-portrait the size of a pea and in the lower-right corner of the paper so that it could barely be seen. At this point, Susie's ADHD had not been diagnosed, and she carried the burden of responsibility for her symptoms.

Contributors to Low Self-esteem

1. Not being effective

According to Dr. Keith Conners, "Being effective is the basis of self-esteem." He says there are a million ways that kids can be effective. For instance, they can dress themselves, play with other children, succeed academically, and experience a sense of accomplishment through sports or the performing arts.

Most children with ADHD do not have the means to feel effective. Their symptoms usually make everything they attempt a hassle. Even their special talents often go unrecognized or undeveloped because many children with ADHD prove unable to practice or sustain interest in their areas of natural talent. Thus the normal means by which most children receive boosts in self-esteem do not exist for these children.

2. Negative feedback

Based on his clinical experience, Dr. Conners says: "Most people either write off children with ADHD as miserable little beings who deserve the negative responses they get, or else they ignore these children." Such responses do much harm to the child's self-image. Dr. Conners reports that long-term follow-up studies of children with ADHD reveal almost a uniform deficiency in self-esteem. Though the academic and behavioral deficits tend to persist as well, he says the low self-esteem becomes a far more serious deficit. After all, success in life is determined by a person's motivation, belief in self, and confidence.

Dr. Welch adds that many children with ADHD become battered by a steady stream of failure, frustration, and disappointment resulting in badly bruised egos. The degree to which the child experiences this emotional beating depends on the degree of severity of the condition. For Peter Rothman, every environment represented a struggle. Even his day camp counselors thought of him as uncooperative. Since he had difficulty going from one activity to the next, ten-year-old Peter turned out to be the last child to get to the starting line and the last one to cross the finish line every day. His mother, Donna, often mistook his uncooperative behavior for obstinacy.

3. The could-if-you-wanted-to myth

Undiagnosed children with ADHD often suffer blows to their self-esteem because of the mythology developed to explain why they do not "get with the program." Faced with a child who does not comply, many parents and teachers often draw the conclusion that the child has control over his or her behavior but *chooses* to misbehave.

As a result of this "you-could-do-it-if-you-wanted-to" myth, many children with ADHD receive a great deal of punishment. Dr. Russell Barkley observes that these children do not want to behave the way they do. By the age of eight or ten, many show signs of poor self-esteem because they really want to behave well. After they are punished for misbehavior, they make great promises to change. These usually turn out to be promises they can't keep because, as Dr. Barkley says, "they are at the mercy of their characteristics."

4. The not-being-able-to reality

Children with ADHD come into the world with the same desires as all other children. They want to be loved, liked, and accepted. So, like other children, they want to please. The behaviors associated with their disability, however, displease themselves and others. They experience failure so frequently, their self-esteem gradually erodes. This sense of failure is compounded in those cases where parents (or teachers) unaware of the child's underlying disorder, decide their son or daughter (or student) is out to drive them over the edge. Actually, frustrated parents (or teachers) often send the child's sense of self on a downward spiral.

Unrealistic Expectations

Furthermore, parents and teachers who do not understand the dynamics of this disorder often have unrealistic expectations. Based on her experience as a former teacher and school psychologist, Dr. Welch notes that many parents and teachers get stuck in the belief that if they really push a child, that child will straighten up and do what is asked. Sometimes when the parents and/or teachers push, the child does perform well, which gives rise to the opinion that if a child with ADHD does something once, he or she should be able to perform accordingly at all times.

Inconsistency

By the way, the child with ADHD often proves equally baffled as to why he or she can get it together sometimes but not others. This "you-could-do-it-if-you-tried-hard-enough" myth and the aforementioned "you-could-do-it-if-you-wanted-to" myth are closely related and are reinforced by the inconsistent nature of the child's ADHD symptoms.

Pediatrician Melvin Levine, director of the Clinical Center for Development and Learning at the University of North Carolina at Chapel Hill, believes inconsistency to be the biggest problem of children with attention problems. Many people act as though the inconsistency of the child's behavior indicates that the child with ADHD really does have control over his or her actions. Occasionally the child does meet expectations without special help, so why not as often as other children?

Why anyone would respond with disbelief and surprise to the idea that ADHD symptoms manifest themselves inconsistently boggles the mind. As Dr. Levine points out, many chronic conditions in medicine are inconsistent in their manifestation. For instance, people with asthma do not wheeze all the time, and people with arthritis may have swollen joints one day and not the next.

But the misunderstandings about the inconsistent nature of

ADHD symptoms take a toll on the child's self-esteem. Instead of allowing the child with ADHD to feel effective when he or she does perform well, these myths and expectations give the child the message that he or she is incompetent.

Incompetency Message

Unfortunately, the most consistent aspect of the disorder proves to be the fact that most children with ADHD receive this "incompetency message" regularly. In fact, this message is so consistent, the child often incorporates it into his or her own belief system. Sometimes the incompetency message is delivered overtly by negative feedback and punishment. Other times, parents in particular, though they do not realize it, develop a demoralizing pattern of response to the child with ADHD. In turn, the negative messages they send to their son or daughter become gradually ingrained within the child.

Dr. William McMahon reports that parents of children with ADHD frequently fall into a condescending pattern of response to the child, which in turn reaffirms the incompetency message. In his practice, for instance, Dr. McMahon has noted some parents who identify the child with ADHD as a social and emotional cripple and overprotect him or her because they feel responsible for the youngster's every move. In other situations, the parents give the child a very wide berth and everyone walks on eggshells around him or her. These responses not only deprive the child of normal consequences for his or her actions but set the child apart from everyone else. Children with ADHD often feel they do not fit in.

Building Good Self-esteem

1. Changing belief systems

Fortunately for children with ADHD, self-esteem increases when the child's circumstances improve. According to Dr. Welch, the most effective remedy for poor self-esteem is changing the child's belief system about him or herself. To do so, we parents and teachers, in particular, need to alter our belief system about the child. Gaining knowledge about the disorder provides a basis to begin changing our point of view.

Parents and teachers must dispel the myth that the child with ADHD is willfully noncompliant. Once we come to view the child as a person with a disability in need of special help, we feel less angry about the child's behavior. As a result, stress level decreases and capability to help the child increases. ADHD affects everyone the child interacts with to some degree; therefore, everyone must learn to cope with the disorder. Changes in approach are required to nurture the child's sense of self.

2. Behavior management

Behavior management is a good way to change what we do and how we do it. These methods, described in earlier chapters, do not change children. Instead, they change how we, the adults in the child's life, respond to our children. They also provide external means for guiding the child. When we use effective techniques as opposed to inconsistency, negative feedback, and excessive punishment, we inflict fewer blows to our children's sense of self. They feel better. So do we, because instead of reacting, we are taking positive action. Teachers will find that behavior management tools have their place in the classroom. In addition to lessening spirit-killing responses, these techniques enable the child to take responsibility for behavior. They do not, however, in and of themselves promote good self-esteem. Instead, they lay the groundwork.

3. Catch the child being good

According to Dr. Conners, the goal of all interventions is to make the child feel good about his or her abilities and to feel effective. To do this, he says, those involved with the child "need to catch the child being good." Throughout the course of most days, children behave appropriately in many instances for which parents do not show approval: for instance, when the child remembers to do his or her chores or to bring home all the necessary homework materials. The child might share a toy or perhaps politely ask for a snack.

4. Praise

None of these appropriate behaviors is above and beyond the call of duty. They are examples of everyday expectations. But even though we expect a child to behave a certain way as a matter of course, we still need to reward the child with ADHD for meeting expectations. Praise becomes the greatest tool a parent or teacher has to help the child carve a positive self-image.

Of course, praise needs to be valid. Furthermore, we parents and

teachers need to know that a child with a poor self-image may initially view even deserved praise as insincere and made-up. Sometimes the child may even act out to try to prove that the praise was
not deserved. Though such a response might provoke an angry reaction, we need to remember that under the circumstances, the child is
coming from a place of low regard. This child needs a lot of positive
feedback to turn that horrible self-image around.

In younger children, Dr. Conners says, blunt forms of praise, such
as "Excellent job" or "That's wonderful," work surprisingly well.
However, he finds older kids to be sensitive to such statements. For
them, praise must be subtly delivered in statements such as "It looks
like you put a lot of work into this."

Dr. Welch tells parents and teachers to think of the child's self-
esteem as a bank account and to make sure there are more assets
than debits. Monitor the number of withdrawals made through negative feedback, and make numerous daily deposits of praise, encouragement, recognition, and positive attention. When a variety of
expressions instead of only one is used, the child knows the praise-
worthy behavior really received consideration. To this end, Dr.
Welch made a list of phrases parents and teachers can use called
"52 Ways to Say 'Good for You.' " Among those included are "I
appreciate your help," "That's a good point," "That's certainly one
way of looking at it," "Good thinking," and "Nice going."

5. Identify strengths and weaknesses

Realistic expectations on the part of parents, teachers, and the child
with ADHD provide the foundation upon which a child can build self-
respect. Thus the child's strengths and weaknesses need to be determined. Dr. Welch has found that the more information parents,
teachers, and the child with ADHD have about the disorder, the
greater their sensitivity to the child's strengths and weaknesses.
Knowledge is like the white plaster cast worn by a child with a broken
arm. The cast conveys the message, "I can't write with this hand, but
maybe I can type with the other one." Once all the people involved
understand the child's problems, they can revise their expectations,
look for constructive ways to overcome the child's difficulties, and
not make unreasonable demands that exceed the child's limitations,
just as they would not demand a child write with a broken arm.

In addition to providing a great sense of relief, knowledge about
the disorder affords the child and the significant others the opportu-

nity to maximize the strengths and compensate for the difficulties. For instance, often the diagnostic evaluation provides teachers with information about the child's learning characteristics. Teachers can use this knowledge to formulate judgments about how long the child can work on a task, how much homework the child can handle, and how the child processes instructions.

Instead of muddling through a haphazard existence, parents as well can plan around the child's strengths and weaknesses. When Paula Anderson and her husband learned their daughter Maggie had no control over her ability to sit still, they stopped expecting her to remain quiet for an hour while the family ate dinner at a restaurant. Even children with ADHD can compensate for their difficulties. For example, ten-year-old John Golding learned to ask his teacher if he could go to a study carrel in the back of the classroom when he needed to have peace and quiet.

In John's classroom, his peers were also taught ways to assist him with class projects. Dr. Welch stresses the important effect peers and siblings have on the way the child with ADHD feels about him or herself. Thus peers and siblings should be encouraged to participate in the boosting of the child's self-esteem by giving positive feedback and not criticism.

6. Accentuate the positive

Children with ADHD, their parents, and their teachers need to look beyond the problems associated with the disorder to its positive aspects. Children with ADHD have many assets they can play to the hilt, but often they need the help of parents and teachers to tap their natural resources. Many successful adults with ADHD note that they have learned to channel their energy, drive, and creativity to a productive end.

7. Build opportunities for success

Parents and teachers can encourage the child with ADHD to develop a special interest. Children feel good about themselves when they find something they can master. Dr. Paul Wender notes that children with ADHD often perform superbly well when given a task of high interest to them. For instance, he notes that boys with ADHD tend to be interested in dinosaurs or in earthquakes, tidal waves, or other miscellaneous catastrophes and will read voraciously on those subjects.

In addition to nurturing the child's special interests, parents and teachers can build opportunities for success into the child's environment. Children feel good about themselves when they feel effective and competent. They develop confidence when they receive positive feedback, meet with success, and fulfill their responsibilities. Since children with ADHD often have difficulty taking and meeting responsibility, parents and teachers need to structure situations so the child can succeed. For example, beginning when John Golding turned seven, he had the responsibility of feeding the family pets. Lack of organization posed a problem for John, so his mother put the food he would need on the kitchen table every morning before breakfast. John proudly reported to me that not one pet, not even a goldfish, had died under his care.

There are a hundred different ways parents can build opportunities for their child to experience success. The following are some suggestions many parents have found to work well. I have arbitrarily divided them into four categories: special jobs, special interests, play, and extracurricular activities. Some of these ideas may work well for your child. Others might be totally disastrous. When you are selecting or devising strategies to build his or her success, the individual child's age, strengths, weaknesses, and interests must be taken into account. At times even the best-laid plans fail. In such instances, don't be discouraged and don't assume that you or your child is at fault. These suggestions, many of which apply to either boys or girls, are intended to spark your imagination.

Special jobs can be a cross between chores and fun and provide an excellent way to develop a sense of responsibility. When presenting a child with the opportunity to do such a task, perhaps we all would do well to recall the example of Tom Sawyer. Because Tom made whitewashing Aunt Polly's fence appear to be so much fun, the other kids became so eager and highly motivated, they even paid money to be allowed to do his work. Special jobs can involve such daily tasks as setting or clearing the table at mealtime, saying grace, emptying the trash, feeding the pets, or making school lunches. On a weekly basis, the child can put away groceries, plan and/or prepare a meal, water plants, or sort objects for recycling. The child can also be responsible for decorating the home for different holidays, helping plan and map out a family outing, or for being the family historian by taking family photos and/or placing photos in albums.

Children usually love to be helpers. They can be encouraged to

assist in special home projects such as building a bookshelf or training a pet. Whenever I wallpapered a room, my children participated
by taking the scraps and wallpapering a cardboard box.

Special interests take advantage of the child's natural tendency
to be curious. The parent can help the child build self-esteem by
encouraging him or her to become expert in an area of interest.
Many children like to start collections of any number of items such
as dinosaurs, sports team memorabilia, stamps, dolls, rocks, or
seashells. For a child interested in birds, the parent can help the
child build a bird feeder and be responsible for keeping it stocked.
Solar-system enthusiasts would enjoy a trip to a planetarium and a
telescope to study the night skies. Other children might like to plant
flowers and tend gardens.

Playing with your child can also foster good feelings, provided
you play a certain way. Dr. Russell Barkley explains that *play* can
take two forms: directive or nondirective. Directive play builds
developmental skills as the parent tries to teach the child something
through the use of a game or construction kit like Legos. Dr.
Barkley says, "Directive play basically involves a lot of teaching,
and this type of play with children with ADHD just gets parents in
trouble."

Instead he advises the use of nondirective play, in which the child
is given full control over what the parent and child will play. The
parent also follows the commands given by the child. Rather than
acting as the leader, the parent's job is observing, commenting,
describing the child's play, and periodically giving positive feedback.

I accidentally fell into nondirective play with my children when
they acquired a Nintendo set and I, of course, could not get past the
first board on Super Mario Brothers. Whether playing Monopoly,
checkers, chess, or cards, the parent does well to structure the game
so the child can win.

Extracurricular activities frequently reported as successful and
of high interest to children with ADHD include team sports such as
basketball, soccer, hockey, football, and baseball. Parents can play a
crucial role in helping the child develop self-confidence by practic-
ing the skills needed for these sports with him or her. For instance,
throw the child balls he or she can catch. Some children might
prefer to participate in sports that require little to no interactions
with peers, such as swimming, skiing, weightlifting, track and field,
martial arts, or gymnastics. The performing arts, such as children's

theater groups or dance classes, offer yet a third type of alternative. Regardless of which activity the child selects, parents need to support the child by attending practices, contests, and performances.

When first developing extracurricular activities, use prudence. Concentrate on activities the child selects, perhaps with your guidance, rather than forcing the child to do something in which he or she has little interest. Chances are, under forced circumstances, the child will do poorly, and that of course defeats the very intent, which is to increase success and thereby build self-esteem.

John Brett, a teenager with ADHD, said to me, "I think when you have ADHD, you need an outlet." He advised parents to find something their child with ADHD can do that makes him or her feel positive. For John, weightlifting boosted both his physical strength and his sense of self. He says that when he lifts weights he also develops his ability to concentrate, because he knows that if his mind wanders he could seriously hurt himself. John also asked me to tell parents that even if their child is failing every class, they should not take away the outlet, which often proves to be the only thing in the child's life that makes him or her feel good. Otherwise, says John, "he'll get more screwed up."

"Can-Do" Kids

Children with ADHD do not have to be beaten down as a result of their disorder. Dr. Welch says, "We can help resurrect a new self-image in our children with feelings of pride, security, and a sense of I-can-do-it-ness through encouragement and praise."

In order to ensure a positive outcome for the child with ADHD, Dr. Conners offers this advice: "Parents need to view ADHD as a chronic disorder. Good things and difficult things about the child will come and go. So you better develop your own sense of equanimity and not give up on the kid, because he will make it eventually, unless the toll along the way proves too high."

Through a concerted effort to boost self-esteem in the child with ADHD, the miserable effects of the condition can be thwarted. Remember, these children are not the children who *can't* or *won't*. They *can* and *do,* but *can* and *do* come harder to them. To succeed, which means to feel competent, they need our special interest and help.

Summary

Self-esteem

- Provides motivation
- Foundation for positive adjustment
- Root of competency

How Self-esteem Develops

- Changes throughout life
- Initially nurtured by parents and then by significant others
- Based on opinions child has of self formed by:
  — messages given to self
  — messages received from others
  — how messages from others are interpreted
- Sense of self characterized by child's attitudes and actions

Factors Leading to Poor Self-esteem

- Belief that child is deliberately noncompliant
- Myths that suggest child could do it if he tried hard enough or if he/she really wanted
- Inconsistency of behavior and performance
- Sending child messages suggesting incompetency
- Negative feedback

Factors That Improve Self-esteem

- Coming to view child as having special needs
- Changes in approach and feedback given to child
- Behavior management
- Changing expectations
- Emphasizing strengths
- Structure environment to build successful experiences
  — create special jobs that child can successfully accomplish
  — encourage special interests and hobbies
  — use nondirective play
  — develop participation in extracurricular activities
  — practice recreational skills with child
- Allow the child to choose the areas of interest

CHAPTER EIGHT

The Elementary School Years and Advocating for Your Child

In May of 1987, I met with our school's child study team to learn the results of the evaluation requested the previous fall. Since David's dad and I had already been through this process two years earlier when David had been diagnosed, I thought the conference would be quite easy to handle intellectually as well as emotionally. Yet the formality of the proceedings caught me off guard, and I felt tense and upset with the dehumanizing nature of this meeting. Except for his teacher, no one spoke about my son David, a first-grader, as a living, breathing soul. Instead, he became a summary of test results.

As a result of the child study team evaluation, David would indeed be eligible for special education services. The evaluation highlighted his difficulty performing to his ability level. Though David's grades were A's and B's, the child study team expressed concern about the *way* our child performed his tasks. Rarely did he use a careful, planned approach. Usually, he did complete his work on time, but at a very high price. David seemingly worked doubly hard to keep on task, which left little energy to cope with frustration. Adding to all the difficulty was his awareness that intellectually he had a brilliance that proved very hard to manifest in day-to-day tasks. That whittled away at his self-esteem.

Even with all our knowledge about ADHD, his dad and I still had a hard time thinking of our son as a child with special education needs. True understanding of ADHD as a serious disorder with a negative impact on all aspects of our son's life took a very long time to register.

A few days after the conference at which we learned the results of the special education evaluation, the postman delivered a copy of each child study team member's written report about David. Of all the reports, the social worker's interview with my then seven-and-a-half-year-old proved to be the most revealing. She wrote, "David describes himself as American. When pressed to describe himself as a person, he says he is nice. David likes that he has a new puppy, Molly, and that he takes care of her well. He states that he is happy most of the time. David does not like the way his brain makes him get into trouble. It tells him to do bad things and when he does them, he gets into trouble. David also doesn't like that his brain does not think too well. He hardly ever gets a 100 on his spelling test. David likes to play games or build things. He does not like to run or do work. David's three wishes were: one, have all the money in the world; two, own this world; three, could have magic."

Based on David's comments, the social worker drew the following conclusions: "David spoke of his brain in the third person, as though it were separate and apart from him, but very much in control. David did not see that he could alter his perceptions or the work of his brain either by studying harder or concentrating on his behavior. David appears to behave in a certain manner and relinquishes blame for his behavior to causes other than himself."

I always knew my son to be very intelligent, but until I read this report, I did not realize his intuitive abilities. In actuality, David described to the social worker, and consequently anyone who read her report, the neurological manifestations of his ADHD disability. He talked about his brain in the third person because he, more than anyone else, knew how little control he had over his behavior. Though he desired to succeed, to be accepted, to have his intentions properly executed, David could not will his brain to do what he wanted. Before the necessary treatment interventions, at most times David had only limited power to regulate his behavior, while at other times regulating the functioning of his brain proved to be completely beyond his control.

At the end of the school year, I received one final note from my son's teacher. "Dear Mary, she wrote. "Wasn't David great today in the play? I'm so proud of him. In fact, his overall behavior has changed in school. His attitude is very positive lately, and several times he has complimented some of his classmates (a real first!). The gym teacher has also noticed the change—and the smiles! I'm just delighted for him. I hope you are experiencing this 'new David' at home, too." Thanks to the behavioral interventions and medication we used to manage our son's disorder, our entire family did reap the benefits of David's improved condition.

I do not mean to imply that all our problems ended. David still needed to learn how to behave appropriately. For instance, one summer evening, he threw a stick into the air, and it accidentally landed on his brother's head. Jonathan landed in the emergency room. I fully intended to be lenient and forgive David for his mistake, but he did not show any remorse for the consequences of his impulsive behavior. Instead, he bounded in the door and screamed at the top of his lungs, "It was his fault! I told the stupid Jon to move and he didn't do what I said. You should punish him."

Maybe my tightly clenched jaw and glowering eyes persuaded him to change his tack. Whatever the reason, David, a survivor, realized this occasion did not lend itself to the "the best defense is a good offense" approach. He said nothing when I sent him to his room for the day, and I felt particularly pleased that my temper did not flare and make things worse.

However, I continued to be disturbed by the thought that maybe David's impulsive behavior would someday push him beyond the horizon and off the edge of the world. Unlike in his toddler days, I could not watch him like a hawk every minute to keep him from going too far. At our next session with the child psychologist, I decided to bring up this stick incident with the hope that perhaps the psychologist could drill into David's head the realization that impulsive acts can lead to serious consequences. I still had not fully accepted that David often had no control over his impulsive acts.

After I recounted the details of that afternoon, Dr. Burke commended me because I gave David an immediate consequence for his action and did not get angry with him. But rather than lecture David about the evils of impulsivity, he asked, "Did you expect the stick to hit your brother?"

"No," replied David in a very soft voice.

The psychologist then queried, "What could you have done differently?" Dead silence.

After fifteen seconds or so I offered, "You could have looked around first to make sure nobody would be in the way."

Immediately Dr. Burke stepped in and told David he should never throw sticks or rocks or anything for that matter. I had missed the point that this child with ADHD could not readily or thoughtfully control his impulses and thus needed strict limits. "No" for David actually proved to be much kinder than expecting him to use appropriate judgment.

That summer between first and second grade, David attended day camp. Since social interactions remained difficult, he continued to be isolated from his peers. Though he did participate in team activities, David spent most of his free time with his twenty-year-old group counselor. Until the winter came, neither my husband nor I realized how the camp experience had benefited our son. David, now eight years old, signed up for swimming and tennis at the YMCA. Such initiative and participation had never before been part of David's style, and in the past, when we forced him into sports activities, our efforts resulted in disaster. For example, we pushed him to play tee ball. During the first game of the season, our pride and joy sat in the middle of the field and repeatedly yelled, "This is boring." He did not play ball after that morning, and his dad and I no longer made emphatic suggestions purportedly for our son's own good.

When school resumed in September, David left the house each morning eager to begin his day. He returned a happy spirit. One of the first papers to come home showed a rocket blasting toward space. Underneath, David wrote, "When I grow up I want to be an astronaut. I want to do that because it is fun." He had neatly formed each letter and spelled all the words correctly. I felt such joy to see my son happy. Finally he had shed the difficult skin that bound him like a tightly wrapped coil ready to spring at the slightest jar.

Second grade obviously agreed with David. In addition to the care and concern of his morning and afternoon teachers, our son also had the support of the program designed specifically for him thanks to the infinite wisdom and mercy of special education. When the school year began, David received supplemental help in the school's resource room for two half-hour periods a week. But by mid-October, both his classroom teachers noted the difficulties that following directions presented for David every day. If a worksheet had multiple directions, David generally read and followed only the first one. Though he understood the concepts being taught, his inability to follow directions seriously affected his performance.

Disorganization proved to be an equally formidable opponent. David's desk looked like a family of ferrets had taken up residence in it. Whenever the teachers asked the class to take out a workbook or hand in a homework paper, our son could not find what he needed amid the varied assortment of crumpled papers and books. When he had more than one worksheet to do independently in class, David often forgot to do them all. Sometimes he brought the wrong materials home for homework. Other times he forgot his assignments altogether.

Since I made a habit of communicating with David's teachers on a regular basis, I learned about his school difficulties and frustrations very early in the year. Both second-grade teachers and I agreed that the special education program designed for David at the end of first grade needed some adjustments. We spoke with the person assigned to manage David's program. She devised a solution: each morning a teacher's aide came to my son's classroom to help him along with four other children identified with similar difficulties. The teacher went over the directions for the day's work, answered any questions the children had, and made a daily schedule for each child to follow. As the child completed a task, he or she crossed it off the schedule list.

At midday, the aide followed the same routine for the afternoon session. At the end of the day, she returned to the classroom and checked each child's backpack to make sure that all the necessary materials went home. If the children evidenced difficulty in any area of instruction, she also gave them tutorial help during the day. The program worked wonderfully and gave David the necessary support. Because the other children were involved as well, David felt "unspecial," which proved to be quite important for his self-esteem. David wanted very much to fit in with the gang.

In addition to this support, David's resource-room teacher devised some creative interventions geared to help him meet success in the regular classroom environment. For instance, David showed an interest in the computer, so the teacher developed tutorial computer games for his use at home. Not only did she make game disks for each week's spelling words, but the second-grade teachers told her what tests they would administer and she made study-guide games as well.

Both David's second-grade teachers also played an important role in his academic and emotional development. They took a special interest in him and communicated with me on a regular basis. Yet even with such care, occasionally unanticipated glitches arose. The worst one proved to be the creative writing project the afternoon teacher assigned in honor of Thanksgiving. She asked each child to "imagine you are a turkey and you have just found out you are going to be Thanksgiving dinner. How do you feel and what are you going to do about it?"

When David's turkey-shaped booklet came home with the smiley sticker pasted on the bird's plumage, I couldn't wait to read his response. Before I even opened the cover, I assumed he probably created a scenario where the turkey escaped by some ingenious method, so I joyously dove into his "Turkey Talk." David wrote: "I just found out I'm going to be Thanksgiving dinner. I think I know what to do. I will bite the farmer. And I'll stab him in the head and put him in a cage and fry him over a fire. And I'll injure his wife . . ." As I read on, I wondered what drove my little boy to such extreme anger.

As luck would have it, the next day his father and I were scheduled to meet with David's teachers at the annual fall teacher's conference. As soon as we sat down, I said, "That was some story David wrote." The afternoon teacher called it "quite descriptive" and said that, because of the violence, she showed David's story to the guidance counselor.

"What did she think of it?" I said, swallowing rather hard.

In reply, the teacher whispered, "The counselor thought it was, um, a little much, unusually violent, quite intense." Everyone fell silent.

Long pauses have always made me uncomfortable. After fifteen seconds or so, I found the silence so loud, I slipped into my "crack a joke" mode and, in an attempt to lighten the moment, rhetorically asked, "Gee, do you think Edgar Allan Poe started out this way?" Everyone sort of smiled. A moment later, David's morning teacher said she had discussed different Thanksgiving rituals with the class the morning before they wrote their turkey stories. One little girl enthusiastically gave a detailed account of her mother's experience growing up on a farm and told how each Thanksgiving her grandfather slaughtered a turkey for dinner. Much to the great disgust and horror of the other children, this classmate described the bloody scene as a headless turkey ran around after it had been decapitated. The teacher reported that eight-year-old David had been quite upset by this information.

Now the violent nature of David's story did not seem quite as inappropriate. In fact, it made great sense to me. This child cried

for days when a goldfish died. On occasion, he still mourns the loss
of two stuffed animals he left in a taxicab when he was six. He even
said to his brother, who had been asking for a hamster. "Why would
you want a hamster? It will just die and you'll be sad." I could now
understand how my son got caught up in the emotion of the moment
as he sat at his desk writing about how he would avoid the evil
farmer's butcher knife.

The remaining months of second grade proved to be a happier
time for all of us. David's teachers called me every Friday to report
about the events of the week. They informed me about any special
projects that might be scheduled so I could monitor their completion
and thereby avoid the 8:00 bedtime "what do you mean you have a
book report due tomorrow?" crisis.

These second-grade teachers also recognized David's lack of self-
esteem and made efforts to boost his opinion of himself. Since he
loved science, they tried to encourage him in every way. One night
one of his teachers even called our home to tell David to go outside
and look at the sky because Venus would soon pass in front of the
moon. That phone call helped David realize how highly his teacher
regarded him.

Besides the genuine and special interest they showed David, the
teachers also had regard for my input. I called one day because
David walked out the door in the morning knowing all the answers
for his social studies test and came home in the afternoon with a
failing grade. The teacher thought he might have had difficulty with
the process of selecting multiple-choice answers and offered to retest
him. He scored 100. The teachers understood that the mechanics of
writing often interfered with David's ability to get spelling words
down on the paper correctly, so each week after he had taken the
written test, they asked him to spell orally the words he misspelled.
Aloud, he usually spelled all the words correctly. David received an
A for the year. I think these teachers would tell you that the special
efforts they made for David took planning and sensitivity, but they
did not take a great deal of time.

I admired these teachers because they openly evaluated their
methods and found ways to make the school environment successful for my son. They accommodated his special learning characteristics and worked to develop his positive qualities. The teachers
never chastised him for his poor social skills or his demands on the
other kids. Instead, they complimented him when he behaved in a

polite and courteous fashion. They understood his need for structure, so they made his day as predictable as possible. They even gave him special jobs to do. When the final report card came home from school that June of 1988, David received four A's, and two B's, and "Outstanding" for effort. More important, young David came home smiling.

Education Outcomes

Due to the early diagnosis of my son's ADHD, I knew the nature of his disability at the outset of his public school career. I had been alerted to the potential difficulties David might face in school as a result. With this knowledge, steps could be taken to protect my son from succumbing to years of demoralizing academic failure. Many children, however, are not diagnosed before they have established a pattern of poor school performance. Some go undiagnosed well into the later elementary, junior high, or senior high school years. In the meantime, these unfortunates experience failure, low self-esteem, and social problems.

Educational outcomes for children with this disability suggest cause for alarm. Results of long-term follow-up studies provide the following data: 30 percent are retained in a grade at least once, with many retained more than once; 46 percent are suspended; 35 percent never complete high school; only 5 percent complete college.

With no wish to create fear or desperation, I share this staggering picture of serious academic failure to underscore the point that if they are left undiagnosed and without appropriate educational interventions, we cannot expect these children and youth to succeed against the odds. Data show they fail.

Typical Classroom Problems

Perhaps one reason the outcomes turn out so poorly stems from a basic misunderstanding about how ADHD affects education. Children with this disorder often do not do what they are supposed to do when they are supposed to do it. Thus schools often see these students as noncompliant, stubborn, willful, or bored. Where ADHD is concerned, schools do not readily understand that educational performance has less to do with an inability to learn and more to do with traits that interfere with doing what is asked in a timely manner. Of course, over time these students develop achievement problems as tasks become more complex and require the efficient use of the "private actions" described in chapter 1.

When a student has ADHD, count on hearing some if not all of the following phrases to describe typical classroom problems:

- seldom starts the task when asked
- doesn't stick with the task
- needs a lot of teacher supervision to finish a job
- can't find books, papers, pencils
- doesn't follow directions
- misses parts of the assignment
- interrupts a lot
- talks a lot
- either moves or fidgets with something constantly
- frustrates easily and lets everybody know it
- can't seem to wait
- interacts poorly with other students
- poor sense of time

At best, students with these types of problems show poor school performance marked by underachievement. At worst, they experience significant academic failure. Unlike their peers without disabilities, these students have significant obstacles that interfere with their ability to benefit from public school education.

Often they meet with a closed-door policy that says, "Do it our way or you are out of luck!" Unfortunately, "our way" requires strengths in the very areas in which these children are weakest. Successful students pay attention, are well organized, think before acting, sit still, and do their work. Without these skills, even the brightest of children with ADHD will do poorly.

ADHD Type Makes a Difference

The diagnostic criteria for ADHD given in chapter 1 describe three different types. These types make a difference in the kinds of problems seen in school. Children with the predominantly inattentive type usually have difficulty with tasks requiring attention. The hyperactive-impulsive and combined types seem to have more problems from lack of self-control.

The inattentive type appear to have trouble with selective and focused attention. Their academic problems come from not directing their attention to the right thing and from being very disorganized. They may also be somewhat squirmy or restless, but not "motor driven," as Dr. Barkley would say. People have described these children as "absentminded professor" types, like Susie White's son, whom I spoke about in chapter 3.

Dr. Barkley describes the hyperactive-impulsive and combined types as "managed by the moment." They usually have difficulty keeping their attention on a task and can be extremely disorganized. While the inattentive type tend to be somewhat invisible and easily slip through the cracks, these types have behavior so visible it's as if they take jackhammers and turn the cracks into canyons.

Ask them to take out a piece of paper, and you might see them accidentally knock everything else off the desk as they rush to do so. Given them deskwork to do independently, and expect you will have to repeatedly bring them back to what they were supposed to be doing. Teachers and parents get frustrated by their lack of self-control. Understandably, the behavior is often viewed as a choice the child makes to be noncompliant. Actually, these children behave in a way that comes naturally to them. They do not have the option of choice. As Dr. Barkley explains, their difficulty is not in knowing the skill but in having enough inhibition to allow them to use the skill effectively. Add to that the problems with seeing tasks through to completion, and it's easy to understand why report cards often say, "Not working up to potential."

Performance Pitfalls

ADHD is a performance disability that interferes with learning. Let's think about some typical school performance requirements. Students are usually expected to be on task, which means they start, stay with, and finish work in a specified amount of time with a reasonable degree of accuracy. Students are asked to follow directions, to organize multistep tasks, to go from one activity to another in an orderly manner, and to produce work at consistently normal levels. Additionally, they are expected to have socially appropriate interactions with others.

To meet these typical school requirements, students with ADHD need to pay attention, plan, and stay in control of activity and impulse. Understandably, these youngsters will have difficulties performing when requirements demand skill and proficiency in precisely those areas where they are compromised. Though excessive activity creates disruption, difficulties with attention and impulse control seem to have a more profound effect on educational performance.

Inattention

Dr. Ron Reeve, associate professor of education at the University of Virginia, explains that attention is not one skill but a process that consists of a series of subskills. When we "pay attention," we choose what to focus on, concentrate, resist distractions, and shift attention appropriately. In trying to locate the root of a child's academic difficulty, each area of the child's attentional process needs to be evaluated. Otherwise, we may waste time having the child work on a nonproblem. For example, we could spend our efforts trying to help the child sustain attention only to find that the student's difficulty was in selective attention. Generally, having the inattentive subtype results in the child not paying full attention to the important features of a task, whereas hyperactivity and impulsivity often interfere with sustaining and completing tasks.

Dr. Barkley's theory about ADHD and self-control explained in chapter 1 presents inattention as a persistence problem. In short, those with the hyperactive-impulsive and combined types of ADHD do not sustain behavior or resist distractions. The reason these people have difficulty staying on track has to do with what they don't do. Why? "They are not internally guided," Dr. Barkley explains.

To resist distractions and thus stay on task, we have to be able to inhibit our behavior and let it be guided by the four internal states that Barkley theorizes are impaired by disinhibition. That is, we have to use sensory imaging to get a picture of what will happen if we do or don't do something, talk to ourselves as we think and reflect about what's in the mind's eye, internalize our emotions, and finally take the information from the first three and recombine it in various simulations, acting on the one that is in our best interests over the long haul.

Think about it! Be a teenager again. You have the choice between talking on the phone with your friends to find out who's wearing what to the dance tomorrow night or doing math. Obviously the phone wins. So how does the math ever get done? Well, some of us are better at resisting distractions because we can use these four internal components of self-control to guide our behavior to make decisions that are better for us in the long run than in the short term. For instance, if you don't do the math, teachers and parents will get on your case. You won't be prepared and may feel embarrassed. You'll get a zero, and chances are the time will come when you can't go to the dance because of your poor grades. So, you bite the bullet—and do the math.

Impulsivity

Impulsivity can be separated into two types: cognitive and behavioral. Dr. Barkley explains that cognitive impulsivity refers to difficulty stopping, thinking, and reasoning through a situation. Behavioral impulsivity is the inability to wait or to delay making a response. Both cognitive and behavioral impulsivity often result in a similar outcome: poor planning or poor approach to a task. Children with ADHD are behaviorally impulsive. They often know how to make a plan, but they are not programmed to wait. Thus they have difficulty delaying a response. Rarely do they use a plan. Instead, they just act.

"ADHD is not a problem of knowing what to do. *It is a problem of doing what you know!*" observes Dr. Barkley. Being able to inhibit your behavior allows you to think to yourself, talk to yourself about the past, and figure out what will happen "if," especially when you look at what happened before. "You can't do what you know if you do not let your past—your knowledge and learning and wisdom—come forward at the point of performance." Therein lies the heart and soul of ADHD. "At the point of performance," explains Dr. Barkley, "out in the real world, when they have to do something, the knowledge they've acquired doesn't come forward in time to instruct them. These executive functions (which do not function appropriately in people with ADHD) allow you to bring the past forward and think about what the future holds if you do or do not do."

Some people have thought that the way to handle impulsivity is to teach "stop and think" skills with the idea that the brain can be trained to wait. Unfortunately, as Dr. Barkley reports, research has shown that these methods do not work for behavioral impulsivity, the type found in ADHD.

Given that self-control appears to be impaired because of a lack of using internal cues such as visual imaging or self-directed speech, it would seem that the best way to manage ADHD is to take what doesn't go on inside and put it out in the open so the person with ADHD is strongly guided. This approach is sort of like putting a spirited racehorse in a starting gate with blinders on. When the gun goes off, at the point of performance, the horse knows exactly what to do and then is driven to do it by a rider who knows how much that horse can give under the specific track conditions.

Motivation

While I'm not much of an equestrian and have rarely played the ponies, I do know that some horses run better on certain types of tracks and under certain conditions. I think most adults know this, yet we seem to forget that children can be like ponies. If the conditions are not well suited to a particular child's needs, you often get poor performance, and, just as with ponies, behavior can run amuck.

When children "know better," adults tend to blame and punish them for their actions, for not having better self-control. Americans are accustomed to believing that willpower drives our self-control. Three hundred years ago, the idea that motivation and inhibition come from biology might have been heretical enough to get us tried as witches. Today, we more readily understand that how we behave has a lot to do with our neurobiology.

Part of self-control has to do with motivation—the ability to delay gratification and work toward a future goal. Dr. Barkley believes motivation, or the lack of it, affects self-control. Consequently, people with ADHD have difficulty sustaining attention, particularly when doing tasks that are boring, repetitive, and lacking in any immediate reward or pleasure—which is how many students view school. Furthermore, this theory also explains why these children perform better when lots of encouragement and immediate incentive are offered. Though the Puritans might call it bribery, neuropsychologists understand immediate rewards as a way of jump-starting the system.

Dr. Barkley believes his theory of self-control makes clear two treatment approaches for guiding behavior:

1. Use external cues
2. Use external rewards

As Dr. Barkley explains, humans are not unlike other species in their reward-seeking behavior. The search for novelty—for the new, the different, the unique—can be rewarding, and novel situations are often stimulating. Dr. Zydney Zentall, an ADHD researcher and professor of special education at Purdue University, believes that people with ADHD are biased toward putting their attention on finding what is new or interesting (novel) in the environment and in tasks. Unfortunately, the most interesting information is not necessarily the most relevant information, so children with ADHD may miss what is important in a task.

According to Dr. Zentall, most academic problems are produced. They are created by tasks with little novelty—that is, tasks requiring repetition, rehearsal, and practice. These tasks, which are basically detail-oriented, change very little. Thus students who need more of the reward that comes from novelty do not sustain attention to such tasks. In addition, students who have difficulty sustaining attention produce more errors and messier work as the task progresses. They also show increased inappropriate activity over the course of a school day and from the beginning of a task to the end. Misbehavior is actually encouraged by tasks and activities that are repetitious and not stimulating.

Children with the impulsive-hyperactive behavior pattern also have difficulty waiting, which results in additional academic and social problems. In order to organize, follow directions, or plan, you have to wait before responding. These children have a hard time waiting, so they act before they should and thus wind up with poor productivity and accuracy. Similarly, in social situations, they may act too soon, winning few friends and influencing ever fewer people—favorably, at least.

To increase task performance, Dr. Zentall suggests the following:

- add novelty to the end of tasks
- get rid of repetition in tasks
- develop routines for work completion
- give the child something to do that involves muscular movement.

Children with ADHD have been called learn-by-doing, trial-and-error learners. Actually, Dr. Barkley notes, we all engage in trial-and-error learning, but most of us do it in the privacy of our own minds. Dr. Zentall says these children will work to *get* something novel, stimulating, and active. They will work to *get away from* something boring and repetitious. The implications for how to teach these students are clear. They require more enriching activities, more hands-on instruction, clear rules and structure, and lots of external rewards and motivators to encourage their use of plans and on-task performance.

Hyperactivity

Do you recall the parental discipline approach of the mid-twentieth century? A parent about to spank a child would say, "This will hurt me more than it will hurt you." Well, hyperactivity is like spanking. It hurts the others in the environment much more than the "hyperactive" child.

Running around the room, climbing excessively, talking loudly and incessantly, and other off-task behaviors are bothersome to those around a hyperactive child. These behaviors do decrease as hyperactive children mature. Actually, hyperactivity is more of a problem in the preschool and very early elementary years. The explanation of why hyperactivity decreases is that inhibition, the ability to control one's behavior, generally improves with maturation. According to Dr. Barkley however, where ADHD is present the process is delayed. Thus, during the stage when most children are able to inhibit their motor behavior enough to meet the requirements of the classroom, children with ADHD will be behind in their ability to do so. Hyperactivity impairs performance to the extent that the child is off task.

Hyperactive children are often held back in a grade "so they can mature." While they may become less hyper over time, the other difficulties persist. Grade retention is not a way to solve ADHD-related problems.

Inconsistency

How often have you said or heard a teacher say, "Tommy behaved one day last week. He should have been able to do that every day. This proves he's doing it on purpose"? Of all the negative comments that dog people with ADHD, remarks about inconsistent behavior and performance have to head the list. We all have good days and bad days. However, when ADHD is present, the bad days tend to be more obvious, and the good days usually come up to what we normally expect from a child. Thus they don't seem like any big deal. We make a lot of assumptions.

For instance, if Susie can remember to bring her book to class one day, she should be able to remember every day. If Johnny can do well in math and spelling, he should be able to do his social studies homework. If Susie and Johnny did not have a disability, these assumptions might be correct. As Dr. Barkley observes, to be consistent, you have to be able to limit impulses; thus inconsistency may be a by-product of this disorder.

I like the analogy Dr. Margolis draws: "Expecting the child to do a great job all the time because he's done a great job once is like expecting an athlete who's broken the world record to equal or better it anytime he participates in an event from then on. It's not going to happen."

Disorganization

Though not listed as a core problem, disorganization is another by-product of ADHD. Not only do these children forget to bring necessary materials to and from school and class, they also lack a systematic approach to tasks. Dr. Zentall notes that they do not easily establish routines. For instance, they may drop their stuff just anywhere when they come in from school. Similarly, when they leave the next day, they not only can't find what they need, they may not even be aware that they are leaving something important behind until they get to class and the teacher asks for the assignment or the book. Difficulty following sequence in four- or five-step processes may also occur.

Information-Processing Problems

"Children who have difficulty sustaining attention, organizing, and concentrating will not learn reliably and efficiently," explains Dr. Zakreski. Research shows that these students do not acquire learning strategies on their own.

Beyond the primary grades, new tasks build on previous skills and become more complex. Dr. Zakreski observes that children with ADHD have difficulty with more complex behaviors like study skills. He explains that most children acquire study skills either when they are shown techniques by teachers and parents or when they develop techniques on their own.

However, children with ADHD given the same models and patterns as their classmates do not acquire these skills without very deliberate instruction. And since study skills are seldom taught in a concrete way, these students frequently do not pick up on any ways to improve their learning efficiency.

Add to poor study skills the tendency these students have to "scatter-shoot" information, as noted by Dr. Reeve. They seem to have great difficulty using metacognitive strategies—which are the outlines and schemes that organize information into hierarchies, like placing apes, dogs, whales, and people into a category called mammals and knowing the particular characteristics that make a mammal a mammal.

These problems probably exist because of difficulties with nonverbal working memory and internalized speech, which Dr. Barkley talks about as part of his self-control theory.

Output Problems

Dr. Barkley notes that ADHD is an output disorder, not an input disorder. Entire books are written about input and output. The information I am about to provide is a very brief distillation of a very complicated subject.

Students with learning disabilities or the predominantly inattentive form of ADHD seem to have information-input problems. The information coming in may not be processed quickly enough or not filtered correctly. At any rate, somehow the initial ingredients aren't quite correct, leading to error.

Students with the disinhibited, hyperactive-impulsive type of ADHD may also have trouble sustaining attention. Dr. Barkley notes that the problem concerns inhibiting, organizing, and executing behavioral responses to the environment. Because of difficulty with the four executive functions (imaging, internalizing language, altering emotional states, and simulating to form new concepts), the output of information is haphazard.

Dr. Keith Conners says, "We often see a distinction between what the child with ADHD knows and what he or she can produce." How many times do we hear people with ADHD say after failing a test, "But I knew that information." Similarly, children with this disorder have been known to jump out of their seats to answer a question in class or share information. Then, when asked to wait or to first raise a hand, by the time they are called on, they have forgotten what they had to say. This, of course, frustrates them, the teacher, and perhaps other students as well. Sadly, as a result, they feel "stupid."

Disinhibition and problems with executive function may also create difficulty with fine motor skills that can lead to information-output problems. In Dr. Barkley's clinic, adults with ADHD had serious problems with a computer-simulated driving test: their motor control over the steering wheel showed impairment. They also had longer reaction times. As Dr. Barkley explained, "It may be a matter of hundreds of seconds, but when hundreds of seconds count, then it's a problem."

These fine motor problems explain why poor handwriting appears in many cases. Besides leading some teachers to complain that the child doesn't care enough to take the time to do the work neatly, messy handwriting causes academic difficulties. For example, numbers illegibly formed or not arranged carefully will lead to math computation errors. Keyboards and calculators can help.

Still, a word of caution. When we see certain behaviors in children, we can jump to conclusions about the underlying cause. For example, messy handwriting could be caused by ADHD, but as Dr. Levine explains, approximately four different causes can result in handwriting difficulties. First, impulsivity may prevent some children from taking special care. Second, to write well, children need to have coordination between the flow of ideas and motor movements; in some children, the flow of ideas is too rapid for their fingers to keep pace. A third problem is that writing is very much a memory task. The children have to simultaneously remember letter formation, punctuation, grammar, capitalization, vocabulary, directions, and ideas. Finally, some children have fine motor dyspraxia, which results in difficulty knowing which muscles to use and in what order to form letters.

Dr. Levine wisely explains, "It is important to pinpoint which particular pathway of writing difficulty is affecting the child, because it will have bearing on which remediation is used."

Reading Problems

As they advance into the middle and high school years, many students with ADHD do not willingly read; in fact, many of them say that they hate to read. Interestingly, they have reading fundamentals. They know how to decode words, understand vocabulary, and are often quite articulate. When it comes to discourse, however—that is, reading larger volumes of text such as novels or articles—these students frequently get lost somewhere in space between the printed word and their brains. They may have trouble stringing together long sequences of events, keeping plots and characters straight, or ordering material that builds on previous information.

Students with ADHD may also experience problems with social language—which in part is the interpretation of others' feelings through written language. Thus, comprehension suffers and the very process of reading becomes a painstaking effort that gives little return. Herein lies a major problem that interferes with academic success.

"The person with ADHD can read and reread passages and get nothing out of them," Dr. Barkley observes. He believes this difficulty arises from problems with working memory and the way it ties in with semantics (word meanings) and comprehension. "To comprehend, you have to be able to read privately and to hold that language in mind while you link it up with semantics." Words get their meanings, he says, because their meanings are linked up with images, sounds, words, and events from the past. He explains, "If you can't hold the words in mind long enough to link them up with their meaning, which is the nonverbal working memory portion of the self-control theory, then the individual is going to be seriously impaired in reading comprehension."

Consider the reading done in junior and senior high literature classes. The text has plots, subplots, multiple characters, often multiple settings. In addition, there is a hierarchy of information within the material. The reader, says Dr. Barkley, has to hold multiple pieces of information in mind at the same time and nest them into hierarchies in order to get the flow of the story and the meaning. His model predicts trouble as reading tasks become more complicated. So, even if there were no reading problems in earlier years, they can and do develop later on.

Alert: Often students with ADHD will develop a progressive problem in reading comprehension.

Additional Disabilities

As mentioned in chapter 5, ADHD can coexist with other disorders. So, in addition to the educational performance problems created by ADHD, children with this disorder can also have other disabilities that affect their education. Among the more commonly co-occurring disabilities are specific learning disabilities, estimated to affect roughly one-third of all children with ADHD. In the past, so little was known about the ADHD that it was viewed as a subtype of a learning disability. Today, most experts agree that ADHD is a distinct disorder. Thus, when assessing school difficulties, evaluators should determine the presence or absence of both conditions.

Your child's school would be the most likely place to have an evaluation for a learning disability. Because so many children with ADHD also have this problem, you might advise them about how important such an evaluation would prove to be. Not only will it provide information about learning problems, the psychoeducational testing will also help the school know your child's potential and particular areas of learning strength.

Essential for Help

The learning problems I have been discussing in this chapter have been problems that arise primarily from ADHD. Please know that I have not exhausted the problems that can occur. Still, all the difficulties mentioned can fall into two main areas: academic productivity problems and information-processing problems. The latter occur more in older schoolchildren, whose task requirements are more complex. Suggestions for educational interventions are provided in the next chapter. The field has a long way to go in creating optimal educational solutions and adaptations for schoolchildren with ADHD. The following information may help you in your efforts to get the school to assist your child.

Educational Planning

Rare is the student with ADHD who does not need some type of modified educational program. The Professional Group for Attention and Related Disorders (PGARD) estimates that approximately 50 percent of children with the disorder can be educated within the regular education program provided their teachers are trained to recognize and make appropriate modifications for their ADHD related difficulties. Examples include:

- adjusting curricula
- altering classroom organization and management
- using behavior management techniques
- increased parent-teacher communication

However, even with these modifications, the middle and high school years prove especially difficult. As our children progress to the higher grade levels, they face ever greater problems meeting the typical expectations of most schools. The amount of work increases. The types of tasks are less and less likely to be those for which our children are well suited; many classes are taught by lecture. Teachers expect students to work independently, and that, coupled with the ADHD student's desire to do it alone like his or her peers, can result in our children not getting or not responding to the assistance they continue to need. The developmental immaturity that goes along with ADHD persists, so that even as our children get older, they tend to remain "younger" than their classmates. I wish I had an easy answer. Of course, a good working plan is needed. It is just as important that you make sure your child finds some speciality, be it academic or extracurricular, that boosts self-esteem.

Beyond modifications and accommodations to the regular program of instruction, the other 50 percent of children with ADHD will require some form of special education intervention. PGARD estimates that 35 to 40 percent of these children will still spend the majority of their day in regular education settings and will additionally require combined services likely to include support personnel and supplementary or resource-room programs. Finally, the remaining 10 percent will probably require self-contained classrooms because they have a severe degree of the disorder and other disabilities as well.

What the Law Says

Unfortunately, this ideal array of services has generally eluded children with ADHD. In 1989, Dr. Barkley aptly observed, "The majority of children with this disability fall through the cracks in the current educational system." Ten years later, as many of us know all too well, educational research is sparse and has not produced consistent, thorough and efficient strategies for dealing with ADHD-related difficulties. Sadly, these children continue to fall through the cracks.

I have spoken with many parents and teachers who have been unable to get special education for children with ADHD because the schools have told them ADHD is not covered under the law. Nonsense. The Individuals with Disabilities Education Act (IDEA) protects children with special education needs. Basically, when a disability has a significant, negative impact on the student's academic performance, this law requires schools to provide tailor-made educational interventions to meet the student's disability-related educational needs.

As parents you need to be have accurate information. Should school officials tell you that ADHD is not covered, hand them a copy of the Policy Memorandum from the U.S. Department of Education Rules regarding the department's position on the school's responsibility. Also, I have included here (see page 178) a copy of part of the U.S. Department of Education's Proposed Rules and Regulations for the latest amendments to IDEA. Please know that all states must have laws that make the same provisions as the federal law. Local schools must obey the law.

If your child has ADHD and is experiencing significant educational performance difficulties, the school must evaluate him or her under the "child find" regulations of this very same law. The evaluation must determine whether a disability exists and adversely affects educational performance. In fact, Dr. Barkley notes from his experience that in the past "many parents had to shop around for the best school district or the best teacher they could find who was willing to be flexible enough to use some of the interventions which work for these children." However, as the paragraphs above declare, ADHD is covered under IDEA, and school districts must comply with the law. If yours does not, you have the right to take the issue to mediation or to court. Obviously, no one wants to expend this effort and energy unless you have to do so as a last resort. Nonetheless, our children's right to a free and appropriate public education should not be relegated to the luck of the draw.

Parent Advocacy

It's a dirty job, but you have to do it. Studies show that the children who have the best outcomes have active, involved parents. The clarification of the responsibility of schools to address the difficulties of students with ADHD gives you some clout.

Being involved with our child's school program is not easy. Not only does it require time, effort, and energy, but many of us feel intimidated by school personnel. We often think we don't know what we're talking about. Even when we do, we sometimes worry

U.S. Department of Education Regulations Governing Individuals with Disabilities Education Act: 34 CFR 300.7 Child with disability, Note 5:

A child with attention deficit disorder (ADD) or attention deficit hyperactivity disorder (ADHD) may be eligible under Part B of the Act if the child's condition meets one of the disability categories described in 300.7, and because of that disability the child needs special education and related services. Some children with ADD or ADHD who are eligible under Part B of the Act meet the criteria for "other health impairments" (see paragraph (b)(9) of this section). Those children would be classified as eligible for services under the "other health impairments" category if (1) the ADD or ADHD is determined to be a chronic health problem that results in limited alertness, that adversely affects educational performance, and (2) special education and related services are needed because of the ADD or ADHD. The term "limited alertness" includes a child's heightened alertness to environmental stimuli that results in limited alertness with respect to the educational environment.

Other children with ADD or ADHD may be eligible under Part B of the act because they satisfy the criteria applicable to other disability categories in 300.7(b). For example, children with ADD or ADHD would be eligible for services under the "specific learning disabilities category" if they meet criteria in paragraph (b)(10) of this section, or under the "emotional disturbance" category if they meet the criteria in paragraph (b)(4). Even if a child with ADD or ADHD is found to be not eligible for services under Part B of the Act, the requirements of Section 504 of the Rehabilitation Act of 1973 and its implementing regulations at 34 CFR Part 104 may still be applicable.

that if we make requests on behalf of our child, the school personnel will come to view the child as that pain-in-the-neck-kid with the pain-in-the-neck-parent. Some of us fear that our efforts to acquire help will backfire, and instead, our child may be made to suffer because we are "bugging" school personnel. Because we have rights guaranteed under the law, should our worst fears come true, such situations can be dealt with fairly.

When parents and schools disagree, sometimes unreasonable requests and frustration are the source. Be sure you know what you are asking for and why. Also, try to appreciate the unique role of your child's teachers and other school personnel. Until proven otherwise, I think it is safe to assume that everyone has the child's best interests at heart and that any disagreement stems from differing points of view over what those interests are and how best to accommodate them. Do make the requests that will get your child's needs met, but be reasonable about your demands. For instance, I know one parent who felt the school district should provide her child with after-school activities in addition to the program the school had in place during school hours, which did address her son's social difficulties.

Effective parent advocacy involves creating partnerships with the school personnel. Though many parents are intimidated by their child's teachers and administrators, many educators are wary of parents. Diplomacy goes a long way toward avoiding many disputes. When meeting school personnel, a good attitude and a courteous demeanor are really important. We want to be problem-solvers, not problem-makers. We must work to ensure that the child receives needed services; at the same time, we need to be certain that we hold realistic expectations for the child. As our child's advocate, we need to be assertive, to ask questions, and to question answers that do not make sense to us. Being assertive, however, does not mean being aggressive. Threats and name-calling do not help anybody.

Sometimes we parents of children with ADHD are just so tired and frustrated, we have a hard time remaining calm and collected. But we really do serve our child and ourselves most productively when we remain nonconfrontational with the school staff. Though we parents and school personnel may have disagreements with each other, we must always agree that we share a common ground, specifically, the child's well-being.

If you try to work with the school and find that you are not getting anywhere in gaining help for your child, you may need to seek help. Appendix B provides an explanation of the laws, rights, and protec tions you and your child have. For now, I offer the recommendations of Dr. Howard Margolis, a professor of educational and community programs at Queens College of the City University of New York who specializes in resolving disputes between school districts and families. If you and your child are refused services, he advises:

1. Find an expert who understands the law, ADHD, and the way school districts operate.
2. Be sure the expert has good problem-solving and negotiation skills.
3. Have the expert meet with you and school district personnel to reach an agreement—which may take several meetings or, eventually, legal proceedings.
4. Obtain additional expertise to shed light on your child and his or her disorder, if you and your expert/advocate think it necessary.

The expert/advocate need not be an attorney, but a person who is very knowledgeable about the law—and not just special education rules and regulations. Dr. Margolis recommends that this person also be very knowledgeable about case law and the development of IEPs.

Finding a person who can do this job is not easy, and it usually takes money. "You have to do a little detective work," says Dr. Margolis, with a slight laugh. Having been there, I know that sometimes you have to do a lot of searching to find additional help.

To find people who do this type of work, Dr. Margolis suggests speaking to people who are involved in private, not-for-profit organizations that represent people with disabilities, such as the Learning Disabilities Association, the Council for Exceptional Children, and ADHD support groups. Also, each state has one federally funded parent training center to assist parents with advocacy questions. To contact the parent training center in your state, call your state department *office of special education* within the state's department of education. Please note: The quality of service varies greatly from organization to organization.

Another resource is the special education and reading department in local universities. Dr. Margolis advises looking for people who either teach special education law courses or who are experts in your child's area of disability—or, if you're really lucky, cover both areas. Chances are that if you find a person with one set of credentials, he or she will know other experts who can fill in the gaps in other areas.

Let's say you find the expert/advocate, meet with the school, and still are forced to take further action. Then you need to find an attorney. Usually the person you've been working with knows lawyers from prior experience and can make recommendations. Dr. Margolis likens the role of the attorney to that of conductor in an orchestra. In addition to masterminding the strategy, his or her primary job is making sure all the parts of the negotiating team "make one sound."

No matter who you use, Dr. Margolis counsels that everyone on your team be truthful. He also recommends that your team provide "the kind of information that the courts need to make an informed decision." Your experts, he says, also have to be willing to tell you when you are mistaken. Not that they are almighty, but as parents we can be so emotionally involved that we miss key points. We have to be willing to accept what we have to change, should the need arise.

The usual steps in resolving disagreements between parents and school districts are negotiation (with just the school district, parents, and possibly their expert/advocate), mediation (with the help of a trained, impartial, state-appointed mediator) and an impartial due process hearing (with attorneys, hearing officers, or judges). Which parts of the process you use and in what order depends on the individual case. Resolution can come at any point in the process. When involved in a dispute, in addition to the financial cost, be aware of the physical, mental, and emotional wear and tear.

I love the advice Dr. Margolis gives parents: *"Be prepared.* Read, read, and read about the area of disability, including the college textbooks." He also advises taking seminars on problem-solving and negotiation. And—extremely important—"get to know the law. Read it at least once every month. Ask questions of your state department of education."

When advocating for your child, bear in mind: *"Knowledge is power."* The more you know about your rights and your child's rights, the better chance you have to see that your child receives an appropriate educational program designed to meet his or her unique learning needs.

Working With Teachers

Parent advocacy involves other skills and techniques that go beyond special education and the law. Though we often think that the teacher should know how to manage our child in school, we need to remember that few teachers have had any formal training in ADHD, though fortunately that training is now beginning to be provided. Nonetheless, in the present state of affairs, in the absence of a diagnosis teachers are often as frustrated and in the dark as we parents are about why the child behaves so poorly or does not perform in school. Thus teachers may make the same false assumptions that we parents make. These are "he could do it if he tried hard enough" or "she could do it if she wanted to." Even when teachers know the child has the disorder, they too often feel helpless and confused about how to help the child with ADHD.

In-service Training

Teachers usually make great students. Rather than complain or get angry, try to work with teachers to be a problem-solver. Offer them literature to read about ADHD. Give them any helpful suggestions you may have picked up along the way. (Some are included in the next chapter.) Since many children with ADHD are served in the regular classroom, you could even suggest that your district use one of the teacher in-service days to present a program about ADHD to the entire staff, not just the special education staff.

Selecting Your Child's Teacher

Many parents find meeting with school personnel to aid in the process of selecting their child's teachers very productive. Parents of children with ADHD, like Jan Lawes and Barbara Chapman, are often heard to say, "My child had a wonderful teacher who really understood him, and he did great last year. This year the teacher is not so willing to help and he's doing a rotten job."

Rather than wait until the school year begins, handle teacher selection before the end of the previous grade. Children with ADHD need teachers who are structured and organized but not rigid, who are patient and willing to take a little extra time to understand the nature of the child, and who will use a little extra effort to help the child succeed. Teachers of these students also need to use a lot of encouragement and praise, because, as we know, children with this disability perform better when they are reinforced for appropriate behavior.

Say Hello

Making an appointment with the child's teachers at the beginning of the school year is also a wise move. At this meeting, we parents need to discuss the concerns we have for our child, as well as the child's strengths and weaknesses. We want to encourage teamwork and let the teachers know that we will support their efforts at home. Suggest frequent and open communication throughout the year, but not only to keep abreast of how the child is doing or to determine if further interventions are needed: we also want to keep track of any special assignments or projects looming in the future. A parent who approaches a teacher in a nonthreatening way, who shares information, and who tries to be supportive will be appreciated by most teachers. If your child's teacher resents parental involvement, then the child has not been placed appropriately.

Keep Good Records

Finally, parent advocacy also involves keeping thorough records. Many parents maintain a file on their child that contains any communications from the school, copies of communications from you to the school, copies of all reports about your child, copies of all report cards and achievement test scores, and records of any phone calls or meetings including the date, the time, and the names of the person or persons with whom you spoke. I also save all my son's school papers until the end of the school year so I can look them over to identify any problem areas before I attend conferences to plan his program. If you keep good records, should disputes arise, you will have a better chance to protect your rights and your child's rights.

Summary

Effects on Educational Performance

- Educational outcomes present a picture of serious academic underachievement
- Typical problems include:
  - attention is not used appropriately or sustained (depending on ADHD subtype)
  - difficulty starting, staying with, and completing tasks
  - difficulty following rules
  - difficulty working independently
  - disorganization
  - excessive activity and vocalization
  - frequent interrupting
  - difficulty waiting turns or delaying responses

- — low frustration tolerance
- — socialization problems
- — messy handwriting
- Problems evident in tasks that:
  - — lack novelty, for example, detail-oriented, lacking in variety
  - — are too long or too hard
  - — require delay in making responses

Performance Pitfalls

- Sustained attention
- Impulsivity
- Motivation
- Hyperactivity
- Inconsistency
- Information processing
- Output problems
- Reading problems
- Commonly co-occurring conditions

Educational Planning

- Regular education modifications and accommodations:
  - — adjusting curriculum
  - — altering classroom organization and management
  - — incorporating behavior management techniques
  - — increasing parent-teacher communication
- Special education services offering a range of placement options and interventions

Parental Involvement and Advocacy

- Better outcomes result when parents are active and involved
- Use diplomacy and assertiveness but not aggression
- Engage in problem-solving, not problem-making
- Provide informative literature
- Participate in teacher selection
- Meet as often as necessary with teaching staff
- Maintain thorough records
- Use professional help when necessary

CHAPTER NINE

Educational Interventions

David's first eight years of life were not the carefree wonder years we associate with childhood. Instead, David's wonder years were filled with tension, with negativity, with not fitting in. But as he entered his ninth year, it was as though he emerged from a chrysalis at peace with himself. David's affect had changed, and this once unhappy child now smiled most of the time. He acquired an enthusiasm for life and a sense of humor, but most important, he liked himself. This change I attribute to his early diagnosis and treatment and his incredible resiliency. Though the entire family has had to deal with the effects of this disorder, the brunt of the struggle is borne by David. He is on the front lines every day.

In July 1988, I took David to the pediatric neurologist for a follow-up visit. After the doctor examined my son, he sat me down in his office and said, "What a wonderful change. You know, I used to worry about both of you and wonder how you were ever going to make it. David's symptoms were so severe. You should be very pleased."

Well, I was more than pleased. I felt such gratitude and such relief that my little boy's symptoms had stabilized.

But the relief did not come from a sense that David had been cured. By now I had come to understand that this disorder has no cure. The neurologist also told me that day in his office that there would always be new issues to deal with, new problems that would arise. Still, the doctor knew and I now knew our entire family had the tools to handle them. One of the tools proved to be the ADHD parent support group a few of us formed with the aid of Dr. Burke, our child psychologist. Through this group we helped and encouraged each other to learn how a family can live comfortably with this disorder most of the time.

By no stretch of the imagination did our family walk off into the sunset, hand in hand, a perfect fifties sitcom family. New stages of life bring challenges. Good periods continue to come and go, as do the tough times. Coping with ADHD requires a lot of hard work and constant effort. Nor was ADHD our only struggle. Shortly after Jonathan, our younger son, entered first grade, we learned he was dyslexic. As a result of his learning disability, Jon too experienced frustration in school. At times, he acted out behaviorally. Often he said to me, "I'm stupid" or "No one likes me."

Clearly, six-year-old Jonathan needed to have his self-esteem bolstered. His dad and I had to find something for Jonathan to excel in that was totally separate from any activity in which David participated. We enrolled him in tennis lessons. At the first lesson, the instructor said, "Put the racket in your right hand, put your left hand over your right, put your left foot forward, then pivot on your right heel and swing the racket."

By the time Jon finished following these commands, he looked like a contortionist. I did not insist he take another lesson. Instead of tennis, Jon, this dyslexic child who wrote all his letters and words backwards and upside down, decided to write and illustrate stories. By the end of first grade, he had a portfolio. Through the help of special education, he also read on grade level.

In addition to his academic struggles, Jonathan also needed to assert himself in the family. For years he had watched David command center stage. He accepted his supporting role passively, it appeared he adapted quite well. In fact, Jon behaved so responsibly, he often seemed like the older brother rather than the younger sibling. But between first and second grade, Jonathan stopped accepting the role of peacemaker. When David tried to monopolize toys, games, Jon's friends, or family members, Jonathan began to fight back. Because of his survival instincts, he has emerged into his own person.

In September 1988, David entered third grade. I assumed his school experience would be as wonderful as the previous year's, but in our district, third graders move to a different school. The teachers in this new school did not know David. They hadn't watched him struggle and grow during his primary school years, nor did they know his capabilities. They did not know me either. So not only did I have to introduce the teachers to my son, the child with ADHD, I had to introduce them to his mother, the woman who watches her kid like a hawk.

As in previous years, I had to make appointments with his teachers to explain the disabling effects of ADHD on my son's performance and to highlight his strengths as well as his weaknesses. Despite the fact that I hate this task, experience has taught me that good and frequent communication between home and school is a necessity. For the most part, David's teachers have been wonderfully supportive.

This third-grade year, however, such communication proved to be crucial. Children in our district change classes in third grade and are grouped by ability in math and reading. David had four teachers. Despite the fact that his second-grade teachers had great faith in my son's ability, his grouping was determined by the placement tests the third-grade teachers gave in early September. Though David's body was present, his mind had not yet fully reported to school. Thus he did not perform well and was placed in groups below his ability level. David came home from school angry because, as he said, "I did this stuff last year." With David's teacher advocating on his behalf, the school staff willingly rethought the situation, and David was placed in groups more in keeping with his capabilities.

No blame attaches to anyone here. Finding the appropriate placement for David is not an easy task. My son's ability is not just a measure of his scores on intelligence or achievement tests. ADHD is a performance deficit. As a child with ADHD, David juggles many balls. In his school program he must be presented with material commensurate with his ability, but not challenged to the point where he experiences so much frustration he shuts down or feels bad about himself because of his performance. David is a perfectionist who sets very high goals for himself. Innate ability and the ability to perform are often separated by a very fine line.

In this third-grade year, though the major battle had ended, new skirmishes developed. David did not want me to be so involved with his school. He resented the extra set of books I kept at home for the times he forgot his homework materials. He did not want the teachers to make any modifications in his program. He just wanted to be like all the other kids. Yet some of the kids called him "loudmouth," and ultimately David did not always feel that he fit in. His dad and

I made special efforts to help David develop some friendships. By the middle of the school year, we often had a house full of boys.

David's confidence eventually grew to the point that he became less guarded about sharing his feelings with us. He even told his dad and me about goings-on in school. The day he came home and said, "Mom, I did something in art today that no one has done in eleven years," admittedly I became a little queasy. I managed to muster some strength and asked, "What was that, dear?" To my relief he answered, "I drew a triangle in a triangle." It seemed the art teacher had not encountered too many third-grade students who could draw two-dimensional triangles.

In May 1989, when I went to the parent-teacher conference, I felt certain that David was in good hands. His teachers opened the meeting by telling me, "You have some smart kid there. I wouldn't worry about him. He's going to run a corporation someday. He just needs to get through school first."

I always worried that David would fall through the cracks, but this comment reassured me that his teachers had taken the time to get to know my child and to appreciate him.

Thanks to the results of his treatment, David made great strides at home too. The scales have tipped, and the days when David cannot control his behavior are few. Sure, new or unanticipated problems arise. There are times when he does not remember to stop, look, and listen before taking action. For example, we went on vacation to an island where farm animals roam freely. David was swimming when suddenly this huge black beast on the beach caught his eye. He excitedly charged out of the water toward the animal. Fortunately, David made a great racket that caught my attention, because the beast he was about to throw his arms around turned out to be a bull who did not appreciate this enthusiastic attention.

But what do bulls know anyway? Both his dad and I have now come to appreciate David's zest for life, his boundless energy, the enthusiasm he brings to tasks that interest him, and the battle he has fought. Though sometimes our son still spins a little, he stays on course, and so do we.

The year I began to write this book, David announced he wanted to be an astronaut. Though I had hoped he would pick a career closer to home, I now felt certain he was not trying to get as far away from me as possible. I even knew he was not playing on my fear of heights and trying to get me riled and scared. When I asked

David if he minded if I wrote this story, his eyes lit up and he danced around the room, chanting, "Oh wow! I'm going to be famous."

As the manuscript progressed, David stole glances at bits and pieces of the earlier part of the text, which did not impress him. My description of him ran contrary to his emerging sense of self. David had just begun to feel as though he belonged, to believe he was a pretty terrific kid and worthy of fame. To think that Mom might make him infamous was not his idea of great literature.

Often he came to my desk early in the morning, before I was awake, and penciled comments into the manuscript. Two particularly compelling notations were "Stoopid" and "Why are you writing this junk?" I tried to explain, but David did not seem to understand. When I referred to the infant as "a baby monkey on its mother's back," he scribbled, "You're a monkey on your own back." After that, I quietly sat with nine-year-old David and asked him if he would like me to stop writing this book. He quickly and emphatically told me he did want me to write this book and then added, "But if you only put the good parts." After a two-day pause, he added, "And I want to read it before anybody else does, because I might have to edit it."

David is a gutsy kid, and I empathize with his defensive instincts. He has had to fight very hard to protect himself in situations that are not always pleasant. On top of that, I sometimes run too much pass interference. I try to overprotect him, which does not help David to feel effective and competent. When I told him I would rather he not sign up for football because I was afraid he might get hurt, David just sighed and said, "Mom, how do you expect me to make the NFL if I don't practice and play?" Who could argue?

Today, my hope for David and for all children with ADHD is that the time will come when the world will stop trying to control these children and stop expecting them to fit into environments too small to appreciate or accommodate their special needs. For now, I know David will land on his feet.

The Student Experience

Other children with ADHD and their families have not been as fortunate as mine. "I've never felt successful in school," seventeen-year-old Louisa Christianson told me. Louisa's ADHD was not diagnosed until she was sixteen. For most of her academic career, Louisa thought she was dumb. She says she was not motivated by much and hated school "because they don't let you take the classes you're good at." Since Louisa is easily distracted, she cannot take a test if the classroom door is open. She says she even gets distracted by her own thoughts.

Louisa is just one of many children with ADHD whose school experience has been predominately negative. Even children diagnosed at earlier ages often feel like failures because they experience such difficulty in the school environment. Ten-year-old John Golding's classmates call him stupid.One of his teachers told him he was a daydreamer. His art teacher marked him down a grade on a drawing because she felt he did not try hard enough, yet John's classmates all said that his drawing was better than anyone else's picture. John felt he did the best he could. Though that teacher made him angry, John also gets angry with himself because he often knows the correct answers to test questions but usually marks the wrong answer box.

Before Gene Conlin's son was diagnosed, he and his wife were advised by the school to take a parenting course. Gene said, "The teacher was convinced that Frank could produce if I exerted my authority as a father and gave him a kick in the pants." The Conlins did take a course and found it helpful, but not for Frank's school performance. When another teacher complained to Gene that his son did not concentrate, did not pay attention, and never finished his work, Gene recalled teachers making similar comments to his parents. He felt overprotective of his son, explaining, "It was so painful to have people yell at me and discipline me all the time. I thought it was so unnecessary, and I did not want Frank to go through all that unnecessary pain. I did not want my son to repeat my life, because my life was filled with loneliness, self-doubt, negativity, and the feeling that I just did not fit."

Much of Gene Conlin's frustration rose out of an overwhelming sense that, as in his own life, Frank's teachers did not realize Frank wanted to succeed but could not. Gene Conlin is not unusual. Often parents complain that teachers do not seem to understand or acknowledge their child's ADHD problems. But, as Dr. Sam Goldstein notes, "it is awfully hard to fault the teacher because he or she is a product of the system that educated him or her." Dr. Goldstein points out that regular education teachers, and often special education teachers, do not have any background in basic neurological processes and problem areas such as ADHD. And many preservice teacher training programs still do not offer instruction about how students learn, why they learn, or why they do not learn.

The Environmentally Dependent Disability

Schools value students with self-control who perform well. In fact, they expect such behavior. But students with ADHD usually fall short of meeting typical classroom demands because their natures do not easily match up to such prerequisites. When presented with a student who has no visible disability, who has ability, who performs sometimes but not always, and who appears to misbehave, many teachers draw false conclusions. The most common is that the child could do well if he or she wanted to. So many students with ADHD go through school experiencing failure and frustration. Sadly, not enough is known about how to effectively educate children with this disability. Still, we do know enough to make some difference.

Perhaps the first step is to change the way schools see and treat these children. Everyone involved needs to acknowledge and understand that ADHD happens to be an environmentally dependent disability. Though ADHD is always present, "environmentally dependent" means that problems do not typically arise until demands are made upon the child to use certain skills that he or she lacks. Case in point: for a long time, researchers have known that when a bunch of children are on the playground, the researchers can't pick out those with ADHD based on activity level.

Classrooms are another story. Think about the whole process of self-control as explained by Dr. Barkley. The child's biologically based problems with disinhibition interfere with his or her ability to use internal actions to guide and control external behavior. Not only do the children behave poorly and, as compared to others of the same age, immaturely, these problems also interfere with the way they do school tasks. Dr. Barkley's research has shown that people with ADHD do poorly at estimating time, creating adaptations out of concrete images, repeating sequences, and using confrontational language. Interestingly, people with ADHD tend to talk a lot unless they are asked to respond to a specific question. Then, they seem to be less able than others to create a variety of responses.

Perhaps the biggest problem caused by poor self-control is that "the future doesn't stand a chance in managing your behavior if you're constantly doing things at the moment," says Dr. Barkley.

Most academic classrooms tend to be the worst places for our children. We keep trying to change the children to meet the demands and expectations of the setting. Instead, we need to alter environmental conditions to accommodate these students. Generally, these children have less difficulty when we do the following:

- provide structured and predictable settings
- emphasize individualized instruction
- make work periods shorter
- develop a highly motivating, interesting, and interactive curriculum
- use lots of positive reinforcement

ADHD is a disability, and we simply have to make accommodations. These types of modifications can be compared to the ramps provided for those dependent upon wheelchairs. As Dr. Barkley observes, remove the ramp and there is no access.

Caution: Expect behavioral difficulties to increase:

- when tasks are difficult
- when work is required for extended periods of time
- when there is little direct supervision

Though the types of interventions recommended below have been demonstrated to be successful, they must be viewed as guidelines. No two children with ADHD are alike. Similarities exist, but still each child is an individual with strengths and limitations, so what we do to help one child may not be what is indicated for another.

Placement Options

Children with ADHD need a range of placement options and services in school. As mentioned in the previous chapter, some will do reasonably well in the regular education classroom with only minor modifications needed, while others might require more extensive accommodations and interventions, including special education services.

The type of special education placement needed depends on your child's individual needs. Some students require time in the resource room; others might need pull-out programs, meaning they spend a portion or all of their school day in a specialized classroom setting. Still others might need special schooling, commonly referred to as out-district day or residential placement; this occurs rarely and usually in cases of students who have other difficulties along with ADHD.

The Teacher's Role

Regardless of what program is used, ultimately all interventions have the same goal: to build the child's sense of competence and self-esteem. Educators, particularly classroom teachers, play a vital role in the network of caregivers that can enable our children to achieve a positive outcome. Thus they need to be educated about the disorder and its ramifications in the home, school, and social environments. They especially need to know the characteristics of students with ADHD, as well as techniques and strategies for effectively educating them. In the absence of a clinical diagnosis, educators also prove a valuable referral source, so they require instruction in methods of identifying children who display ADHD characteristics. This important training can take place through in-service programs, recertification programs, and college curricula for educators in training.

Teacher Selection

Placing the student with a teacher who can deal with your child's special needs often makes a major difference in how the child feels about him or herself. While self-esteem is not the goal of education, we can hardly overlook its importance in helping a child with a disability to beat the odds. A good teacher for a student with ADHD has at least these four qualities:

- understands the nature of the disorder
- appreciates the child's struggles
- changes conditions to meet individual needs instead of trying to change the child to meet conditions
- welcomes parental involvement

What I call teacher affect can prove equally important. The research literature consistently points to positive reinforcement as the best medicine for these students. Teachers who give the best medicine tend to act with a certain style. In general, children with ADHD do well with teachers who have these characteristics:

- are loving, kind, supportive
- recognize, reward, and encourage positive behavior
- create a safe classroom atmosphere in which all ridicule is absent
- respond calmly to inappropriate behavior
- use positive commands and actions that tell the child what is expected
- act instead of reacting to behavior

Classroom Strategies

Add Structure

Our children need to be told very specifically about what can and cannot happen in situations. To meet expectations, they need a structured and predictable environment. Teachers cannot assume the child knows how to behave. Expectations must be clearly stated by the teacher and understood by the student. Frequent praise and even specific rewards must be given when expectations are met. Taking such steps may seem excessive, especially when the other kids generally behave well on their own. Still, it falls to the classroom teacher to provide the necessary organization that will give children with ADHD every opportunity to succeed. As they have proven time and again in classrooms all over the world, these students do not do well without this helpful guidance.

Specific classroom management techniques provide another form of structure. Some suggestions:

- display classroom rules
- post a schedule and homework assignments in the same place each day
- provide separate and specific places for completed and uncompleted work
- set aside specific work periods for specific tasks
- ease transitions between activities
- seat away from extraneous noise

- seat near teacher
- seat with positive role model or cooperative learning partner

Two of the biggest problems these students experience are desk fatigue and loss of interest. They also tend to be more productive earlier in the day and more accurate at the beginning of an assignment. Knowing this, teachers can structure tasks and lessons to address ADHD-related difficulties.

- schedule academic subjects for morning hours
- give regular and frequent breaks
- minimize the amount of written work
- alternate types of activities
- divide tasks into multiple, easily completed parts

Provide Routines

Whether children or adults, people with ADHD do not easily develop routines. Imagine going through life without a place you "always" put your car keys! How often would you be late? Miss important meetings? Get in trouble? Routines eliminate some of the problems caused by impulsivity and disorganization. Here are some possible school routines:

- guidelines for arranging work on paper
  — placement of headings
  — spacing
- signals
  — to begin work
  — to complete work
  — to put work away
- notebook organization
  — date all papers
  — place in date order
  — put in sections by topic
- locker organization
  — books on top shelf
  — lunch on top of books
  — binders upright on locker bottom
  — extra supplies on locker bottom
  — coat on hook
  — gym bag on hook

As these recommendations indicate, students with ADHD require a considerable amount of teacher involvement—much more than most students.

Remember, the types of interventions described above *do not cure* the disorder. They *manage* ADHD-related difficulties. Consequently, when these types of supports are withdrawn, though your child may have developed some compensating skills, in all likelihood academic and behavioral difficulties will increase and your child may even revert to preintervention levels.

Teachers and parents tend to become frustrated doing all this behavior management stuff—behavior charts, structuring the environment, et cetera. I certainly understand why. So does Dr. Barkley. "They're not getting the yield," he says.

His group at the University of Massachusetts ran an experimental kindergarten program a couple of years ago. For an entire year, staff highly skilled in the use of behavior management techniques used a very intense and systematic behavior approach with the entire class. During the time the program was in operation, the children with ADHD in the control group did great. Then the researchers stopped the program and followed the kids through first grade and into second grade.

The result: "All the gains were lost. Every one of them. There's absolutely no difference between the people who went through our program, and the kids who never did," Dr. Barkley reports.

The moral of this story is that behavior management works when you do it. So do it. But do not blame the child or yourself when you let up and the results go south. Remember, people with ADHD have trouble with their internal guidance mechanism. It's as if they're flying in bad weather without instruments. The clocks, timers, coaches, charts, rule lists, daily reminders, Post-it notes, color coding—these replace their instrument panel. They provide the external guides to behavior.

As one mother reported, under the guidance of a thoughtful teacher who tried different strategies to help her son, Steven, whose favorite book was *Leo the Late Bloomer,* bloomed. He earned straight A's in second grade. In third grade, he floundered. At the midyear conference, the teacher reported to his mother that almost every day, twenty minutes after she had handed out an assignment, Steven's page was blank. Both the teacher and his mother told

Steven that he simply had to do his work. One day after the conference, Steven came home from school teary-eyed and told his
mother, "Mommy, I'm trying. I just don't know what to do." Now in
fourth grade, Steven is receiving the necessary support, and once
again he is achieving.

Next year, what happens to Steven will be anybody's guess.
Hopefully his teacher will be one who understands and knows what
to do with ADHD problems, and hopefully he will be placed in the
best setting. But parents need to understand that teachers cannot
solve ADHD and may, in fact, be held entirely too responsible for
what happens to these students. First of all, the individualized attention required is practically a superhuman feat given the fact that
most regular education teachers have classes with far too many students who all have different needs and varying ability levels.
Second, the challenge faced by most teachers in educating students
with ADHD goes far beyond the environmental manipulations I've
explained. What we teach and how we teach need to be changed.

Modify Curricula

I believe that if educators designed curricula to ADHD specifications, all students would benefit. Too often, accommodating ADHD
means reducing the amount of work and lowering performance
expectations. This "remedy" reminds me of the old saying, "Give
me a fish and I eat for a day. Teach me to fish and I eat for a lifetime." I'm not suggesting that reduction in work isn't appropriate.
For example, if a child can demonstrate command of a concept after
doing ten math problems, making him do fifty seems ridiculous. But
to modify curricula also means to change the types of tasks, the
approach to tasks, and the methods used.

Overall, the fact that children with ADHD lack internal guidance
systems suggests that a direct instructional approach is best for
them. With this method, tasks are broken down into a series of
simple parts. The student masters one part, gets feedback about what
he or she has done, and then goes on to the next part. Dr. Barkley
recognizes that "this approach has been criticized for being mecha-
nistic," but people with ADHD need that kind of structure. He notes
that part of this method's success is due to the great amount of feedback the student gets as he or she proceeds through the curriculum.

An adaptation of direct instruction is mastery learning. In this approach, not only are tasks broken down into their parts, but the student proceeds to the next level at his or her own pace after achieving a minimum of 80 percent mastery.

The worst instructional approaches for these children are ones that use a lot of talking. Children with ADHD tend to be interactive learners. They require a lot of hands-on activities and novelty in tasks. Yet teachers do not have to be stand-up performers. Tasks can be made interesting by using color to emphasize key elements and phrases. Lectures can be brief and followed with learn-by-doing activities. The computer as an instructional tool has great potential. Clearly, curricula can be modified and made more interesting in a myriad of ways. The point here is that children with ADHD require schools that will work outside the status quo.

Even with a good modified curriculum, some children with this disability have significant impairments that require intensive levels of help. Regardless of placement, such students may require highly individualized direct instruction, or an aide working as an assistant to the regular classroom teacher. In still other cases a trained behavioral specialist using a chart system within a regular or special education classroom might be needed. What the child needs and how to get those needs met requires an individualized assessment and plan. There are no standard, one-size-fits-all answers for any type of disability.

Use Behavior Charts

Many teachers are familiar with the use of behavior charts. Like many parents, they also find them intrusive. Still, as demonstrated in the University of Massachusetts kindergarten program, when used properly and while in use, they get results.

There are many different styles of school charts. In general, Dr. Richard Zakreski describes a well-designed school charting system as having the following components: The child should know ahead of time what behavior is expected. He or she has the choice to decide to meet or not meet the expectations. Feedback is then provided about how well he or she met expectations. Finally, the child receives consequences, either positive or negative. Usually the consequences are meted out by the parents, but school-based responses can also be used.

Sample school charts are included in appendix C. The charts not only provide the child with feedback about his or her school performance, they are also an effective way for parents and teachers to work as a team and to communicate frequently.

Besides the valuable feedback charts offer, Dr. Zakreski explains, school charts serve other useful functions. First, they help the child overcome problems with sustaining attention by providing motivation to stay on task and finish. When a child completes work, he or she gets a reward. For instance, a primary-grade child who finishes all his or her seatwork on a given day might earn a trip to the park. An elementary-age boy might opt for a pack of baseball cards.

Second, the school chart helps organize the child. Most of these charts include a space for the child, or teacher if need be, to record homework assignments. The child, with or without teacher direction, can then use the chart as a guide to gather the necessary homework materials before leaving school at the end of the day. At home, the parents review the chart to check the daily progress and that evening's assignments. Since forgetting to bring completed homework back to school happens quite frequently, the child, with the help of the parent if need be, can use the chart to reorganize his or her backpack so the completed work gets back to school.

Medication and Education

As explained in chapter 6, medication often proves to be a valuable intervention for children with ADHD. In fact, according to Dr. Zakreski, the use of medication has been associated with improved academic performance. This is not to say that all children with ADHD should be given medication. As explained earlier, this decision must be made by a competent physician in each individual case. However, through altering the child's abnormal biology, medication often lessens the ADHD symptoms that interfere with the child's ability to learn.

Professionals suggest a behavior chart be used for a few weeks before a child with ADHD takes medication. The chart will provide a baseline that indicates what the child is able to do when a formal systematic approach is employed. It also serves as a guide about whether to use medication. Should medication be indicated, Dr. Zakreski says, "some type of rating scale should be used to document the effects of medication and the dosages which prove to be most effective for a given child."

Though medication can be of enormous benefit to many children with ADHD, caution is advised. We do not want to provide medication without careful consideration, nor do we want to give the child the wrong message about the medication. First, we do not want the child to think that medicine alone makes him or her function appropriately. These children need to know that medication is only a support and that they have control over their behavior. Second, when a child is having a bad day, the teacher should not publicly ask whether the student took the pill that day. Not only does such an insensitive question single out the child and humiliate him or her; it also verifies to that youngster that he or she is different from peers and incompetent. Finally, medication should never be the sole course of intervention.

The Homework Blues

One of the nicest aspects of summer vacation for many parents of children with ADHD is that they don't have to think about homework. Without question, this task has driven many parents and the children themselves to utter desperation. Homework requires a considerable degree of self-direction and motivation. It also requires the child to perform after an entire day of trying to energize him or herself to regulate behavior so as to follow rules, concentrate, and inhibit impulse. It creates tension and frustration. Gene Conlin, a father I interviewed, called it "a confrontation." Gene explained, "Every night I used to spend three or four hours yelling at my son until I was red in the face because it took him that long to complete a fifteen-minute homework assignment."

This experience is not unique to the Conlin family. Donna Rothman told me that night after night her son Peter sat in the kitchen chair spinning around while she tried to help him get his work done. She would say, "Peter, pick up your pencil." But Peter would just spin some more. Then she would plead, "Peter, please pick up your pencil and just write the answer down. You just told me the answer. Now write it down." When the interchange reached the yelling point, sometimes Peter would scream back; other times, he would be passively defiant. Donna would start to shake, then give up and tell Peter to pack up his books. Many days Peter went to school without his work completed.

Teachers and parents need to ask if homework is work or torture. As Dr. Margolis points out, if someone by definition has trouble concentrating, organizing, and resisting distractions, homework can be counterproductive. In fact, he says that very little research strongly supports homework for elementary students, especially those with learning problems. Poorly designed or overwhelming amounts of homework create conflict within families and between parents and schools. Another unintended consequence of inadequately personalized homework assignments is that the student learns the wrong things. This "wrong" learning requires unlearning and reteaching.

Fortunately, there are ways to tone down these nightly horror shows. Dr. Barkley recommends these general guidelines for managing the homework hassle, with consideration given to your child's age and attention span. Of course, you will want to meet with your child's teacher and come to an agreement.

1. *Amount:* Make homework appropriate to the child's age and ability to stay on task.
2. *Legitimacy:* Do not assign uncompleted classwork as homework. Dr. Barkley points out the unfairness of expecting a child to complete in a few hours at home all the work he or she was unable to do during the entire school day. In fact, he emphatically states: "Unfinished classwork is the teacher's jurisdiction. It is corrected by changing its management at school and not by dumping it into the home."
3. *Size:* Microsize assignments. Break work into smaller units. Have your child work for a preset time period, take a break, then come back to finish. A timer helps the child know the amount of time he or she has to complete the task.
4. *Consequences:* If your child completes work on time, you can give tokens such as points or stars, to be used for a reward like pizza or extended television time later on. Not finishing on time would result in a loss of tokens.

In addition, some children receive a checklist to keep alongside their homework. This checklist offers a step-by-step procedure for the child to recheck his homework. For instance, the child would be directed to look over the instructions for an assignment, reread the action words, and then check to see that the directions were followed correctly.

In keeping with the positive response children with ADHD have to have structure and routine, a specific place and time should be established for the homework task.

Dr. Barkley notes that adolescents have longer attention spans than younger children and therefore can do more homework. Still, the homework needs to be legitimate homework and not unfinished classwork. Timers are also used, set for six periods so the youth can move around between assignments and not get frustrated or bored. A checklist, individualized for each student, directs him or her to double-check the work and make sure the directions were correctly followed.

Dr. Barkley acknowledges that most teenagers are not thrilled with these interventions, but as he says, "our goal is not so much happiness as success." With both younger and older children, parents are asked to check the completed assignments against the assignment sheet to make certain the child has accomplished the assigned tasks.

The goal of the homework program is to increase productivity, says Dr. Barkley. Once your child has gotten better at getting work done on time, then accuracy becomes the goal. At first, reward the child when 70 percent of the homework is done correctly. After that, the standard should be gradually increased until the child achieves 85 percent accuracy.

Students with ADHD are usually quite disorganized. Lockers have been the undoing of many middle and senior high schoolers with a disability. In addition to being unprepared for class, materials needed to complete homework often stay behind. A very successful and simple remedy is to keep a second set of books at home; request these from the school.

When parents have to be so involved with their child's homework, hassles happen. Whenever possible, use a tutor. It can get you out of the middle and also lessen the emotional element for your child. Some schools also offer after-school homework programs. Maybe you can interest your district in starting one, if it isn't already available.

Should your child have a teacher who refuses to modify the homework program, you need to get help. Please understand: I don't want to encourage unnecessary parent-teacher conflict, but when the difficulties threaten to ruin home life, something must be done. Dr. Barkley does the following, and any specialist working with your child can do the same.

First, he informs the teacher about the amount of homework the child is likely to be able to do given his or her difficulties. He then instructs the parents to write the teacher a note when, in their judgment, the amount of work on a particular day is too great. If the teacher—for whatever reason—does not believe the homework should be modified, you may have to call the teacher's supervisor. On occasion, the child needs to be placed in a different classroom. "Sometimes," says Dr. Barkley, "the parents have to move to a better school district." Of course, special education law provides rights and protections for children and their parents. However, some districts are so incompetent, and so unwilling to do what they should, that a parent must decide between rights and sanity. It's like planting a garden. If the conditions are bad—poor soil, no water, no sun—it doesn't matter how good the seed is. The plant will not grow. No matter how hard you try, sometimes you cannot improve conditions—even with the law on your side.

The idea that a family might need to move to obtain an appropriate education for their child raises *justified anger*. But it also makes me think about one aspect of intervention that is frequently overlooked. Children with ADHD often feel that they do not fit in, and many of the things we do to intervene inadvertently—and unfortunately—reinforce that belief. Some children and youth come to resist efforts to intercede because they view them "as just another way for me to be labeled as a bad kid." Interventions designed to change children to "fit in" tend to create that impression.

We need to understand that the child's behavior is but one part of the equation. Antecedents and consequences are the other parts. Antecedents set the stage for behaviors to occur. Consequences provide either the reward or the punishment.

Too often, children and youth with this disability are held accountable for not fitting in, when in actuality we adults in their lives perpetuate their behavioral difficulties by not changing our behavior, meaning we rely on the same antecedents and consequences we would for children without the disability. This phenomenon reminds me of a popular quip: "What's the definition of insanity? Doing the same thing over and over and expecting a different result!"

Summary

Providing Environmental Access

- Structured, predictable settings
- More individualized instruction

- Shorter work periods
- Highly motivating, interesting, and interactive curriculum
- Lots of positive reinforcement

Improving Performance

- Requires educator training, including knowledge of:
  — ADHD and its manifestations in educational environment
  — methods of identifying children with the disorder
  — characteristics of these students
  — techniques and strategies for dealing with ADHD in the school setting
- Requires careful teacher selection
  — willing to change conditions to meet child's needs
  — uses a lot of positive reinforcement
  — encourages parental involvement
  — actively involved with students during work periods
  — has patience, humor, and a positive attitude
- Structured learning environment and tasks: specific schedules, routines, tasks that include novelty, hands-on activities, programmed learning materials, et cetera.
- Use of behavior management techniques
  — provides positive feedback
  — implements preset rules and consequences
  — behavior charts that list expected behaviors, provide feedback about student's choices, provide consequences, help organize the student
- Do not rely on medication as only intervention

Handling Homework Hassles

- Make sure homework is legitimate and not uncompleted classwork
- Reduce amount to reasonable expectations
- Provide frequently scheduled breaks
- Provide rewards for completion
- Focus first on productivity, then on accuracy
- Provide a checklist for following directions
- Establish a specific place and time to work
- Keep an extra set of books at home
- Use a tutor when necessary

CHAPTER TEN

Adolescence and Adulthood

As of this edition, we are about to close the chapter on David's teenage years. I have not written in depth about these past ten years; so much has happened that they are another book. Yet people who have read this book often ask me how he is doing, so without going into great detail, I give this update. I continue to believe, as I did through the first and second editions, that knowing about ADHD, parenting with information, being my child's advocate, and helping him to become his own advocate have made a difference. All in all, the early diagnosis and management have helped him negotiate what has to be one of the most difficult developmental stages—adolescence! Aside from the usual wear and tear of added responsibility and independence, of greater consequences for deeds done and not done, our family added divorce and the death of loved ones to the mix. Through it all, though David had times when he rocked and reeled, he never sank.

Admittedly I might be prejudiced, but many people tell me what a remarkable young man my son is. David did not change the scholastic achievement record books. He did, however, find his passion in running. He built on that avocation, gained success in school, received the Reach for the Stars athletic scholarship, and was given an athletic award for leadership, cooperation, and spirit. He has held an after-school job for three years. He goes to work when expected and has a good rapport with his customers and employers. I can depend on my son—maybe not to clean his room regularly or get his homework done on time, but for the big things in life, I can count on him. More important, *he* knows he can count on himself.

Many children with this disability will not be as fortunate. They will go undiagnosed and untreated, and so they will go through life barraged by negative and demoralizing feedback because their behavior, though the outward manifestation of a disability, is seen as a deliberate choice to be difficult, a way to get attention, or whatever. Their lives will be painful and, in too many cases, tragic as well.

Anecdotal reports of people with ADHD diagnosed as adults bear witness to this outcome. Unlike the children, who lack the insight or verbal ability to tell the world what growing up with this disorder is really like, thanks to public awareness, adults with ADHD are finally realizing the root of their troubles. They are coming forth in record numbers to tell us what happened to them, how they have suffered, and that they continue to be challenged by this disability.

Many of these adults learned about their ADHD after having a child diagnosed. This was the case for David's dad, who did not view young David's behavior as out of the ordinary. To the contrary, David Sr. often commented that our son behaved much better than he had as a child. For many years, David Sr. thought of himself at worst as a "bad seed" and at best as "just not good enough." But never until the diagnosis of our son did Dad realize that he too had been at the mercy of the symptoms of ADHD.

By the age of ten, David Sr.'s life was darkened by a steady stream of frustration and failure. In elementary school, he could not concentrate, had difficulty following instructions, persisted in doing the first thing that came to his mind, and could seldom sit still. Yet at times he would "ace" a test, which led everyone to believe that he just did not apply himself. Though most adults viewed him as polite, well-mannered, and articulate, problems with peers proved to be a constant source of disappointment.

Academic and social problems stayed with him through adolescence. He continued to show poor judgment and never really thought about the consequences of his actions until he landed in the thick of trouble. Sometimes his impulsive actions were dismissed under the guise of the exuberance of youth, yet most times he felt remorse and bewilderment about what might have possessed him to behave so poorly. Nonetheless, his difficulties led to harsh consequences. By his teenage years, David Sr.'s sense of self had hit an all-time low, and he always felt depressed.

In early adulthood David Sr. was still immature. He wanted immediate gratification and often felt bored with life in general. He changed jobs and relationships frequently. Many times his significant others questioned why this nice, capable guy did not live up to his potential. Here is his account of life with ADHD as he told it to me.

Elementary school is a blur, but I do remember that my parents moved a lot, and I never attended the same school for any substantial period of time. I can remember not grasping what was going on in class. As early as kindergarten, I got into trouble for doing things like walking on tables, wandering off during recess, and having problems with the other kids. I remember being unhappy when I had to go to school, and I used to stall by not eating my breakfast. School was a fearful place for me. I felt scared by the size of the place and the authoritative teachers who disciplined me because they had to, I guess. I knew I didn't do well and did not like feeling that humiliation. I got left back in kindergarten.

Life at home was not much better. Even as a real young kid I got into a lot of trouble. I actually remember playing with matches and accidentally setting some curtains on fire in my mother's room when I was five. In that same house I also pushed my older sister through a glass door, which cut her wrists and scarred her. I never meant to do any harm. For some reason, I either did not or was not able to operate within the rules. I felt very lonely and very much like an outsider, even in my own family.

My two sisters were successful students and people. I was the boy with a lot of promise who was going to be a late bloomer. In fourth or fifth grade my parents sent me to some special classes after school for reading and writing. I had to spend hours writing on a blackboard to try and improve my penmanship.

In junior high school, my good experiences were few and far between. How afraid I was of the teacher determined whether I pretended to pay attention. With a teacher who cut any slack, I behaved like a real wise guy, a troublemaker. Some teachers hated my guts because as soon as they turned their backs I threw something. I usually behaved that way with the teachers who gave me no encouragement.

But I did do well with some teachers. They understood me as being a sharp kid and allowed me to express the things I knew. And I knew a lot. My seventh-grade geography teacher was a jazz buff who always hummed jazz in class. One day he said, "Does anyone know what song that was?" Of the entire class, I was the only kid who knew it. I not only knew that song, I knew as much about jazz as the teacher. From that day on, he and I talked jazz. We developed a rapport, and I did pretty well for a couple of marking periods, but I could not sustain the effort.

During the time I did perform well in his class, that teacher realized I had a lot going for me. So I had a good experience with him and with a few other teachers as I went along. But for the most part, I met with alienation, with comments like: "Why aren't you more like your sisters?" "Why don't you try harder?" "You're bright, but you're just lazy."

I have a short attention span. In those days, unless something really interested me, my attention span was horribly short. I knew the batting averages of every baseball player, and every singer and song on the charts. I did not necessarily have an interest in the things other people liked, but still I could sit and study those things that interested me for a long time and understand them. To this day, if anything I don't have a terrific interest in goes on longer than a short period of time, I'm lost. That holds true from cocktail party conversations to lectures. I can tune in with the best of them for the short haul, but I cannot stay with it.

During junior high school, my group of friends and I began to get into trouble. This group I hung around with didn't have any wimps. It didn't have any Rhodes scholar types either. We used to let the air out of tires and rip antennas off cars. We even went as far as to break into the houses of people we knew. We'd find a window or door that could be opened and raid the refrigerator. We never took more than a can of whipped cream. I never thought about the consequences. It just seemed like fun.

Eventually the police caught up with us. No charges were pressed. But the embarrassment deterred me from ever doing those things again. We lived in a small neighborhood, so everyone knew what I had done. My parents moved to another community shortly after that.

In this new school, my problems with studies persisted. Though I was basically a terrible student and a disciple problem, I did develop some friends who were good students and athletes. I wanted to be an athlete too, but I was afraid I would fail and afraid I would succeed. I had no idea what to do with success. I lived a kind of double life that eighth-grade year. In school I hung around with the president of the student council and dressed well. My after-school friends barely made the fringe of acceptability.

During eighth grade, I spent many long periods sitting in classrooms without the vaguest idea of what was going on. Most times, this confusion concerned me. I remember being fearful because I was failing, but I didn't know what I could do about it. I didn't think I was dumb, but I began to believe that I just did not want to succeed. I spent so much time worrying about why I didn't want to succeed that I became a nervous wreck and very depressed. One marking period my sister forced me to work, and I wound up getting very good grades. Of course, this said to all the teachers and my parents, "You can do it if you want to." But without my sister's help, I slipped back into my old ways, and left to my own devices, I just did not get the work done. I had to go to summer school that year.

Around this time, I began lying to my parents a lot. I think in the beginning I lied because it seemed easy to do and my parents never challenged me much. My lies were really exaggerations of how I did in school. As I got older my exaggerations became more elaborate. For example, whenever we moved, I told the new kids what life was like in the previous city. I would tell them I had been a star athlete or that I got into a fight with another kid and inflicted serious damage. That kept the new kids at a distance. And I wanted things that way because I knew that I had lied about how successful I was and I knew damn well that if you hung around me long enough you would find out that my story was not true.

While my classmates didn't like me much, adults and older kids did. I think maybe they saw me as bright and appealing, which are things kids don't necessarily see. When I was fourteen years old I had a job as a batboy for a minor-league baseball club in the town where we lived. The players let me tag along when they went out socially. I loved that. Being a batboy was ironic because I got cut from Little League my first time out.

When I entered ninth grade, even though I had done so poorly in school, people still thought I was college material. In those days, you were either in college prep or dummy classes. So at that point I had mainly college prep courses, but I also had a few dummy courses because I couldn't pass subjects like basic algebra. I hated Monday mornings. They meant school. I only got by in ninth grade because of some benevolent teachers.

After ninth grade, my parents decided to put me in private school. As a requirement for acceptance, I had to start again as a freshman. I bombed out of that second-rate prep school, and then I went back

to public high school. That public school had a lot of tough characters, and I had my usual problems, but I was happier in that school
than I had ever been anywhere else. I made some friends. My football playing improved to the point that I showed real promise. The
teachers did not ask much from me—or from any of the students,
for that matter. Though I didn't do much academically, they passed
me. I actually got a few C's and a B or two.

While at this school, I did not set the world on fire, but I was
acceptable. Once again, I had a dual life going. My girlfriend went
to a prestigious private school, so when she was home, I turned my
belt from the side to the front, buttoned my shirt, and went to see
her. With my friends I dressed punk. With my coach I was a different way. I just was not the same with anybody.

Meanwhile my father was worried about how I would ever get
into college. Somebody suggested to him that I needed to go to this
school where they used a lot of discipline, straightened out kids with
problems, and got them into college. So I changed schools for the
millionth time and went to this place that was just short of being a
military school. I had a terrible year there and did not go back.

From there, I went to another second-rate prep school. That environment was not too demanding. I played football and actually made
all-state that year. I didn't do any studying, but two months shy of
turning twenty, I graduated from this place. Still, I had a lot of sleep-
less nights because I certainly shouldn't have passed. I even went
into a couple of final exams and didn't bother to look at the questions. But they passed me, probably because I had been accepted to
a college for my football ability. Not too many kids from that school
got accepted to college. Needless to say, I was not at all prepared for
college and had serious academic problems. I left as soon as football
season ended.

I felt very depressed, empty, and afraid, like the jig was up. I had
no idea what would happen to me or where I would end up in life.
I tried some different things, and nothing panned out. I felt more
and more frustrated. I considered enlisting in the service, but I knew
I didn't really want to do that, so I joined the reserves. For active
duty, I played football. I didn't have to go to boot camp, so I just
slept, ran, and chipped a little paint for the rest of my time. Back
then, I thought I had pulled a great coup, but now I wish I had gone
through the regular program, because I didn't learn anything that
the other guys did.

After active duty, I got a job selling advertising. My boss thought I seemed like a nice, bright guy but unsure of myself and always uptight. Still, he liked my work and advanced me. My father, however, got a lot of good feedback, and I got panicky. I felt so afraid that somebody would ask me to do something I couldn't and that I would fall flat on my face. This fear was terrible. Even though I had a job and a car, I had no confidence and didn't feel good about myself. So I decided to quit and move to the West Coast.

I had a similar experience there. My life was a farce. When I decided to move back east and leave my new job, my boss told me the same thing I'd heard before: "It's too bad you're leaving, because it seems like you're at the point where you understand what we want and you're doing a good job." But I never felt a sense of permanence. Instead, I always felt like "This good stuff is gonna pass, and then what?" I always worried about tomorrow.

Then I reached a point where I tired of dodging bullets. All the time I felt my life had no purpose, that it would always be painful, and that I would never be able to keep fooling everybody. I was at the point of totally bagging it when somehow, around the age of thirty, I got into counseling. Some of that helped, though I never felt like I really had a good sense of why I was such a mess.

But I did start to realize that I was succeeding somewhat in life. I think slowing down and maturing helped me to see that I had actually been doing better than I thought. I built on that realization a bit. I have always had a competitive nature and a high energy level. Where at times those traits had been destructive, they turned into positive factors. I had some more success, and like anything else, success leads to more success. Even before I had a real sense of myself and knew that I had problems not of my own making that caused many things to be difficult for me, I started to get better.

Between the ages of thirty and forty, I made real strides in life. Though I changed jobs a lot, each move meant more responsibility and improved salary. The year I turned thirty-three, I got married, and in addition to my son from my first marriage, I had two more boys. Finally, I felt part of a family.

When my son David started to have his difficulties, I had a hard time believing he had a problem. Maybe one of the manifestations of this condition is not believing it exists or denying it. For as long as I could remember, there was always a lot of noise in my head. But I thought this was normal. I always thought of ten things at a time instead of one and could never focus. But I didn't know that made me different from anyone else. Whenever I got something right, it was always a great relief. You know, "Boy, I got through that," or "I hope I don't have to do that again."

I knew that my son and I had a bond of similarity and that many of the problems he had were like the ones I'd had. But when I had to learn about ADHD and go to professionals with David, I began to realize that maybe this life of fear and inability to get with the program and do what everybody else was doing might have been caused by something other than the fact that I'm a no-good person.

Beyond Childhood

Whenever I told people that my son had attention deficit hyperactivity disorder, invariably they asked, "Is this ADHD something new?" As David's dad's story demonstrates, generations of children with ADHD have passed through the stages of life never quite knowing why they had so much trouble or why they underachieved. Thanks to more public awareness and more recognition by the medical and mental health communities, children with ADHD are being diagnosed and offered treatment.

As a result, their parents with ADHD are also learning for the first time that they were not problem children but rather children with a problem. In fact, Kevin Murphy, chief of the Adult ADHD Clinic at the University of Massachusetts Medical Center, reports that the majority of his patients are referred to the clinic after they have brought their children in for evaluation, subsequently learned about ADHD, and then associated it with difficulties in their own lives.

Sometimes the similarity in presentation of ADHD difficulties between parent and child is uncanny. Joe Curran, a father I spoke with, has never been diagnosed with ADHD, but he told me, "When I read the neurologist's and psychologist's reports about my son, all I had to do was change the name of the patient, and they described me as a kid exactly. Then when a note on a report card came home from my son's teacher that matched word-for-word one of my report cards at the same age and the same grade level, I knew my school problems had been related to ADHD."

At one time ADHD was considered to be a self-limited disorder, which meant that like an ill wind, it would blow away with puberty.

Recent years have brought an explosion of interest in the diagnosis and management of ADHD in an adult population estimated at between five and eight million people. Today, researchers know that approximately one-half to two-thirds of children with this disorder carry ADHD symptoms into adolescence and adulthood. Each of these life phases raises its own unique set of challenges, complicated by ADHD.

Adolescence: Expectations and Risks

Adolescence as a developmental stage poses worrisome aspects to parents regardless of whether their son or daughter has ADHD. The adolescent quest for independence and freedom often results in experiments, choices, and judgments that can lead to potentially damaging outcomes. Add to that the impulsivity and poor self-control characteristic of the disorder, and the combination can be devastating.

Consider the risks associated with the disorder during this developmental stage. According to Dr. Russell Barkley, the incidence of car accidents is three to four times higher for teenagers with ADHD, so parents might want to postpone the child's acquisition of a driver's license or supervise the use of the car much more than they would do otherwise. Children with ADHD are likely to begin smoking and using alcohol earlier than their peers. The risk of suicide, though very low among teenagers with ADHD, is nonetheless higher than that of their peers.

Jean Bramble, a former caseworker at Primary Children's Medical Center in Salt Lake City, is also concerned that "raging adolescent hormones combined with the drives to be social and accepted by peers, the use of alcohol, and the characteristic impulsivity are a setup for unplanned pregnancy." Recently completed studies at the University of Massachusetts seem to validate her concern. Dr. Barkley reports that these adolescents are at a higher risk than the normal population for sexually transmitted diseases. His study did not find teens with ADHD to have intercourse any more than the normal control group. However, "they were having more partners, staying in relationships for shorter periods of time, and having more unprotected sexual activity," he reported.

Furthermore, though people without ADHD tend to wait until their late twenties to have children, Dr. Barkley's group found that many teens with ADHD were having children. Also, 54 percent of the teens who became parents did not have custody of their children. Ms. Bramble believes parents of children with ADHD vigilantly need to provide sex education.

These cautions are not meant to cause alarm but rather to encourage parents to be "overly involved" with their adolescent's comings and goings. Even teens diagnosed and treated during childhood may experience extraordinary adolescent adjustment problems. As explained by Dr. C. Keith Conners: "Kids go through phases of this disorder in which the intensity of it may be more apparent. For example, they often have a terrible time in the early years when they first go to school. They might settle down a little, but then suddenly as they go to junior high school, the rules of the game change and they become disoriented again."

Furthermore, Dr. Conners notes that as physiologic developmental changes occur, where before these children had little sense of self, they now begin to experience internal states. Dr. Conners says, "The adolescents with ADHD I talk to are full of fear and anxiety, which I believe have been accumulated over time. They find they're in a heck of a mess because in school they have not been able to learn." Academic achievement often worsens.

Adolescents with ADHD have good reason to feel so anxious. According to Dr. Sam Goldstein, "The American education system is designed with the best interests of the adolescent with ADHD at the bottom of the line." He cited typical performance expectations of junior and senior high schools that require adolescents to have more internal responsibility, which is lacking in students with ADHD.

These students experience even more trouble operating within the system because now they have a different teacher for each subject and must get from class to class with the appropriate materials. Because they are in a larger system where their teachers may be responsible for a hundred or more children in the course of a day, the undiagnosed adolescent has to be "a real screwup" in order to be identified. By the high school years, Dr. Goldstein reports, 80 percent of kids with histories of ADHD are behind at least one year in one basic academic subject. Follow-up studies indicate an estimated 10 percent drop out of school. Only a small percentage complete college.

As a result of her difficulties negotiating within the junior high school setting, as an eighth-grader Christine McLean did get diagnosed as having ADHD. Chris is adopted. Her mother, Sally, explained to me that she and her husband did not have any information about their daughter's biological background. Chris's biological mother had also been adopted. When their daughter was younger, the McLeans had no idea why Chris was such an emotional and impulsive little girl. However, Sally McLean reported that Chris's serious school problems did not begin until she got into junior high school. When Chris was faced with the task of getting from class to class and keeping track of her belongings, she fell apart. She also started to "pick the wrong kind of friends," her mother told me.

Cumulative Effects

By junior or senior high school, the cumulative effects of undiagnosed or untreated ADHD can reach critical mass. Adolescents often suffer from depression, anger, and very low self-esteem. Signs of conduct disorder may also arise. When making a diagnosis, Dr. Conners finds these secondary problems hard to separate from the primary ADHD problem. "If you take the history carefully," he remarks, "you'll see the antecedents to the behavior patterns are the impulsive, restless, inattentive, poor learning style culminating in rebellion and rejection of the things around them."

Dr. Conners believes teenagers with ADHD are often aggressive because they have developed a lot of anger over their failure to adapt to the home, school, and social environments. Consequently, the adolescents he observes are often "angry, defeated, and demoralized to the point where they openly rebel or get in trouble."

Some adolescents with ADHD develop a pattern of lying and stealing. Dr. Conners explained that all kids lie occasionally. However, he observes that some kids with ADHD appear to keep lying continually because they always get themselves into situations where they feel the need to cover up for something they did without thinking. Sometimes, Dr. Conners says, adolescents with ADHD will steal something because they are immediately attracted to it, but afterward they realize they were wrong.

Dr. Conners strongly believes that these behaviors in adolescents with ADHD are very different from an antisocial behavior disorder pattern in which deeds are more calculated and premeditated. He says, "Kids with ADHD are not sociopaths. They make a lot more mistakes and get into a lot more trouble, but this behavior comes more from an inability to restrain themselves than out of calculated wantonness. Parents need to understand that the kid with ADHD is not a bad kid."

Small wonder that adolescents with ADHD are at risk for more serious problems. By the teenage years, as Dr. Goldstein so sympathetically describes, "if you have ADHD, you are at greater risk because you've gotten a lot more quit it, stop it, cut it out, don't do it, just a lot more negative reinforcement than everybody else."

Teen Management

According to Dr. Paul Wender, "Nobody knows for sure whether early treatment prevents subsequent psychopathology." He believes, however, that parents and practitioners alike have to operate on the assumption that early treatment will prevent future behavior problems and psychological scarring. He says it seems logical that if a child gets treatment, he or she performs better in school and gets along with parents, siblings, and peers. Thus, Dr. Wender said, "you would expect a good psychological experience, rather than the bad one the child is likely to have without treatment."

The treatment for adolescents with ADHD is much the same as it is for children. They require a modified school program, behavior management, psychotherapy, and sometimes medication. Given the adolescent need for autonomy, a wise practice is to involve them actively in the decision-making process regarding the management of their ADHD-related difficulties.

A common misconception about stimulant medications is that they are ineffective for adolescents. Dr. Wender reports that stimulant medication is effective for the treatment of ADHD in adolescents, and in adults for that matter. As is the case for children with ADHD, the use of stimulant medication with adolescents needs to be carefully monitored.

Dr. Bennett Shaywitz notes that monitoring the clinical effects of medication with college students poses problems. He explains that given the college student's erratic schedule, it is hard to pinpoint the student's target symptoms and when the student should take medication. Furthermore, in the absence of a teacher or parent to report about the medication's effects, the clinical response proves hard to measure. For one patient, Dr. Shaywitz tailor-made a rating scale for which he and his patient selected six areas requiring intervention. The scale rated the effectiveness of medical management in those areas.

Medication, the potential for abuse, and other related issues have been discussed in depth in chapter 6. For now, the primary problem for adolescents using stimulants seems to be complying with the recommendation to take the medication.

Adult Identification

By the time many people with ADHD reach adulthood, their overall functioning shows significant impairment. Dr. Edward Hallowell cites the following as typical among the population of adults with ADHD: a sense of underachievement, even in high achievers; disorganization; impulsivity either verbally or in action, evidenced by such things as career changes, geographical moves, and spending money excessively or pathological gambling; a tendency to be drawn toward highly stimulating activities, whether dangerous pastimes or high-pressure jobs; a propensity to get involved in many projects simultaneously, often without completion of any; chronic ruminative worrying over nothing in particular; difficulty maintaining relationships; poor self-esteem and feelings of incompetency; problems with accurate self-observation; and a tendency to self-medicate, which leads to substance abuse or dependency.

According to Dr. Hallowell, frequently women with ADHD often have different difficulties than men with the disorder do. Often they seek treatment for depression, but upon inquiry, they report disorganization, not being able to complete tasks, and feeling like a "space shot."

Judy Woodruff learned she had ADHD after her daughter had been diagnosed. With the information came relief. She explains, "From the time I was very young I knew I had something wrong with me, but I always blamed all my problems on my home life. When I saw the same symptoms in my daughter, I realized I was not neurotic and that something else caused my problems. When I learned about ADHD and that it was a genetic disorder, I felt so relieved to have a label and to know that this problem can be surmounted."

Adult Diagnosis

Diagnosis of ADHD in adults can be complicated. As Dr. Hallowell points out, "So much ADD among adults is out there masquerading as something else." Adults can present symptoms suggestive of other disorders such as depression, dysthymia (a milder form of depression characterized by an overall sense of malaise), anxiety, substance abuse, eating disorder, bipolar or manic depression, and obsessive-compulsive disorder. As with childhood assessment, clinicians must make a differential diagnosis, through which they attempt to determine the presence or absence of other disorders.

Dr. Wender, who pioneered much of the research in adult ADHD, maintains that identifying the ADHD disorder in adults is fairly easy provided the practitioner knows that the disorder can exist in adults and that an adult can have more than one disorder. "We certainly see people with combined major biological depression and ADHD," he explained.

Dr. Murphy as well notes that patients in his clinic rarely have just ADHD, so an issue in diagnosis is determining whether ADHD is a problem, and if so, whether it is the primary problem. The most commonly co-occurring conditions he finds are anxiety, depression, and substance abuse. Approximately 60 percent of his adult patients with ADHD have at some time in their life had either a major depressive episode or dysthymia.

"That these adults feel depressed makes sense," says Dr. Murphy. "Often they've grown up with a history of failures and frustrations in school, work, and social arenas. They have internalized all kinds of negative messages about themselves and their abilities." These adults quite often suffer from generalized anxiety about meeting performance expectations. Substance abuse problems, which commonly co-occur, are thought to arise from the tendency to self-medicate.

An In-depth Evaluation

Dr. Murphy's Adult ADHD Clinic at the University of Massachusetts Medical Center follows a very thorough evaluation process, which incorporates many of the same tools used in childhood diagnosis.

Some of this information is used for research purposes. Your private practitioner may not gather so much data, but this discussion can serve as a guide to inform you about the types of assessment tools your evaluator may use. Dr. Murphy's evaluation includes the following:

- assessment of prior school functioning through questionnaires and rating scales
- reports from others such as spouses and parents
- work and social history
- a careful medical history
- in-depth, structured interview focusing on various life areas including the core ADHD symptoms
- a structured diagnostic interview that screens for other possible psychiatric difficulties
- intelligence testing

Forms to be filled out by the patient, his or her parents if possible, and the spouse are sent ahead of time. These include behavior rating scales to determine the presence of the core symptoms in the present and in the past. ADHD does not have an adult onset, which means that the diagnosis cannot be given to an adult unless a childhood history of the disorder can be documented. Patients are encouraged to provide any available objective data such as school records, which often reveal a history of ADHD-type problems.

Often the information given by the patient will differ from that given by family members and significant others filling out the forms, especially when rating childhood symptoms. Dr. Murphy has found that the parents of the adult being assessed who are asked about the existence of the core symptoms in childhood do not rate their adult son or daughter as severely as the patient does in a self-report. Interestingly, Dr. Murphy points out, just the opposite occurs in child clinics, where "parents primarily complain that the child is a behavior problem in school and a discipline problem at home."

We can only guess why adult patients and their parents see things so differently. Nevertheless, examiners should be aware that differences may exist. Dr. Murphy generally finds more consistency between reports by patients and their spouses.

Among the forms and questionnaires the patient fills out are an employment history and a social history. These provide information about adaptive functioning and problems potentially related to

ADHD such as frequent job changes, problems at work, difficulties with relationships, temper problems, incidence of speeding tickets and car accidents, and the number of residence changes made since high school. Clients are also given the Michigan Alcohol Screening Test, which assesses for alcohol abuse.

A careful history both of the patient and his or her extended family is taken. The history delves into prior evaluations and diagnoses, psychiatric problems, learning problems, drug or alcohol abuse, and the presence of ADHD in the patient's immediate and extended family.

Of course, the patient interview proves to be a critical element of the assessment. The interview has two parts. First, the assessor asks a variety of questions to document the presence of ADHD symptoms. Dr. Murphy finds that when given an open-ended question about why the patient thinks he or she may have the disorder, those who turn out to have it usually provide "a richness of response," graphically describing ADHD difficulties and the sense of chronic frustration they have experienced in their lives. Moreover, the language these patients use when answering assessment questions is often quite similar. In contrast, he notes that patients with psychiatric difficulties and not ADHD tend to respond less readily and much less specifically.

For the second part of the interview the assessor uses the Structured Clinical Interview. This is a standardized and structured interview that helps to determine the presence of other psychiatric disorders.

Dr. Murphy also does a brief assessment of intellectual functioning. Achievement tests are given when learning problems are suspected. The clinic does not focus on this type of testing because, as Dr. Murphy explains, "the diagnosis is not made on the basis of test results." As with the diagnosis of children, to date, no specific test or test battery has been shown to determine who has ADHD and who does not. Testing can add some useful information, but by itself, it is not a valid way to diagnose.

Management

Once the diagnosis of ADHD is made, the adult's treatment begins, as it does for children, with education about the disorder.

Medication

Many patients are also given medication, which of course is never recommended as a sole course of treatment. Generally, the guiding principles for children, described in chapter 6, apply to adults. However, adults may have unique circumstances, such as a history of substance or alcohol abuse, which warrant additional guidelines for the safe and effective medical management of ADHD.

To date, no clear-cut consensus exists among practitioners regarding whether or not patients with a history of substance abuse or dependency problems should be given medication. Some physicians will prescribe, others will not. At the University of Massachusetts Adult ADHD Clinic, Dr. Murphy reports, some patients with episodic substance abuse problems have shown improvement both in their ADHD symptoms and in their substance abuse problems when given medication. However, if a patient is determined to have a primary substance abuse or substance dependence disorder, then he or she is referred to an appropriate treatment facility to deal with this problem first. In contrast, for those who are episodically abusing or self-medicating and do not have a primary substance abuse problem, medication may be quite helpful. These patients need to be monitored very closely. Dr. Murphy emphatically advises, "If somebody is not prepared to follow up closely when prescribing medication to a substance abuser, then they should not do it."

Awareness

For adults who have suffered their entire lives from ADHD-related difficulties, the diagnosis can bring a great deal of relief. "I can't tell you how many successful adults come to my office and just break into tears when they realize they've had ADHD all their lives," says Dr. Hallowell. "They talk about their struggle of always knowing something was wrong with them and the secret life they've lived trying to cover up," he adds.

Dr. Hallowell, who also has ADHD, strongly believes that initially the focus of treatment has to be on helping the adults get past their negative feelings and poor self-esteem. "The treatment process," he maintains, "is not just taking medication. It's an education process that creates a reunderstanding of oneself and a restructuring of one's life."

Dr. Hallowell views diagnosis and patient education aimed at changing the patient's belief system as the first two treatment steps. He finds many patients frustrated by their inconsistent performance, a phenomenon dating back to childhood. Because of impulsivity, distractibility, and the inability to focus and finish, Dr. Hallowell says, "they've never been able to harness the engine they've got, so even though they may have achieved a lot, there's always a sense that they could do better."

Generally, these adults seek high-intensity situations as a way of focusing themselves, Dr. Hallowell has observed. He describes one patient who did vertical skiing, which entails being deposited on top of a mountain by a helicopter, pointing the skis downhill, and then basically gliding on sheer ice at speeds upward of 100 mph. The patient told him, "The only time I feel truly focused and relaxed is when I'm vertical skiing." Dr. Hallowell does recommend an aerobic exercise activity at least four times a week or other heart-rate-raising pursuits.

Coaching

This technique is used to aid in redefining one's self and in restructuring one's life. Just as implied by the term, coaching involves having someone provide direction, encouragement, and reminders to the adult with ADHD. Dr. Hallowell finds group therapy with these adults to be a tremendously effective coaching tool. Group members validate and encourage each other, as well as provide help in defining goals and working toward them.

Many an adult with ADHD has sunk in the quicksand of details that come from having too many projects started at one time. In such cases, coaching can be extremely useful for redirecting focus. Dr. Hallowell finds that large organizing principles provide immense structure. "These adults," he explains, "need what Alfred North Whitehead called 'an habitual vision of greatness,' a banner posted in the front of their minds showing what they are working toward." There are coaching organizations nationwide (see appendix A).

Adults with ADHD can benefit from developing an arsenal of organizational tools. These include learning to prioritize, setting deadlines, breaking down large tasks, and using pocket reminders, calendars, notepads, color-coding, rituals, reminders, et cetera. These organizational techniques can help considerably with improving job-related performance.

Regarding employment, the adult with ADHD might need other

accommodations as well. In the lead article of the January 1993 issue of *CHADDERbox,* published and available through CH.A.D.D. (see appendix A), Edward Hallowell and John Ratey provide fifty tips for management of ADHD in adults. Some of these tips relate to life in general; others relate specifically to performance management.

Americans With Disabilities Act

As Dr. Murphy notes, many adults are reluctant to seek accommodations from employers because doing so can work against them. The passage of the Americans With Disabilities Act (ADA) in 1990 prohibits discrimination against persons with disabilities regarding employment and accommodations. Thus this law provides rights and protections to people with disabilities. The act defines a person with a disability as one who has a physical or mental impairment that substantially limits one or more of the major life activities, who has a record of such impairment, or who is regarded as having such impairment. For such individuals, employers must provide reasonable accommodations. (See appendix A for agencies and free publications that can answer questions you might have about the ADA.)

Undoubtedly, ADHD has great potential to create misery in an individual's life. The disorder poses a lifelong challenge. Yet Dr. Hallowell emphasizes that ADHD has a positive side, which he feels does not receive the attention it deserves. He cites as examples creativity, energy, intuitiveness, and openness with people. These qualities, when combined with life-management strategies, can be the driving force to success. There's the hope. As Dr. Hallowell said to me, "I'm at the point where I would rather have ADHD than not have it, because I think the assets outweigh the liabilities."

Summary

Difficulties in Adolescence

- Increased desire for independence combined with impulsivity, poor planning, and attentional problems leads to poor choices and judgments
- Associated risks include:
  - higher incidence of auto accidents
  - propensity to earlier alcohol and substance use/abuse
  - though very minimal incidence, higher suicide rate

— unplanned pregnancy
— secondary problems such as conduct disorder
- Careful parental supervision required
- Continuation of educational performance problems resulting from
    — increased expectations for self-control and responsibility
    — larger system, more classes, multiple teachers, less task supervision
- Higher incidence of grade retention, dropping out, suspension, and expulsion
- Less completion of college
- Managed as in childhood (see chapter 6)

Problems in Adulthood
- Overall functioning can be significantly impaired
    — underachievement in employment
    — more career changes and geographical moves
    — disorganization
    — engagement in high-stimulus activity often involving risk
    — involvement in too many activities at once, often without completion of any
    — chronic worrying
    — difficulty in interpersonal relationships
    — tendency to self-medicate; may lead to episodic substance abuse
    — higher incidence of substance/alcohol abuse or dependence

Issue and Methods of Diagnosis
- Must have childhood history of the disorder (can be documented retrospectively)
- Commonly co-occurring with symptoms of anxiety, depression, substance abuse, or dysthymia
- Symptom presentation must be differentiated from other psychiatric disorders
- Assessment includes
    — careful history
    — in-depth, structured clinical interview
    — questionnaires and rating scales
    — reports from others, including parents and spouses
    — objective data, including school records and prior psychiatric evaluations

Treatment Approaches

- Education about disorder to change self-concept
- Restructuring methods of operation and situations
- Medication
- Coaching to provide direction, encouragement, and helpful reminders; done through group therapy or individual counseling
- Developing organizational tools
- Employee assistance
- Accentuating the positive

CHAPTER ELEVEN

In Appreciation of Individuals With ADHD

Over the last two decades, research has generated a great deal of knowledge to add to the understanding of attention deficit hyperactivity disorder. Yet at this point in time, though much is known about the way the disorder manifests itself and about its probable basis, any explanation about its actual neurological pathology remains theoretical. Over the course of writing this book, I learned that ADHD is as multifaceted as a prism. Though general patterns exist, each child is imprinted with environmental circumstances and varying degrees and symptoms of the disorder so that no two children with ADHD are exactly alike. Still, in speaking with the authorities on the subject, I found some of the analogies they made to describe the "generic" child with ADHD helpful in conceptualizing the struggle these children, as well as adolescents and adults, face daily.

Dr. Melvin Levine explains the child's deficits in terms of an unskilled pilot who must manage the multitude of controls in an airplane's cockpit with such precision that the plane flies effectively and evenly. He developed a chart called the Concentration Cockpit, which has a series of meters and dials depicting the various thought processes and/or behaviors the child with ADHD must regulate in order to fly straight. Among them are the selective focus control, the consistency control, the tempo control, the motivational input control, the arousal control, the mood control, the memory control, the social control, and the motor/verbal control. Understandably, a child innately deficient in the skills needed to operate these controls will experience difficulty adapting to the myriad demands placed upon him or her by the environment.

Dr. Russell Barkley views the disorder as an inability to motivate and regulate behavior. He describes the child with ADHD as a company highly motivated to maximize profits for immediate gain and not so motivated to plan for future development. According to Dr. Barkley, our society has a hard time accepting the notion that an individual's biology rather than one's willpower is in control of one's motivation. Perhaps that is why children with ADHD are often blamed for their characteristic inability to "get with the program."

Dr. C. Keith Conners says the child with ADHD is like a company with too many workers managed by an ineffective boss. Because the child with ADHD suffers from a lack of appropriate energizing ability, he or she cannot arouse him or herself to the level necessary to effectively order the mind's workers, who need a lot of executive input.

Though each of these analogies is different, a common thread runs through them. Children with ADHD are not the children who won't. It may be that we do not need to know any more about ADHD than that. Instead, maybe we need to know how to adjust our attitudes about the disorder. Like everyone else, individuals with ADHD thrive on love and acceptance given freely, unconditionally, and with no demands attached. Unfortunately, for children, adolescents, and adults with ADHD, approval, acceptance, and love often come with a price tag.

Psychologist Sam Goldstein believes, "As a society we need to recognize that the demands of the culture actually play favorites with our kid's lives." He points out that one hundred years ago, these children who could not sit still and listen to the teacher, who did not fit into the school system, were probably sent out to work the land or roam the frontier. While this alternative may not have been the best, at least a place existed where people with ADHD could tap their potential.

"But, unlike a hundred years ago," says Dr. Goldstein, "we have no place to send these people. Today, we have no wilderness where they can go and be fur trappers, no farms they can work. We are between frontiers. Yet the demands of the culture are such that these people have a real hard time fitting in. When we do finally open up space, the last frontier, maybe we'll send these people out to be explorers, trappers, and miners on the moon. And some of them will probably want to go. But why? Maybe the kid who wants to be an astronaut is saying, 'Gee, get me the hell out of here. I need a new frontier. I want to go someplace where I won't bump into somebody all the time.' "

I think we need to ask ourselves if we view the children who do not "fit the mold," the children who cannot "get with the program," as square pegs. Rather than search for their intrinsic value, do we try to force these people into round holes? Maybe ADHD is not necessarily something gone amuck that needs to be fixed. Many of the traits associated with this condition can be either assets or liabilities.

Consider perseveration. Dr. Goldstein says, "Being perseverative when you're a kid means you're a pain in the neck. Mom tells the child that she will take him or her to the park in half an hour, and the child asks every thirty seconds if it is time to go. But being perseverative, which is rooted in the word 'persevere,' is a valuable trait when you find something that interests you and you are willing to stick with it. Maybe a child with ADHD might someday find a cure for cancer because he or she has extraordinary energy and curiosity and is willing to stay up all night and test a million different hypotheses until the cure is found."

Admittedly, when my child was first diagnosed, I had no concept that this disorder might have a plus side. Then a parent sent me an article from *Pediatric Clinics of North America* (February 1982) titled "The Unhappy Wanderers: Children with Attention Deficits" by Melvin Levine and Raun Melmed. The authors discussed the potential dividends of ADHD. They suggested that the highly distractible child with the wandering mind might see things others lacking this trait might never perceive. The wandering mind may represent creativity. The child who is insatiable may become the adult with ambition. The trait of egocentricity may form the foundation of leadership. They also cautioned, "Environmental circumstances, patterns of nurturance, critical life events, and educational experiences can minimize or aggravate the effects of attention deficits. It is likely that the responses of adults have a significant impact on prognosis."

When I interviewed Dr. Levine for this book, he expressed his dissatisfaction with the ADHD label given these children. He explained why. "One of the remarkable things about kids with attention deficits is that they have extraordinary strengths and affinities. For that reason, I do not like to take a fully pathological view of them. We need to at least consider the possibility that the word 'deficit' is wrong. Maybe ADHD is just an alternative way to be wired. I am worried that with the current label of the disorder we may be creating a self-fulfilling prophecy in which these kids feel they have brain damage, which is sort of implicit in the name."

Dr. Levine acknowledges that applying some type of label to describe these children and adults leads to recognition and help. But he observes, "So many kids we see with attentional problems are highly entrepreneurial and creative people who have certain foci of interest that are very sophisticated and exciting. Perhaps we need to direct our energies to help the child recognize the existence of these traits. It would be so much better for them to think they just see the world differently from a lot of other people and there are good advantages to that and there are problems created by it. The child needs to see his or her potential value." And so does the adult.

Dr. Levine's point of view raises an important consideration. We know that ADHD presents a unique set of challenges both to the individuals who struggle with its manifestations and to those who care for them. But when does a challenge become a disability? Certainly many people with disabilities lead happy, well-adjusted lives despite, or perhaps because of, their struggles. My hope for my child and those individuals with ADHD I have come to know is that as a society, we come to understand our role in cultivating a playing field where the challenges of ADHD do not become insurmountable obstacles that break the spirit. In nature there is no right or wrong. There are only consequences. Maybe the label for these individuals should be HANDLE WITH CARE.

National Organizations for Information, Support, and Advocacy

CH.A.D.D. (CHILDREN AND ADULTS WITH ATTENTION DEFICIT DISORDERS)
National Headquarters
8181 Professional Drive
Landover, Maryland
(301) 306-7070
www.chadd.org

ADDA (NATIONAL ATTENTION DEFICIT DISORDER ASSOCIATION)
9930 Johnnycake Ridge Rd.–3E
Mentor, Ohio 44060
(440) 350-9595
www.add.org

AMERICAN COACHING ASSOCIATION
P.O. Box 353
Lafayette Hill, Pennsylvania 19444
(610) 825-8572
www.Americoach.com

CEC (COUNCIL FOR EXCEPTIONAL CHILDREN)
1920 Association Drive
Reston, Virginia 22091
(703) 620-3660

LDA (Learning Disabilities Association)
4156 Library Road
Pittsburgh, Pennsylvania 15234
(412) 341-1515

(NCLD) NATIONAL CENTER FOR LEARNING DISABILITIES
381 Park Avenue South
Suite 1401
New York, New York
(212) 545-7510
1-888-575-7373
www.ncld.org

NICHCY (NATIONAL INFORMATION CENTER FOR CHILDREN
AND YOUTH WITH DISABILITIES)
P.O. Box 1492
Washington, D.C. 20013-1492
1-800-695-0285 (voice and TT)
www.nichcy.org
(Information specialists on hand to provide assistance, send free and low-
cost publications, and make referrals to organizations nationwide for specific types of needs.)

NPND (NATIONAL PARENT NETWORK ON DISABILITY)
1600 Prince Street
Alexandria, Virginia 22314
(703) 684-6763
(Every state has a federally funded parent training and information center
that helps with advocacy issues. Call NPND to access the name and
number of your state's parent training center.)

United States Government

For questions about IDEA and special education:

U.S. Department of Education
Office of Special Education Programs
400 Maryland Avenue S.W.
Washington, D.C. 20202
(202) 205-5507
www.ed.gov/offices/OSERS/OSEP/index.html

For questions about Section 504:

U.S. Department of Education
Office of Civil Rights
400 Maryland Avenue S.W.
Washington, D.C. 20202
1 (800) 425-3481
http://www.ed.gov/offices/ocr

For questions about Americans with Disabilites Act (ADA):

EEOC (Equal Employment Opportunity Commission)
1801 L Street N.W.
Washington, D.C. 20507
1 (800) ADA-EEOC (232-3362)

Web Sites of Interest

www.wrightslaw.com
www.cec.sped.org/ericcc.htm
www.ldonline.org
ods.org/about_dy.stm#what_is_
(part of the Orton Society site)
members.aol/lepmom/index.html
(Raising Special Needs Kids)
www.bridgetounderstanding.com

Publications

The *ADHD Report,* ed. Russell Barkley
Guilford Publications
72 Spring Street
New York, New York 10012
(800) 365-7006
(bimonthly updates on ADHD issues and latest research findings)

Education Rights and Protections Under Federal Law

Local school districts have a legal responsibility to provide a free, appropriate public education to students with disabilities. When a student has a disability and that disability adversely affects the student's educational performance, then schools must follow two laws to meet the educational needs of the child. Those laws are the Individuals with Disabilities Education Act, Amendments of 1997 (IDEA), and Section 504 of the Rehabilitation Act of 1973 (In some instances this may also have to comply with the Americans With Disabilities Act.)

Many parents have had great difficulty with their local school districts because the districts have not been clear about their responsibility to meet the educational needs of students with ADHD. Consequently, in 1991, the U.S. Department of Education (USDOE) issued a policy memorandum notifying all state departments of education that, under IDEA and Section 504, they and the local districts must provide special education and related aids and services to children with ADHD who were in need of these services.

IDEA

The primary law that mandates what schools must do to serve the needs of students with disabilities who are eligible is IDEA. Education advocate Fran Rice explains that "special education and related aids and services" was intended to mean very specialized instruction to meet the disability-related needs of the child. Furthermore, "special education must be sufficiently personalized," says Dr. Howard Margolis, coordinator of reading for the Educational and Community Programs department at Queens College.

To understand special education, it is important to know about the intent of Congress in creating IDEA. Prior to this law's passage, no uniform standard existed in this country to meet the educational needs of children who had disabilites. Congress wanted to assist these children to become as independent as possible, Dr. Margolis notes. Thus, he adds, Congress intended them to make "real, substantial, meaningful progress." To do so, through the creation of IDEA and its subsequent amendments, Congress established six principles that are the superstructure of this law.

The most recent amendments are those of 1997. Congress has always taken the position that children with disabiites are entitled to a free, appropriate public education. As noted by Robert Silverstein, director of the Center for Study and Advancement of Disability Policy at George Washington University and the former staff director and chief counsel for the U.S. Senate Subcommittee on Disability, the 1997 amendments underscore the point that appropriate education means genuine, effective, and meaningful.

Every five years amendments are made to the IDEA to keep up with changes in special education practice. "The law was strengthened in terms of parent participation and the individual education plan. Kids with disabilites will now have a better chance of partipating in the regular curriculum," Silverstein explains. Furthermore, he adds that "a notion of high expectations" now exists. In fact, students with disabilities whose scores on national assessments were usually not counted or included in reports will now figure into the assessment picture. Additionally, families will now receive regular progress reports.

Silverstein explains, "This reauthorization moves the country to the next level in ensuring equal education for the children with disabilities." First, in addition to providing access, it tries to ensure quality outcomes. Second, it increases the likelihood that, to the extent appropriate given the unique needs of the individual child, children with disabilities will participate in the general curriculum that applies to children without disabilities. Third, it calls for increased parent participation in critical decisions including placement and the individual education plan.

The basic entitlements of the law remain unchanged. These are:

1. free, appropriate public education
2. appropriate evaluation
3. individual education plan
4. education in the least restrictive environment
5. parent participation in decision-making
6. procedural due process

Following is an explanation of each of these six principles with some commentary based on my interview with Dr. Margolis and on my prior knowledge. Your state has and, upon request, will give you a copy of its rules and regulations regarding special education. These are written in legalese, but you should read them regardless. The states also have booklets specifically written for parents which explain your rights and the special education procedures that pertain to you and your child.

1. Free, appropriate public education

This provision is the heart of the law. Basically it means that the education provided to a student with a disabilty must be meaningful and of no cost to the parents. Our country provides free public education to all students. Prior to this law, many students with disabilites were unable to take advantage of that free public education because of the nature and severity of their disabilites.

2. Appropriate evaluation

When a child is known or suspected to have a disability, schools must evaluate the student to determine the need for special education and related aids and services. Prior to evaluation, schools must provide the parents with written notice and get the parents' fully informed consent to do the evaluation. "Fully informed" means that the parents understand the implications and agree to the action. Further, the evaluation must be done in *all* areas of suspected disability. As you know, many children have more than one disabling condition.

When the disability in question is ADHD or a learning disability, schools may not move quickly to evaluate or provide services. This has led some advocates to dub this law the "fail first" law because schools often do not act until there is a major gap between the child's ability and performance. When this happens, Dr. Margolis reports, "there are major, negative emotional and social consequences, which make remediation far more difficult." He cites recent statistics that indicate when districts wait until the third or fourth grade to provide appropriate remediation for students who have reading or writing disabilities, there is a 73 percent chance such a child will continue to struggle in ninth grade.

I know too many parents who have sought help for their children only to be told, "Let's wait and see what happens." This 73 percent figure indicates that to wait and see is to let the problem get worse. As Dr. Margolis points out, in many cases, the social and emotional consequences of doing poorly in school eventually become the primary problem, because these students then become poorly motivated and develop a negative or self-defeating attitude about learning. "There's the idea of having the skill," he says, "but associated with that is the will."

A few other points must be made about evaluations (also see chapter 5). If you have an evaluation of your child done privately, schools have a legal obligation to consider that evaluation and its recommendations. If they disagree, they have to put in writing why they are not accepting it. Schools and parents can agree to have an independent educational evaluation done by an outside professional with no connections to either party.

Evaluations must be conducted by a multidisciplinary team. *No single test or measure or procedure can determine a child's eligibility.* The educational evaluation should include:

- interviews with teachers and parents
- social history
- norm-referenced testing (for example, WISC-R Wechslr Intelligence Scale, Revised or standardized achievement tests)
- in-depth observations
- functional evaluations of academic performance

Too often schools use the results of annual achievement tests as a preliminary screening measure. Besides being a violation of the law, this practice doesn't work where ADHD is concerned, because ADHD does not show up as a discrepancy between the student's ability and achievement on standardized tests. It is a problem of ability and underperformance—the consistent act of not working to capability on a daily basis, which causes academic failure.

3. Individual Educational Plan

Once a student is found eligible for services, the school must design an individual educational plan (IEP). In fact, information acquired in the assessment forms the basis for the program. "Individualized does not mean identical," says Dr. Margolis, referring to the practice some schools have of using a one-size-fits-all approach based on the type of disability and not on the individual student's needs.

Please keep in mind, *education does not mean academics only.* When we are talking about a child's unique needs within special education, we are also referring to the social, emotional, and behavioral difficulties that arise as part of his or her disability. Learning goes beyond the three *R*'s.

According to Fran Rice, "The IEP is a very important legal document which parents should not enter into lightly." Once in place, the IEP cannot be significantly changed without parental approval. Ms. Rice advises parents to learn all they can about their child's impairments before they enter into IEP development. Parents are supposed to be part of the process. Often, schools develop the IEP without parental input, have an IEP conference with the parents, give them the plan, and then ask for a signature. Guidelines for participating in IEP meetings are included at the end of this appendix.

Your child's IEP should have the following components:

A. *Educational status section*: In order to prepare an individual program for your child, those involved must really know the youngster. This section includes all the relevant information about your child to provide a comprehensive, functional picture—strengths, weaknesses, skills, abilities, accomplishments, frustrations. In general, it should describe what your child knows and what he or she needs to learn in order to function effectively in life. It is from this section that the next two IEP areas are developed.

B. *Annual goals*: Basically the goals should be what the child is expected to accomplish in a year with good instruction and a reasonable amount of effort. The goal should be *measurable*. Ideally it should contain a performance standard (for example, remain on task when reading, for thirty minutes). It should not be *vague* (for example, "pays attention"), which makes it *un*measurable.

C. *Objectives*: The objectives are the steps taken to achieve those goals. You can view objectives as mini-goals that are achieved along the way. These should be meaningful, measurable, and aligned with marking periods. At the end of each marking period, parents should be able to see where their child stands in terms of achieving the annual goals based on whether or not the objectives are being met. Assessing step-by-step progress is extremely important. It lets the school and parents know if changes need to be made to the IEP. Under the IDEA Amendments of 1997, schools have to inform parents if their child's progress for each marking period is sufficient for the child to achieve the goals in his IEP by the end of the year. This makes it imperative that the goals be precise and measurable.

Part of creating objectives is designing the teaching methodologies and related services necessary to help the child achieve the objective. Related services are any nonmedical services the child requires to benefit from special education. "Nonmedical" means that a physician does not need to perform the service.

If objectives are vague, measuring them can be difficult. Too often grade or achievement test scores become the measurement. These are often unreliable and unrelated to objectives. They do little to tell you whether a student has made actual progress in specific areas of functioning. For example, if an objective is to increase the amount of homework assignments submitted on time, measurement must take into account how many were given and completed. The marking-period grade for the course or an achievement test grade equivalent does not provide that information.

D. *Transition*: The federal law calls for IEPs of students sixteen years old to include a transition plan. That plan is supposed to "get them ready for the 'world of work' or post-secondary school, or independent or supervised living," says Dr. Margolis. Developing transition plans involves finding out what some of the student's hopes, aspirations, and goals are, and speaking to the parents about their goals for their child. Outside agencies may be enlisted as necessary to help the student achieve the goals in the transition plan.

4. Education in the least restrictive environment

A central feature of IDEA is to educate the student in the least restrictive environment (LRE). This concept has been much misunderstood and misapplied. LRE does not mean that the child is always placed in the regular education classroom. The law requires that schools consider a continuum of placement options. Placement is determined by looking at the unique needs of each child with a disability in determining how to best help the child achieve the goals and objectives of the IEP. Placement may be in regular education classrooms, resource-room pull-out programs, special classes, special schools, or at home. Which one or which combination depends on the child's individual needs, not on some arbitrary decision. I have found that school officials sometimes misapply this provision by assigning a child to what they think is the least restrictive environment and then not changing that placement until the child fails. IDEA calls for a continuum of placement options, not a continuum of placement failures.

5. Parent participation in decision-making

Not only are you supposed to partipate in decision-making, your participation is supposed to be meaningful. Being presented with an IEP in which you've had no input is not meaningful participation. Nor is a phone call telling you that a change in the IEP is needed and has to be made immediately. You must learn to ask questions and keep in mind the main point: how will this action or decision further my child's education?

6. Procedural Due Process

IDEA has procedural safeguards to help both the parties resolve their differences when parents and schools disagree over any part of the evaluation/IEP/placement process. These safeguards require the following of formal procedures: When either party, parent or school district, decides that they cannot resolve their differences, they have two options. One option is mediation. This process involves the use of an independent third party to help the parents and the district personnel achieve a mutually satisfying resolution to their conflict. Mediation does not have the same weight as a court proceeding. Thus, if the parties cannot come to agreement, then they usually have to proceed to the other option, impartial due process. In this case, both the parents and the school go before a hearing officer or judge who decides for them. These are legal, court proceedings. In impartial due process hearings, the ruling of the hearing officer or judge is considered binding and must be followed. School districts have school board attorneys who represent them in impartial due process hearings. Dr. Margolis believes parents who attempt court proceedings without an attorney are at a big disadvantage.

"Going to court is miserable for everybody," observes Dr. Margolis. In his experience, many due process hearings happen because the parties do not listen to each other, or are not interested in solving problems and resolving issues. Due process hearings are an extremely burdensome process that exact a heavy price in terms of money, emotions, and time. They often create or increase bitterness and distrust. Whether you represent the school district or the parent, if the other side is unwilling to listen or problem-solve, then you may have no choice but to use mediation or initiate a due process hearing. Please be aware that you do not have to follow these safeguards in a sequential manner. You can begin with requesting a due process hearing and then use mediation any time before the hearing. Should the disagreement become so difficult as to require either of these measures, you must decide which to use first based on individual case circumstances.

Section 504

Section 504 of the Rehabilitation Act is a civil rights law. It says that a person with a disability cannot be discriminated against on the basis of that disability. As in IDEA, all children with ADHD are not automatically protected under this law. They must meet the definition of a handicapped individual as set forth in the law. Section 504 defines a "handicapped person" as any person with a physical or mental impairment that substantially limits a major life activity—for example, learning. Depending on the severity of the child's ADHD, the child may or may not fit within the definition.

Under Section 504, school districts have to evaluate a child when the parents believe their child is handicapped because of ADHD and consequently may need special education or related services. School districts can use the same process as under IDEA for evaluation or a separate process. Children with ADHD who are not eligible under IDEA may qualify under Section 504. If a child is found qualified, the school district must provide special education and related aids and services to the child.

Fran Rice notes that Section 504 protects children in regular and special education. The child is entitled to an individual educational program designed to meet the child's individual educational needs. The IEP can be used for this purpose. Additionally, Section 504 requires the following:

• The quality of services must be equal to that of services provided to students without handicaps; thus the teacher must be trained in the instruction of persons with the handicap in question, and appropriate materials and equipment made available.

• The child's education must be provided in the regular education classroom unless it is demonstrated that education in that environment cannot be achieved satisfactorily without the use of supplementary aids and services.

Even with an understanding of the rights and protections guaranteed under both IDEA and Section 504, many parents need the assistance of trained advocates or lawyers to help when schools and parents disagree. Appendix A lists advocacy organizations that can assist in the process. Parents can also contact the U.S. Department of Education for IDEA concerns and the Office of Civil Rights for Section 504 concerns. See appendix A.

Establishing a Record

You may have little time or perhaps you just hate the tedious job of keeping notes and records about your child and the interactions with your school district. Be on guard. Should a disagreement arise, you want thorough records.

When dealing with any agency, including the public schools, your chances are better if you have a written record of all communications with that agency. The following suggestions should increase your chances in getting action and will strengthen your positions when confrontations arise.

WHAT SHOULD BE IN A RECORD
- A. *All* letters *from* you to the school district and other agencies about your concern.
- B. *All* letters to you from the school district and other agencies about your concern.
- C. *All* reports from the school, doctors, other agencies, and others including: report cards, parent-teacher conference reports, diagnostic reports, minutes or reports of meetings with persons involved with your concerns, IEP recommendations, etc.
- D. *A lot of telephone calls* giving the dates and time and length of the call, who initiated the call, who participated in the call (i.e., sometimes calls are transferred to more than one person or are conference calls), a summary of the conversations (i.e., who said what, what conclusions were reached or what action was promised, etc.).

HOW TO DEVELOP AND KEEP A RECORD
The following are suggestions for establishing and maintaining a record of contacts with the schools or other agencies.

1. Purchase a three-ring notebook, pocket folder or small file. This will be the one location where you will keep all information related to the record.
2. Organize the record in whatever way helps you to locate the information quickly. (It is suggested you use reverse chronological order with latest information on top.)

3. Place all written reports, minutes of meetings, letters, etc., in the record. (See C above.)

4. Write down all phone calls (see D above). You may want to have the telephone log as a separate section in your record.

5. For meetings and phone calls for which there is no record, ask the school or other agency people to supply a summary of the meeting or call. If you agree with the summary, file it.

6. If you do not agree with the record or summary of a meeting or phone call, put your own interpretation in writing, and send it to the persons who chaired the meeting and wrote the minutes or summary. Ask that person to respond if they disagree with your interpretation.

7. Make your own notes at every meeting. If you have trouble writing notes during the meeting, *use a tape recorder* and transcribe your notes later.

8. Write out a summary of your interpretation of each meeting or phone call. Send your summary to the chairperson and minute taker and ask that person to react to your interpretation if he disagrees with it.

9. Make enough copies of all your correspondence so that you can send copies to all persons related to your concern. Always keep a copy for yourself.

10. Always send copies of your complaint letter to the following people:
    a. Local Superintendent
    b. Local Director of Special Education
    c. School Principal
    d. Local School Board President

11. Notifications of formal action such as requests for a hearing or filing of a complaint should have copies sent by certified mail to all those listed in 10 above.

12. If your initial letter is not answered or responded to, you may wish to follow up by doing any of the following:
    a. Make a telephone call to any of the above listed persons
    b. Make a direct phone call or in person visit to your local Superintendent of Schools.

13. *Never* let anyone have the master copy of your record except your legal counsel. You may want to have photo copies made and sent to others to help make your point.

By Harold W. Spicknall
Provided to the author from:
Fran Rice
Advocacy Associates of Northern New England
Montpelier, Vermont

Telephone Log

PERSON I TALKED TO	TELEPHONE	DATE

QUESTION/INFORMATION

FOLLOW-UP:
- I PROMISED TO —

- HE/SHE PROMISED TO —

- ADDITIONAL ACTION NEEDED —
(i.e. letter documenting phone call,
others to contact, etc.)

PERSON I TALKED TO	TELEPHONE	DATE

QUESTION/INFORMATION

FOLLOW-UP:
- I PROMISED TO —

- HE/SHE PROMISED TO —

- ADDITIONAL ACTION NEEDED —
(i.e. letter documenting phone call,
others to contact, etc.)

Provided to the author by Statewide Parent Advocacy Network SPAN
516 North Avenue East, Westfield, New Jersey 07090

Guidelines for Being
an Effective Participant
in the IEP Process

How Should Parents Prepare for the IEP Conference?

Although parents may not be experts in the area of special education, they are experts on their child's strengths, weaknesses and learning patterns. Therefore, the full participation of parents is important in developing an appropriate IEP. Further, the parents' knowledge of their child will help them in deciding whether a proposed IEP is "appropriate." Parents should not be afraid to ask questions at the IEP conference or to speak up if they disagree with the educators.

If the parents have an IEP for their child from the current or previous school year, they should review each section of that IEP prior to the conference. Do they agree that their child requires special education in each goal area listed? Are the "objectives" or tasks appropriate, or has the child already learned these skills? Should other areas be included? Are all necessary related services being provided and are the type and amount listed sufficient? Do the parents believe the child could spend more time in class with non-handicapped students? If no IEP yet exists, the parents should think about these IEP areas prior to the conference. The checklist below provides other areas for all parents to consider before, during and at the end of the IEP Conference.

IEP Checklist

Before Attending an IEP Conference:
- review all school records, including school district evaluations;
- review the results of any outside evaluation done on the child;
- talk with people who have worked with or evaluated the child;
- identify those areas in which the child needs special attention, including, if appropriate, vocational areas;
- identify and/or review the goals (both long- and short-term) for the child and the type of educational setting the child needs.

During the IEP Conference:
- get an explanation of all evaluation results, terms and recommendations;
- find out how much progress the child made in achieving the goals and objectives in the previous IEP (if one exists), which teaching methods and materials worked and which did not;
- review each aspect of the district's proposals, including current levels and goals, and compare these to the parents' own observation of their child;
- discuss parents' academic and vocational goals for the child and the types of skills they want their child to learn;
- make known any agreement or disagreement with the district's recommendations and ask that any modifications or additions be included in the IEP;
- discuss the type and amount of any related services the child requires;
- discuss the amount of special education and regular education the child requires;
- discuss any modifications to the child's regular education classes that may be necessary.

At the End of the IEP Conference:
- make sure that the type and amount of all related services appear on the IEP;
- make sure that the amount of time the child will participate in regular education appears on the IEP.

The Surefire Four-Step Record Decoder

STEP I: ORGANIZE

1. After obtaining the *complete set of records* from the school system, separate reports about your child (teacher reports, psychological evaluations, social history, etc.) from the correspondence.
2. Make an extra copy of the records in order to have an original and a working copy you can mark, cut, paste and use in any way that will help you.
3. Arrange each set, reports and extra documents, in chronological order.
4. Secure the pages in a folder with a clip or in a loose leaf notebook.

Excerpted from *The Right to Special Education in Pennsylvania: A Guide for Parents,* published by The Education Law Center, 225 South 15th Street, Philadelphia, Pennsylvania 19102.

5. Number each report and make a chronological list that can be added onto as new records are generated.

STEP II: READ

1. Read through the entire record to get overall impressions, tones of the school's view of your child.
2. In the margins of your working copy, mark with a "?" the statements or areas of the reports with which you disagree or do not understand.

STEP III: ANALYZE

1. While re-reading the reports, underline the phrases or sentences, you feel best describe *both* your child's strengths and your child's problems. Put an "S" in the margin opposite a description of your child's learning strengths, a "P" opposite problems.
2. Using a worksheet, place the phrases or sentences about your child's strengths and problems within the categories of Oral Expression, Listening Comprehension, Basic Reading Skills, Reading Comprehension, Mathematical Calculation and Mathematical Reasoning, and Social Perception.
3. After each piece of data put the *source* and *date*. Often you will find trends beginning to emerge. The same observation, said in similar language, may occur in several reports over a period of time. You can indicate this by simply recording additional sources and dates to the original data.
4. List *recommendations* in the last section of the analysis sheet that are made by each evaluator; for example, services needed, classroom environment, class size, type of school setting, recommendation for further testing, specific teaching materials or methods.

STEP IV: EVALUATE

Using the question mark quotations you have made in the margins and your overall sense of the records from your analytical work with them, evaluate their accuracy against the following criteria:

ACCURATE—   do these reports and portions of the records correspond with your own feelings, perceptions, observations and assessments of your child?

COMPLETE—   are all the documents required by the school system for the Eligibility, Individualized Education Plan (IEP) and Placement decision available in the file? For example, medical

	report, psychological examination, educational report and others as required.
JARGON-FREE—	do the reports describe your child in non-technical terms and/or language you can understand and use? In a good report diagnoses and technical language will be used and defined within the report.
CURRENT—	are the dates on the records recent enough to give a report of your child's present behavior and functioning?
CONSISTENT—	are the reports contradictory? Is there consistency between the descriptions of your child by each evaluator?
UNDERSTANDABLE—	is the language used meaningful, clear and understandable to you? Example of an unclear statement: "She appears to have a psychological learning disability, calling for treatment involving a moderation of the special focus on interpersonal sensitivity she has received so far." "WHAT DOES THAT MEAN?"
OVERALL INTEGRITY—	considering the records as a whole, do they make sense and lead to the given recommendations?

Provided to the author from Fran Rice, Advocacy Associates of Northern New England, Montepelier, VT 05602

U.S. Department of Education Policy on ADD

UNITED STATES DEPARTMENT OF EDUCATION
OFFICE OF SPECIAL EDUCATION AND
REHABILITATIVE SERVICES

THE ASSISTANT SECRETARY

MEMORANDUM

DATE   : Sep. 16, 1991

TO   : Chief State School Officers

FROM   : Robert R. Davila
                  Assistant Secretary
                  Office of Special Education
                    and Rehabilitative Services

                  Michael L. Williams
                  Assistant Secretary
                  Office for Civil Rights

                  John T. MacDonald
                  Assistant Secretary
                  Office of Elementary
                    and Secondary Education

SUBJECT   : Clarification of Policy to Address the Needs of
                  Children with Attention Deficit Disorders within
                  General and/or Special Education

I. *Introduction*

There is a growing awareness in the education community that attention deficit disorder (ADD) and attention deficit hyperactive disorder (ADHD) can result in significant learning problems for children with those conditions.[1] While estimates of the prevalence of ADD vary widely, we believe that three to five percent of school-aged children may have significant educational problems related to this disorder. Because ADD has broad implications for education as a whole, the Department believes it should clarify State and local responsibility under Federal law for addressing the needs of children with ADD in the schools. Ensuring that these students are able to reach their fullest potential is an inherent part of the National education goals and AMERICA 2000. The National goals, and the strategy for achieving them, are based on the assumptions that: (1) all children can

---

[1]While we recognize that the disorders ADD and ADHD vary, the term ADD is being used to encompass children with both disorders.

learn and benefit from their education; and (2) the educational community must work to improve the learning opportunities for all children.

This memorandum clarifies the circumstances under which children with ADD are eligible for special education services under Part B of the Individuals with Disabilities Education Act (Part B), as well as the Part B requirements for evaluation of such children's unique educational needs. This memorandum will also clarify the responsibility of State and local educational agencies (SEAs and LEAs) to provide special education and related services to eligible children with ADD under Part B. Finally, this memorandum clarifies the responsibilities of LEAs to provide regular or special education and related aids and services to those children with ADD who are not eligible under Part B, but who fall within the definition of "handicapped person" under Section 504 of the Rehabilitation Act of 1973. Because of the overall educational responsibility to provide services for these children, it is important that general and special education coordinate their efforts.

II. *Eligibility for special Education and Related Services under Part B*

Last year during the reauthorization of the Education of the Handicapped Act (now the Individuals with Disabilities Education Act), Congress gave serious consideration to including ADD in the definition of "children with disabilities" in the statute. The Department took the position that ADD does not need to be added as a separate disability category in the statutory definition since children with ADD who require special education and related services can meet the eligibility criteria for services under Part B. This continues to be the Department's position.

No change with respect to ADD was made by Congress in the statutory definition of "children with disabilities"; however, language was included in Section 102(a) of the Education of the Handicapped Act Amendments of 1990 that required the Secretary to issue a Notice of Inquiry (NOI) soliciting public comment on special education for children with ADD under Part B. In response to the NOI (published November 29, 1990, in the *Federal Register*), the Department received over 2000 written comments, which have been transmitted to Congress. Our review of these written comments indicates that there is confusion in the field regarding the extent to which children with ADD may be served in special education programs conducted under Part B.

A. *Description of Part B*

Part B requires SEAs and LEAs to make a free appropriate public education (FAPE) available to all eligible children with disabilities and to ensure that the rights and protections of Part B are extended to those children and their parents. 20 U.S.C. 1412(2); 34 CFR §§300.121 and 300.2. Under Part B, FAPE, among other elements, includes the provision of special education and related services, at no cost to parents, in conformity with an individualized education program (IEP). 34 CFR §300.4.

In order to be eligible under Part B, a child must be evaluated in accordance with 34 CFR §§300.530–300.534 as having one or more specified physical or mental impairments, and must be found to require special education and related services by reason of one or more of these impairments.[2] 20 U.S.C. 1401(a)(1); 34 CFR §300.5. SEAs and LEAs must ensure that children with ADD who are determined eligible for services under Part B receive special education and related services designed to meet their unique needs, including special education and related services needs arising from the ADD. A full continuum of placement alternatives, including the regular classroom, must be available for providing special education and related services required in the IEP.

B. *Eligibility for Part B services under the "Other Health Impaired" Category*

The list of chronic or acute health problems included within the definition of "other health impaired" in the Part B regulations is not exhaustive. The term "other health impaired" includes chronic or acute impairments that result in limited alertness, which adversely affects educational performance. Thus, children with ADD should be classified as eligible for services under the "other health impaired" category in instances where the ADD is a chronic or acute health problem that results in limited alertness, which adversely affects educational performance. In other words, children with ADD, where the ADD is a chronic or acute health problem resulting in limited alertness, may be considered disabled under Part B solely on the basis of this disorder within the "other health impaired" category in situations where special education and related services are needed because of the ADD.

C. *Eligibility for Part B services under Other Disability Categories*

Children with ADD are also eligible for services under Part B if the children satisfy the criteria applicable to other disability categories. For example, children with ADD are also eligible for services under the "specific learning disability" category of Part B if they meet the criteria stated in §§300.5(b)(9) and 300.541 or under the "seriously emotionally disturbed" category of Part B if they meet the criteria stated in §300.5(b)(8).

---

[2]The Part B regulations define 11 specified disabilities. 34 CFR §300.5(b)(1)–(11). The Education of the Handicapped Act Amendments of 1990 amended the Individuals with Disabilities Education Act (formerly the Education of the Handicapped Act) to specify that autism and traumatic brain injury are separate disability categories. *See* section 602(a)(1) of the Act, to be modified at 20 U.S.C. 1401(a)(1).

III.   *Evaluations Under Part B*

A.   *Requirements*

SEAs and LEAs have an affirmative obligation to evaluate a child who is suspected of having a disability to determine the child's need for special education and related services. Under Part B, SEAs and LEAs are required to have procedures for locating, identifying and evaluating all children who have a disability or are suspected of having a disability and are in need of special education and related services. 34 CFR §§300.128 and 300.220. This responsibility, known as "child find," is applicable to all children from birth through 21, regardless of the severity of their disability.

Consistent with this responsibility and the obligation to make FAPE available to all eligible children with disabilities, SEAs and LEAs must ensure that evaluations of children who are suspected of needing special education and related services are conducted without undue delay. 20 U.S.C. 1412(2). Because of its responsibility resulting from the FAPE and child find requirements of Part B, an LEA may not refuse to evaluate the possible need for special education and related services of a child with a prior medical diagnosis of ADD solely by reason of that medical diagnosis. However, a medical diagnosis of ADD alone is not sufficient to render a child eligible for services under Part B.

Under Part B, before any action is taken with respect to the initial placement of a child with a disability in a program providing special education and related services, "a full and individual evaluation of the child's educational needs must be conducted in accordance with requirements of §300.532." 34 CFR §300.531. Section 300.532(a) requires that a child's evaluation must be conducted by a multidisciplinary team, including at least one teacher or other specialist with knowledge in the area of suspected disability.

B.   *Disagreements Over Evaluations*

Any proposal or refusal of an agency to initiate or change the identification, evaluation, or educational placement of the child, or the provision of FAPE to the child, is subject to the written prior notice requirements of 34 CFR §§300.504–300.505.[3] If a parent disagrees with the LEA's refusal

---

[3]Section 300.505 of the Part B regulations sets out the elements that must be contained in the prior written notice to parents:

(1) A full explanation of all of the procedural safeguards available to the parents under Subpart E;

(2) A description of the action proposed or refused by the agency, an explanation of why the agency proposes or refuses to take action and a description of any options the agency considered and the reasons why those options were rejected;

(3) A description of each evaluation procedure, test, record, or report the agency uses as a basis for the proposal or refusal; and

(4) A description of any other factors which are relevant to the agency's proposal or refusal. 34 CFR §300.505(a)(1)–(4).

to evaluate a child or the LEA's evaluation and determination that a child does not have a disability for which the child is eligible for services under Part B, the parent may request a due process hearing pursuant to 34 CFR §§300.504–300.513 of the Part B regulations.

IV. *Obligations Under Section 504 of SEAs and LEAs to Children with ADD Found Not To Require Special Education and Related Services under Part B*

Even if a child with ADD is found not to be eligible for services under Part B, the requirements of Section 504 of the Rehabilitation Act of 1973 (Section 504) and its implementing regulation at 34 CFR Part 104 may be applicable. Section 504 prohibits discrimination on the basis of handicap by recipients of Federal funds. Since Section 504 is a civil rights law, rather than a funding law, its requirements are framed in different terms than those of Part B. While the Section 504 regulation was written with an eye to consistency with Part B, it is more general, and there are some differences arising from the differing natures of the two laws. For instance, the protections of Section 504 extend to some children who do not fall within the disability categories specified in Part B.

A. *Definition*

Section 504 requires every recipient that operates a public elementary or secondary education program to address the needs of children who are considered "handicapped persons" under Section 504 as adequately as the needs of nonhandicapped persons are met. "Handicapped person" is defined in the Section 504 regulation as any person who has a physical or mental impairment which substantially limits a major life activity (*e.g.*, learning). 34 CFR §104.3(j). Thus, depending on the severity of their condition, children with ADD *may* fit within that definition.

B. *Programs and Services Under Section 504*

Under Section 504, an LEA must provide a free appropriate public education to each qualified handicapped child. A free appropriate public education, under Section 504, consists of regular or special education and related aids and services that are designed to meet the individual student's needs and based on adherence to the regulatory requirements on educational setting, evaluation, placement, and procedural safeguards. 34 CFR §§104.33, 104.34, 104.35, and 104.36. A student may be handicapped within the meaning of Section 504, and therefore entitled to regular or special education and related aids and services under the Section 504 regulation, even though the student may not be eligible for special education and related services under Part B.

Under Section 504, if parents believe that their child is handicapped by ADD, the LEA must evaluate the child to determine whether he or she is

handicapped as defined by Section 504. If an LEA determines that a child
is not handicapped under Section 504, the parent has the right to contest
that determination. If the child is determined to be handicapped under Section 504, the LEA must make an individualized determination of the child's
educational needs for regular or special education or related aids and services. 34 CFR §104.35. For children determined to be handicapped under
Section 504, implementation of an individualized education program developed in accordance with Part B, although not required, is one means of
meeting the free appropriate public education requirements of Section 504.[4]
The child's education must be provided in the regular education classroom
unless it is demonstrated that education in the regular environment with
the use of supplementary aids and services cannot be achieved satisfactorily. 34 CFR §104.34.

Should it be determined that the child with ADD is handicapped for
purposes of Section 504 and needs only adjustments in the regular classroom, rather than special education, those adjustments are required by Section 504. A range of strategies is available to meet the educational needs of
children with ADD. Regular classroom teachers are important in identifying the appropriate educational adaptions and interventions for many children with ADD.

SEAs and LEAs should take the necessary steps to promote coordination between special and regular education programs. Steps also should be
taken to train regular education teachers and other personnel to develop
their awareness about ADD and its manifestations and the adaptations that
can be implemented in regular education programs to address the instructional needs of these children. Examples of adaptations in regular education
programs could include the following:

> providing a structured learning environment; repeating and simpli-
> fying instructions about in-class and homework assignments; sup-
> plementing verbal instructions with visual instructions; using
> behavioral management techniques; adjusting class schedules; mod-
> ifying test delivery; using tape recorders, computer-aided instruction,
> and other audio-visual equipment; selecting modified textbooks or
> workbooks; and tailoring homework assignments.

Other provisions range from consultation to special resources and may
include reducing class size; use of one-on-one tutorials; classroom aides
and note takers; involvement of a "services coordinator" to oversee imple-

---

[4]Many LEAs use the same process for determining the needs of students under Section 504
that they use for implementing Part B.

mentation of special programs and services, and possible modification of nonacademic times such as lunchroom, recess, and physical education.

Through the use of appropriate adaptations and interventions in regular classes, many of which may be required by Section 504, the Department believes that LEAs will be able to effectively address the instructional needs of many children with ADD.

C. *Procedural Safeguards Under Section 504*

Procedural safeguards under the Section 504 regulation are stated more generally than in Part B. The Section 504 regulation requires the LEA to make available a system of procedural safeguards that permits parents to challenge actions regarding the identification, evaluation, or educational placement of their handicapped child whom they believe needs special education or related services. 34 CFR §104.36. The Section 504 regulation requires that the system of procedural safeguards include notice, an opportunity for the parents or guardian to examine relevant records, an impartial hearing with opportunity for participation by the parents or guardian and representation by counsel, and a review procedure. Compliance with procedural safeguards of Part B is one means of fulfilling the Section 504 requirement.[5] However, in an impartial due process hearing raising issues under the Section 504 regulation, the impartial hearing officer must make a determination based upon that regulation.

V. *Conclusion*

Congress and the Department have recognized the need to provide information and assistance to teachers, administrators, parents and other interested persons regarding the identification, evaluation, and instructional needs of children with ADD. The Department has formed a work group to explore strategies across principal offices to address this issue. The work group also plans to identify some ways that the Department can work with the education associations to cooperatively consider the programs and services needed by children with ADD across special and regular education.

In fiscal year 1991, the Congress appropriated funds for the Department to synthesize and disseminate current knowledge related to ADD. Four centers will be established in Fall 1991, to analyze and synthesize the current research literature on ADD relating to identification, assessment, and interventions. Research syntheses will be prepared in formats suitable for educators, parents and researchers. Existing clearinghouses and networks, as well as Federal, State and local organizations will be utilized to

---

[5] Again, many LEAs and some SEAs are conserving time and resources by using the same due process procedures for resolving disputes under both laws.

disseminate these research syntheses to parents, educators and administrators, and other interested persons.

In addition, the Federal Resource Center will work with SEAs and the six regional resource centers authorized under the Individuals with Disabilities Education Act to identify effective identification and assessment procedures, as well as intervention strategies being implemented across the country for children with ADD. A document describing current practice will be developed and disseminated to parents, educators and administrators, and other interested persons through the regional resource centers network, as well as by parent training centers, other parent and consumer organizations, and professional organizations. Also, the Office for Civil Rights' ten regional offices stand ready to provide technical assistance to parents and educators.

It is our hope that the above information will be of assistance to your State as you plan for the needs of children with ADD who require special education and related services under Part B, as well as for the needs of the broader group of children with ADD who do not qualify for special education and related services under Part B, but for whom special education or adaptations in regular education programs are needed.

Behavior Management Charts

Many variations of behavior management charts exist as do books to explain their use. The following charts are provided as samples. The home management chart depicts the type of chart we used with our son. The daily and weekly school charts have been used successfully by some of the parents I interviewed. For more information about the theory behind behavior management, see chapters 3 and 6.

Chart #1   Home Management Behavior Chart
Chart #2   Daily School Chart
Chart #3   Daily School Record Chart
Chart #4   Weekly School Chart

Sample Home Management Behavior Chart

CHILD'S NAME _____   WEEK OF: _____

	Sun.	Mon.	Tues.	Wed.	Thur.	Fri.	Sat.
NIGHT BEFORE BEDTIME ROUTINE: washes, takes bath, brushes teeth, changes into pajamas, gets into bed, turns lights out on time	3	2	3				
MORNING ROUTINE: gets up, washes, brushes teeth, gets dressed, eats breakfast, is ready on time	2	2	3				
BEDROOM: makes bed, puts books, toys, clothing neatly away by (time)	1	0	3				
HOMEWORK: brings home all necessary materials, completes all assignments by (time) without delays or arguments	3	2	2				
GENERAL COOPERATION AND RESPECT: listens to and follows house rules and directions, cooperates with requests, speaks to and treats other family members nicely	2	2	3				
TOTAL	11*	8*	14**				

RATINGS
Excellent = 3
Good = 2
Needs Improvement = 1
Poor = 0

DAILY TOTALS AND CONSEQUENCES
Excellent Day (12-15 points) Bed 9:30, unrestricted TV/Nintendo time, 50 cents, 2 stars
Good Day (8-11 points) Bed 9:00, 1 hour of TV/Nintendo time, 25 cents, 1 star
Poor Day (0-7 points) Bed 8:30, no TV/Nintendo, no money, no stars

WEEKEND PRIVILEGES = STARS
Excellent week (10-14 stars) = Super Special (e.g. sleep over)
Good week (6-9 stars) = One Special (e.g. rent video tape)
Poor week (0-5 stars) = No Specials

This chart is for an elementary age child whose normal bedtime is 9:00. For younger children—preschool through kindergarten age—it is often best to use a "sticker" or "star" chart. A younger child's chart would have only three behaviors list Similarly, rewards would be age-appropriate, e.g., ice cream cone.

Sample Daily School Chart

DATE:		DAY: MONDAY '89	
SUBJECT	DO YOU HAVE BOOKS/MATERIALS YOU NEED?	HOMEWORK ASSIGNMENTS	
PERIOD 1 READING:	YES/NO HOMEWORK? ☐	ASSIGNMENT:	PAGES:
PERIOD 2 SPELLING:	YES/NO HOMEWORK? ☐	ASSIGNMENT:	PAGES:
PERIOD 3 PENMANSHIP:	YES/NO HOMEWORK? ☐	ASSIGNMENT:	PAGES:
PERIOD 4 MATH:	YES/NO HOMEWORK? ☐	ASSIGNMENT:	PAGES:
PERIOD 5 COMPUTER:	YES/NO HOMEWORK? ☐	ASSIGNMENT:	PAGES:
PERIOD 6 SCIENCE:	YES/NO HOMEWORK? ☐	ASSIGNMENT:	PAGES:
PERIOD 7 SOCIAL STUDIES:	YES/NO HOMEWORK? ☐	ASSIGNMENT:	PAGES:

RESOURCE ROOM:	ARE THERE ANY NOTICES TO GO HOME? YES/NO

COMMENTS:

POINTS TODAY:	POINTS TOTAL:	TEACHER(S):	PARENTS:
			89P1DEMO

Sample Daily School Record Chart

NAME: _____   DAY/DATE: _____

SUBJECT	WORK COMPLETION				CLASS BEHAVIOR			
Language Arts	3	2	1	0	3	2	1	0
Math	3	2	1	0	3	2	1	0
Science	3	2	1	0	3	2	1	0
Reading	3	2	1	0	3	2	1	0
Social Studies	3	2	1	0	3	2	1	0

RATINGS - Please Circle

Total = _____

3 = Excellent
2 = Satisfactory
1 = Needs Improvement
0 = Poor

Language Assignment:
_____

Teacher initials: _____
Test/Quiz Grades: _____
_____

Reading Assignment:
_____

Teacher initials: _____
Test/Quiz Grades: _____
_____

Social Studies Assignment:
_____

Teacher initials: _____
Test/Quiz Grades: _____
_____

Previous Assignments overdue:

Math Assignment:
_____

Teacher initials: _____
Test/Quiz Grades: _____
_____

Science Assignment:
_____

Teacher initials: _____
Test/Quiz Grades: _____
_____

Richard S. Zakreski, Ph.D.

_____
_____
_____

Sample Weekly School Chart

Name: _____ Date: _____

Ratings
3 = Excellent   2 = Satisfactory   1 = Needs Improvement   0 = Poor

Subject	Work Completion				Class Behavior				Teacher Initials
Language Arts	3	2	1	0	3	2	1	0	
Math	3	2	1	0	3	2	1	0	
Science	3	2	1	0	3	2	1	0	
Reading	3	2	1	0	3	2	1	0	
Social Studies	3	2	1	0	3	2	1	0	
Subtotal									
Total									

Missing Assignments
English/L.A.
Social Studies
Math
Science
Specials

Test/Quiz Grades or Upcoming Tests
English/L.A.
Social Studies
Math
Science
Specials

Index